OLIVER'S BRITAIN

This book is dedicated, with gratitude, to all those
past and present who have helped Oliver reach
the point where he can say "I am a professional
Landscape and Wildlife Photographer."
Thank you.

OLIVER'S BRITAIN

Photographs by Oliver Hellowell

Foreword by Iolo Williams

ACC ART BOOKS

CONTENTS

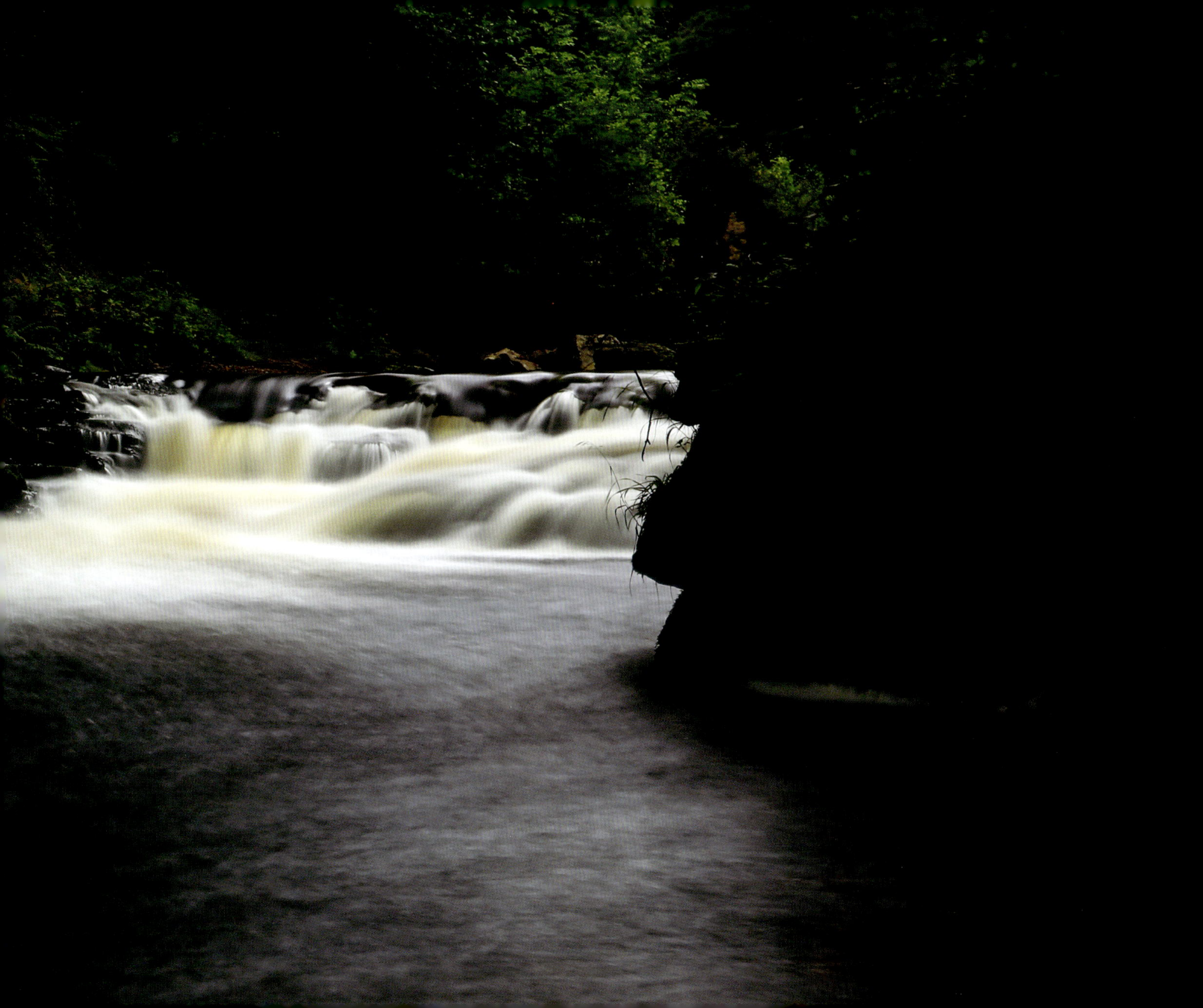

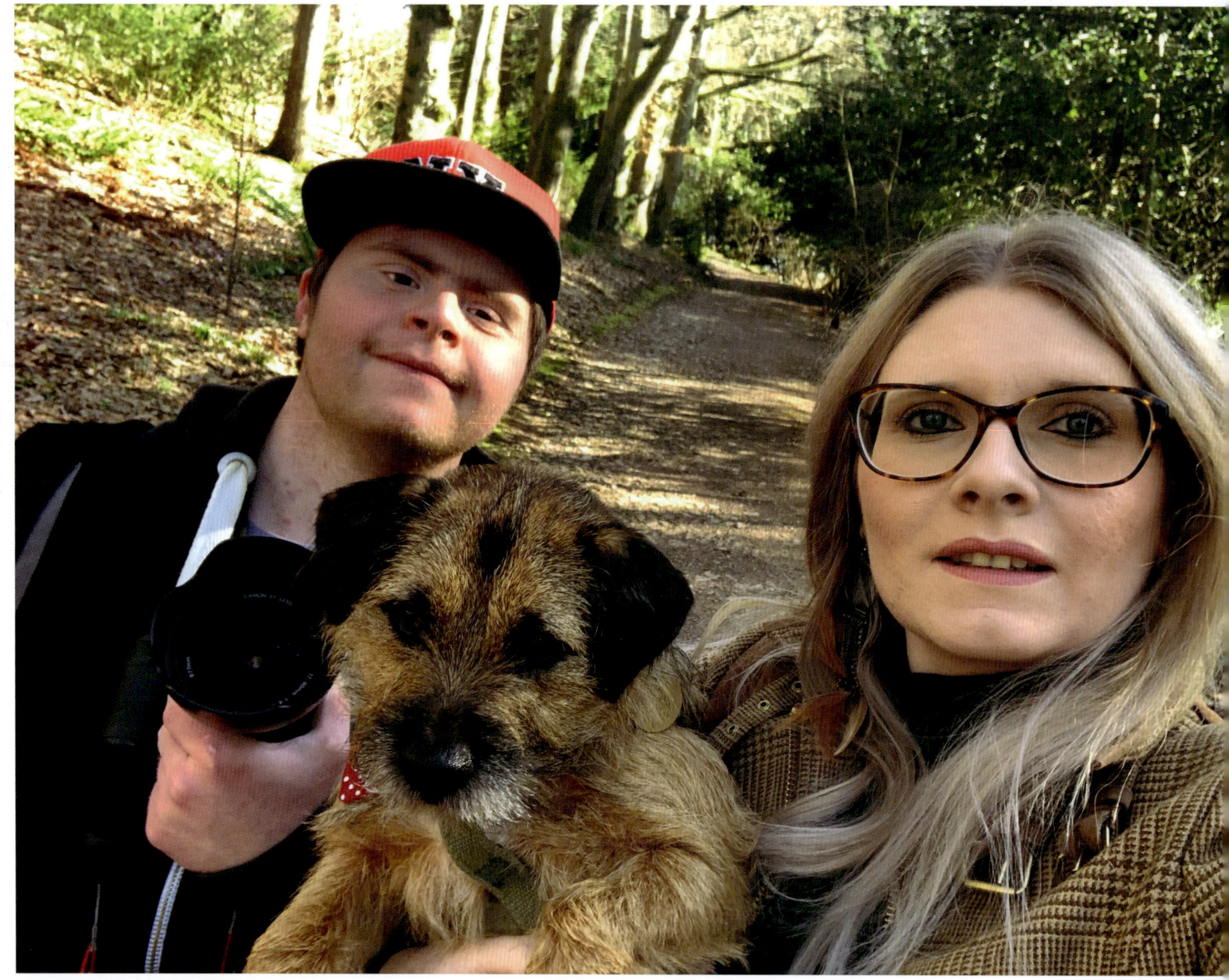

OLIVER HELLOWELL
PHOTOGRAPHER

Oliver is a young man who is well known for his ability to notice and take pictures of things other people don't appreciate, or from angles they might not usually adopt. Born in 1996, Oliver happens to have Down Syndrome. If anything, he has used this to his advantage. He does not 'obey the rules' usually self-imposed by your average photographer and does not concern himself with the technicalities or complex jargon that most photographers employ. His picture taking is simple and refreshing, yet has within it Oliver's own unique view of what constitutes a 'good' picture. Very simply, Oliver takes pictures of things he likes. Born in Somerset, he has lived and holidayed in Britain all his life. Fortunately, Britain is an extremely green and pleasant land, and so affords Oliver exactly the kind of environments he loves best. You will notice there are no cityscapes within these pages, no Tower of London or London Bus, which to so many would be truly iconic British images. Oliver can find cities and busy loud places a bit overwhelming and prefers to enjoy life and time in rural areas, where he can operate at his own speed and in his own way. Oliver has always loved the great outdoors. When he was very young, he used to ask, "Can we go to the wild?" when he wanted to go off exploring the countryside.

Oliver was born with three serious cardiac defects, for which he underwent life-saving surgery at 3 months old. During his early years, he was diagnosed with additional difficulties, resulting in varied extraordinarily negative predictions by speech and language therapists and physiotherapists.

However, with a very determined and optimistic mother Wendy, and much encouragement from his elder sister Anna, Oliver grew up enjoying all manner of activities, hobbies and interests, and

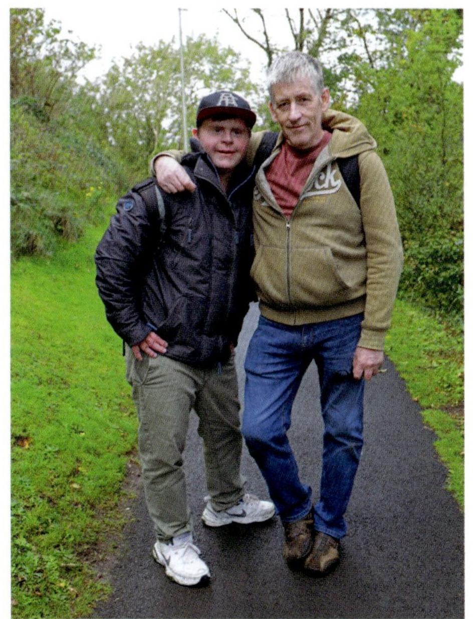

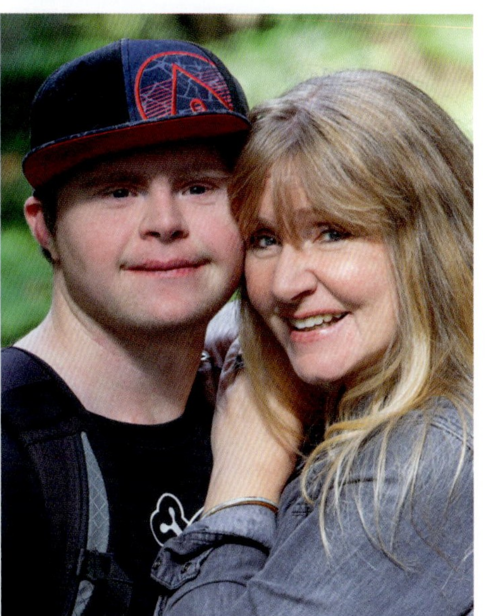

became a happy, healthy and fit young man. At the age of 11 he became fascinated by photography and wanted to be able to 'take pictures like Mike', his stepfather, who came into Oliver's life when he was nearly ten years old. With Mike's patient mentoring and instruction, Oliver learned to use a camera, and very quickly developed his own unique style and view of the world through his lens. Photography has certainly played a large part in enabling Oliver to completely smash professional medical predictions whilst at the same time, through his Facebook page, encouraging and inspiring thousands of people all over the world.

Oliver has an innate talent for framing and composition, frequently capturing smaller and more detailed fragments of a picture rather than seeking to seize an image of the 'whole'. (He has, for example, taken many hundreds of images of bits of castle wall!) A camera allows him to filter out the rest of the world and concentrate on just the piece he's interested in. He constantly refers to the rear screen, checking after almost every click of the shutter, to see if he has caught exactly what he intended to.

Wherever he goes, he always takes his camera, whether on a 'drive-around' with his mum Wendy, an early morning sunset trip or a fishing outing with his dad Mike, a day out with his big sister Anna, a day with his best mate Stuart (both with camera in hand), or on holidays to Wales and Scotland. One of his favourite subjects has already been covered with his previous book, *Oliver's Birds*. In this book, we have endeavoured to give you a glimpse of *Oliver's Britain,* showing a few of his most cherished images from England, Scotland and Wales. (Ireland is still on the bucket list!)

We sincerely hope that as well as bringing inspiration and encouragement to young people with disabilities and everyone involved with them, these images will strike a chord with all those fortunate enough to live in Britain,

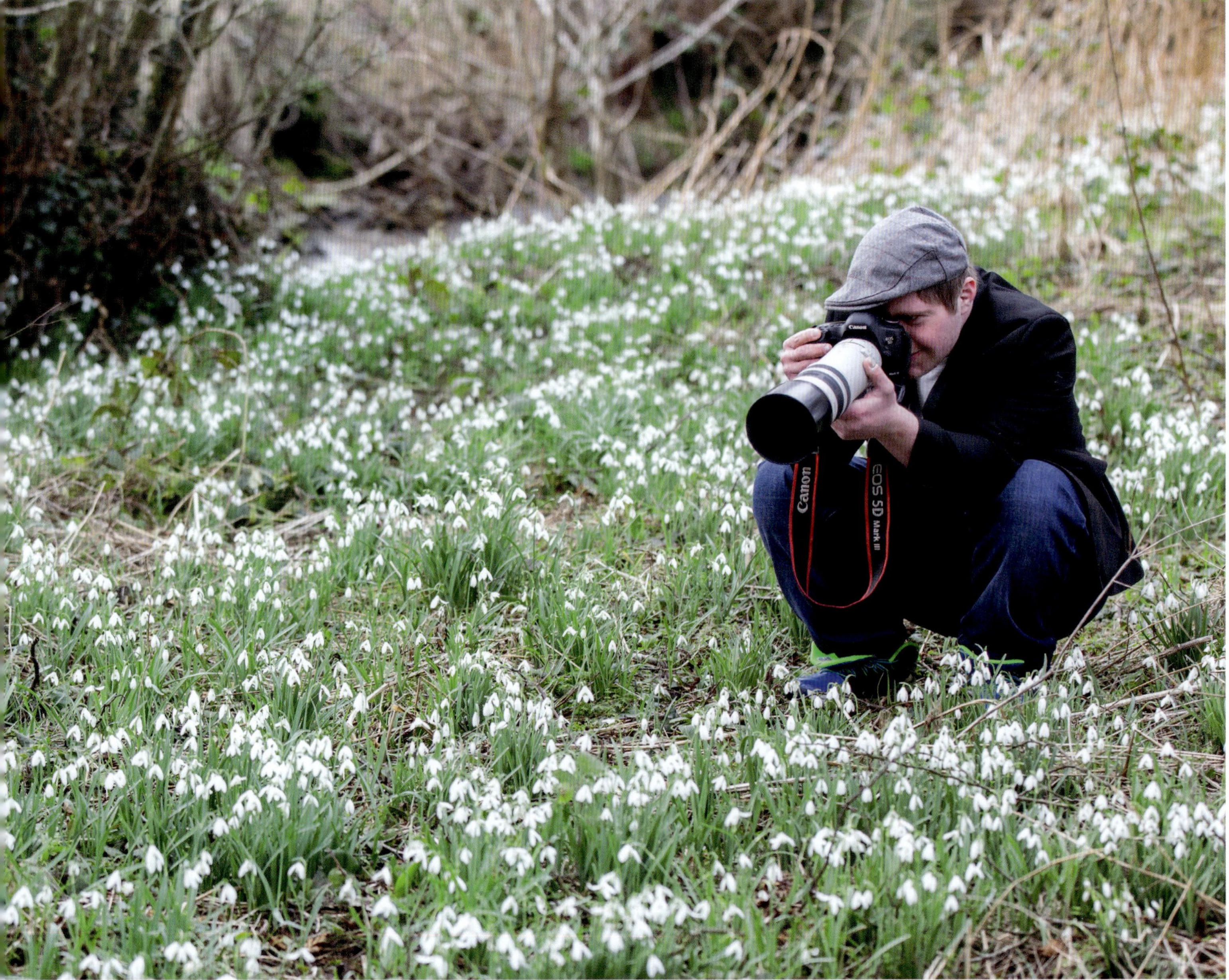

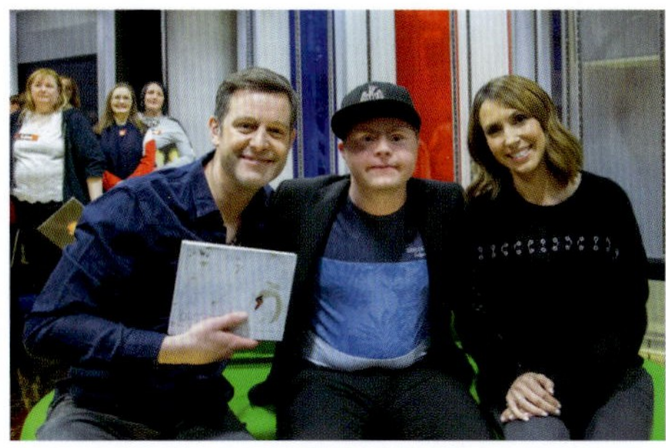

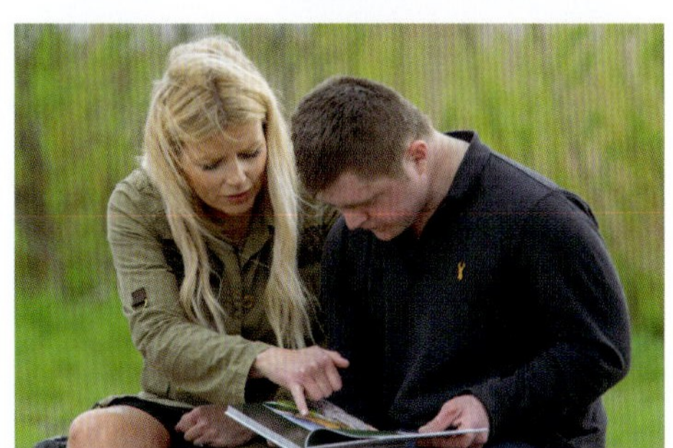

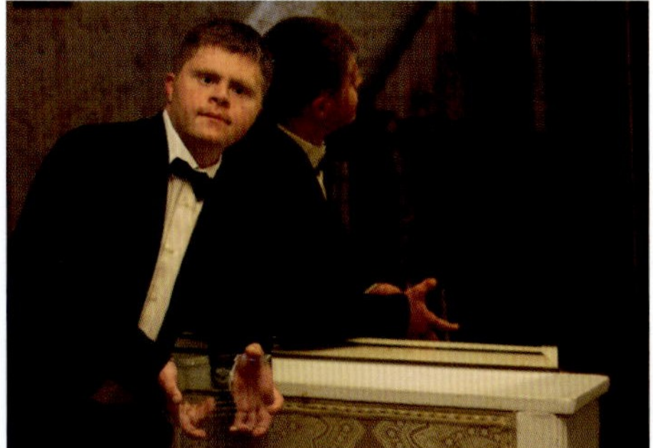

remind 'ex-pats' of home, and encourage those who have never visited our shores to come and see us!

On Facebook, Oliver has a following of over 65,000 people from around the globe and receives orders to his website every week from all over the world. Their comments and support mean a lot to him and to us as a family. A selection of quotes is included on the opposite page and more are scattered through the book, next to the images that inspired them.

Oliver is an extraordinary young man, completely unaware that he is changing the world and making it a better place – one picture at a time.

Throughout this book, Oliver's favourite images are highlighted and his comments on the reason for choosing them are directly quoted for your enjoyment.

www.facebook.com/OliverHellowellPhotographer
www.oliverhellowell.com

A few quotes from Oliver's followers:

Penny Armstrong: 'I love Oliver's photographic perspective of Britain! He hones in on the hidden unique beauty of English countryside and draws it to our attention. It gives me a yearning to return to Britain again and truly see its gems with "Oliver's perspective"! Truly talented.'

John Parry: 'In a stressful world Oliver reminds me of the intense beauty we have all around. This amazing man offers a unique perspective through his lens, seeing the world in marvellous detail and colour. I am calmed and love to retreat into the pictures.'

Lisa Farley: 'Oliver's ability to capture an instant of beauty gives me insight into my daughter's perception of the world and reminds me how important it is to pause and wonder at moments in daily life.'

Sarah Jetley 'Oliver's pictures epitomise everything that is so beautiful about our green and pleasant land. His astonishing photographic ability never fails to capture the beauty of our natural world.'

David Parkes: 'Love seeing Oliver's work, he has gone from being Oliver Hellowell – photographer with Down Syndrome to Oliver Hellowell – photograher. And a damned fine one.'

Carol Himmelman-Christopher: 'With every photograph, Oliver takes me on an instant vacation to magic places. I find, too, that on my daily walks through Berlin, I stop and look at small details of gardens, hedges, buildings. Oliver teaches us all to slow down, concentrate, and open ourselves up to the places we pass through.'

Grace Jarvis: 'Oliver has given me loads of inspiring ideas on how to view the world in a truly different way, to look at the ordinary and see something extraordinary. His work has changed my perspective on photography and in my personal life. Thank you so much.'

Sonia Mitchell: 'When our son was born, Oliver's success as photographer showed us that everything was going to be ok. Oliver is not just a talented photographer, he's also a fantastic role model for our son.'

Suzanne J. Dean: 'I've lived away from the UK for 23 years now and as I get older I miss it more and more... just looking at Oliver's photos takes me back home... just being able to drive "down the road" and seeing all the beauty of a castle, a church, the beach makes me yearn for the UK.'

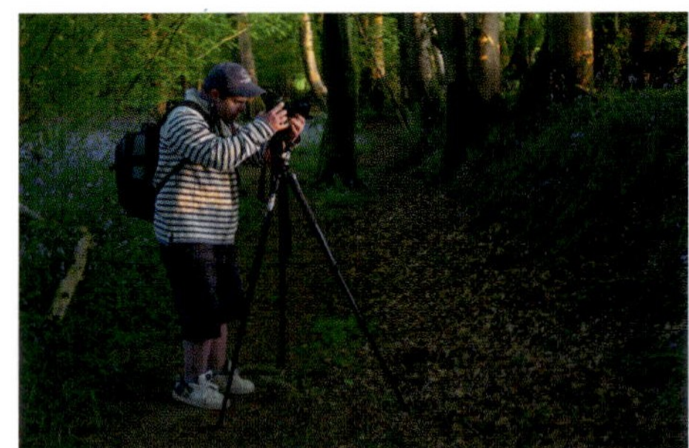

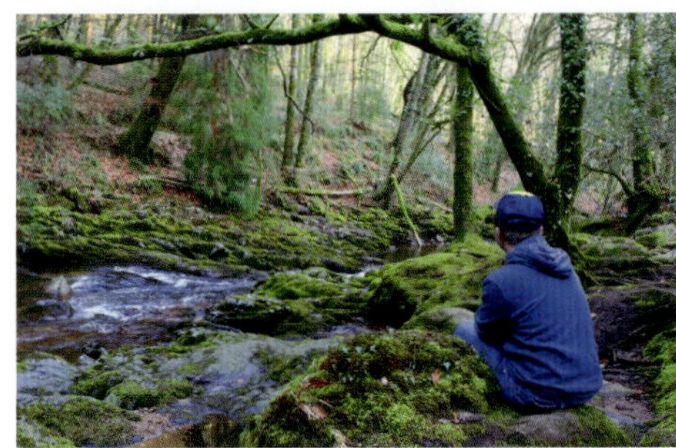

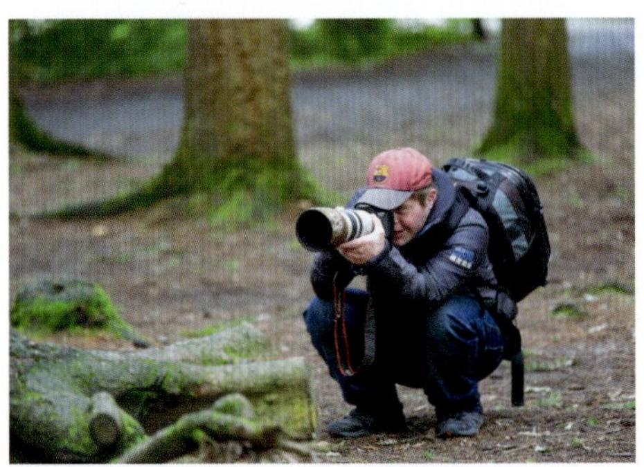

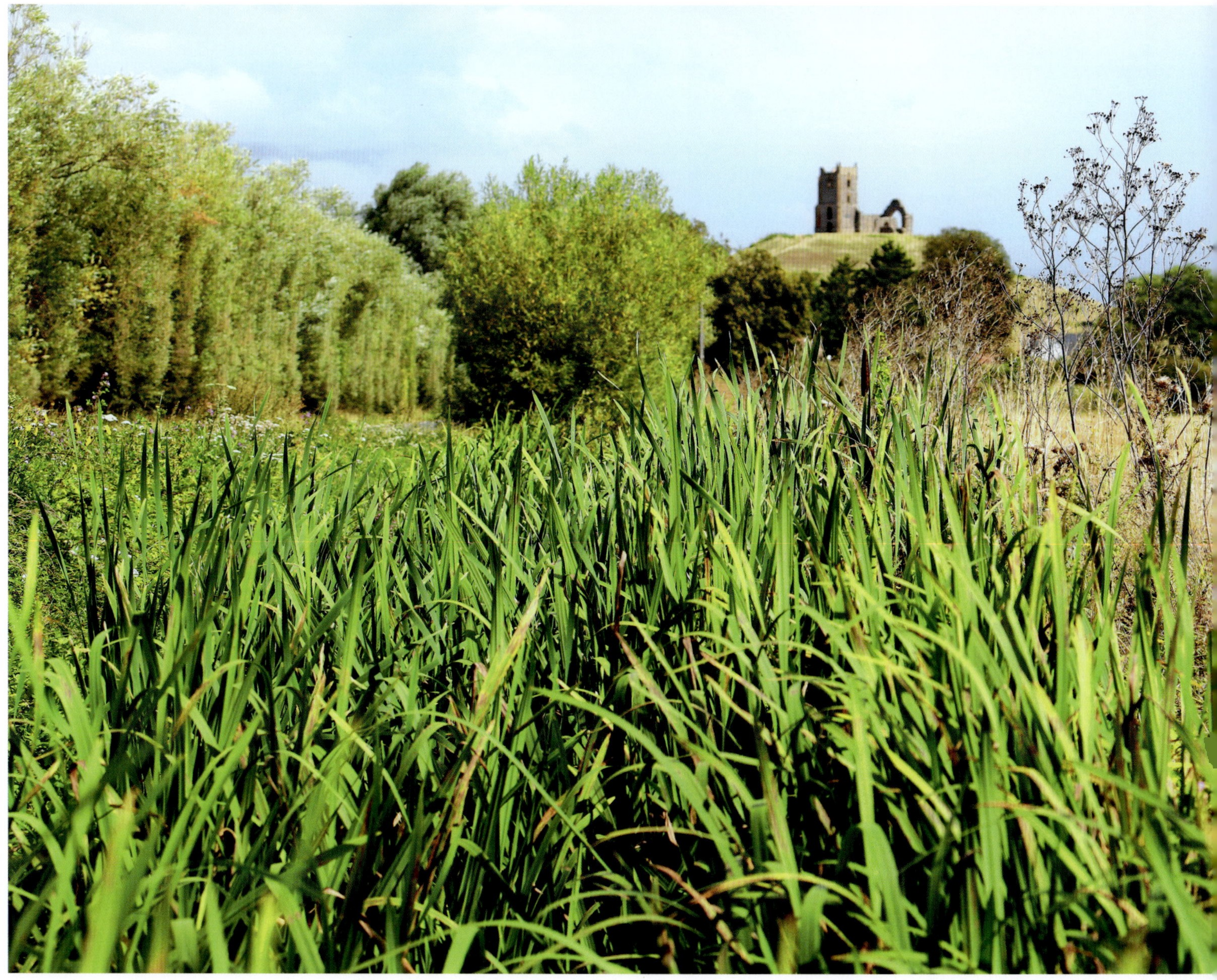

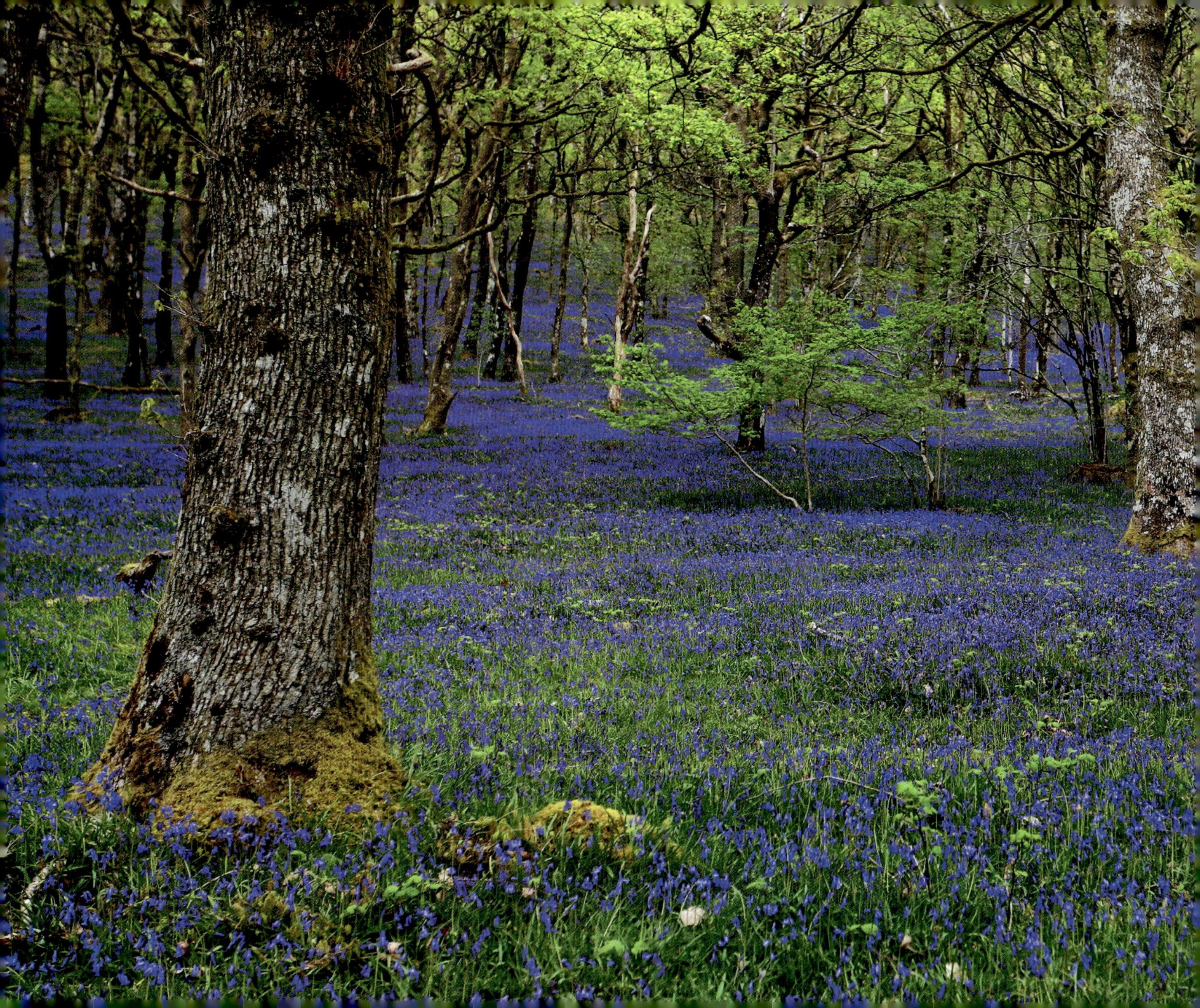

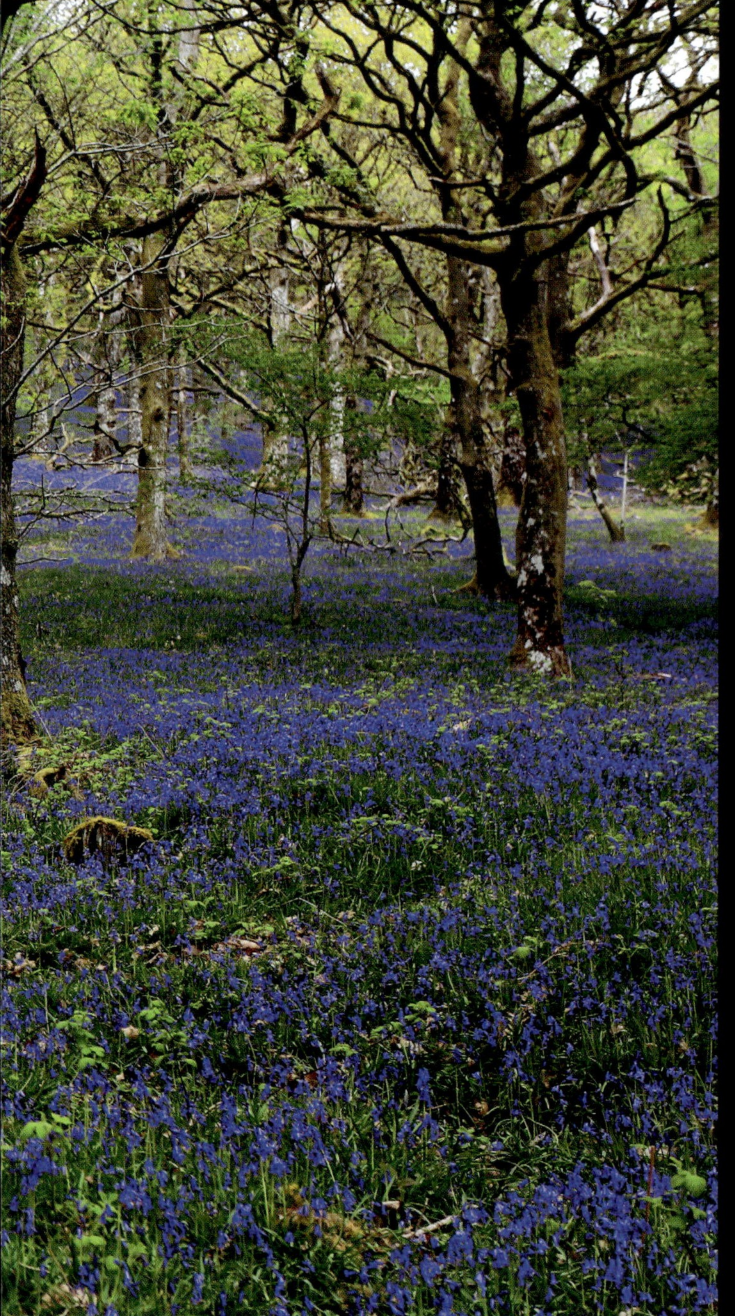

BLOOM WHERE YOU'RE PLANTED

In Britain we are very fond of our gardens and our flowers. Almost everyone has a favourite. Oliver really loves to take pictures of all flowers, everything from the humble daisy and dandelion through to a beautiful scented rose. He does not distinguish flowers by their beauty, stature or rarity, but by their shape and form. In fact, the more humble and common the flower, the more likely Oliver is to be captivated by it. He is often found flat on the ground, taking pictures of daisies; he has hundreds of beautiful images of this cheery little wild flower. While everyone else is cursing dandelions as a weed, he loves their bright vibrant yellow and loves to take pictures of them too. One day we will need to produce a book of *Oliver's Flowers* so you can all see a small sample of his *massive* library of truly beautiful flower images!

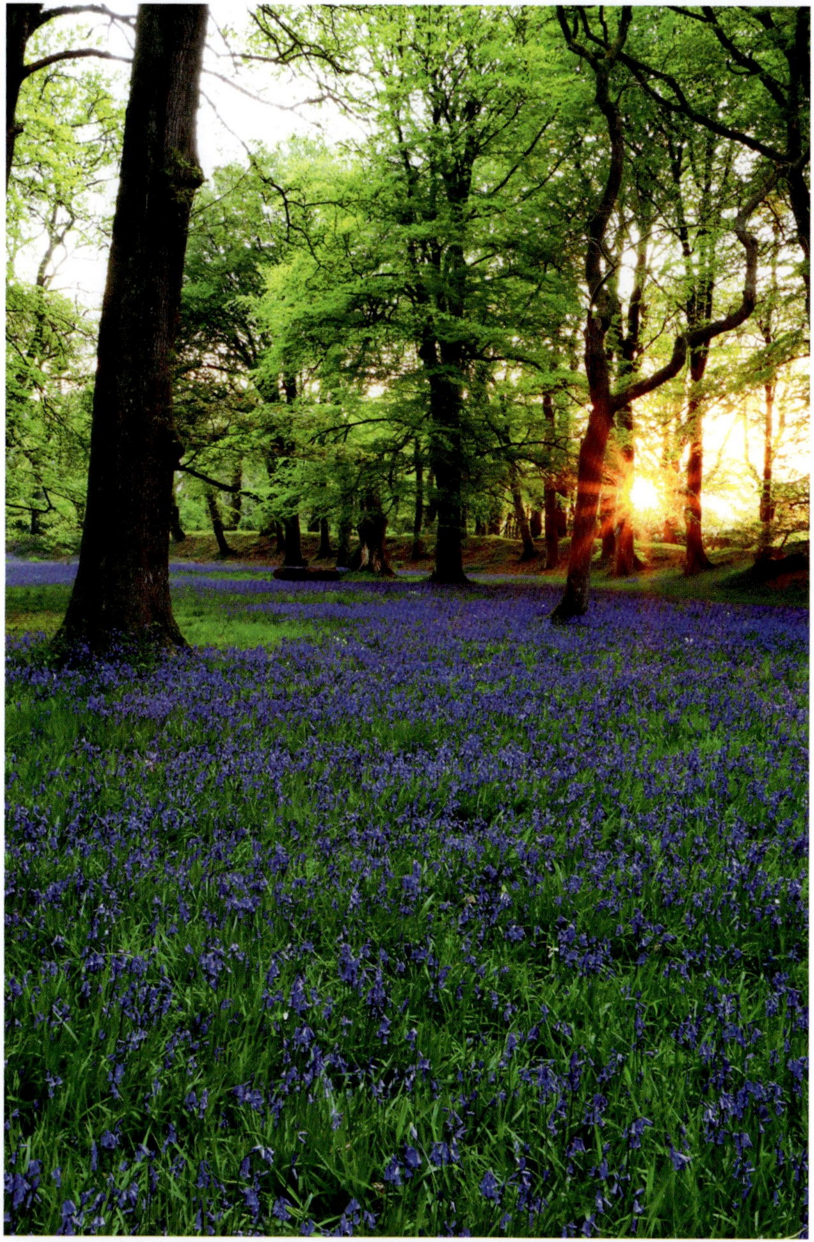

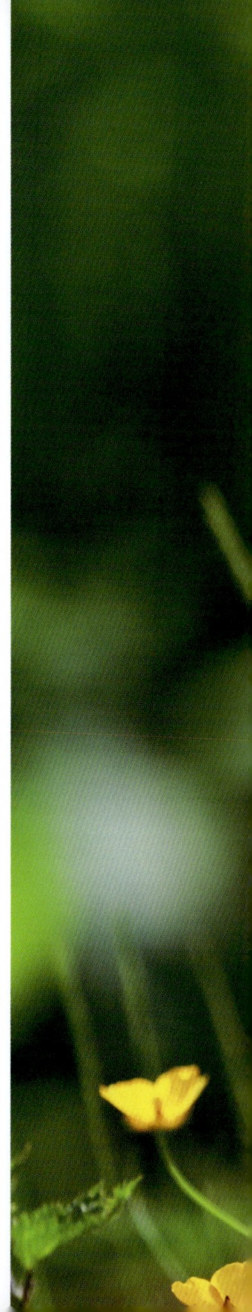

SUNSET OVER NATIVE BLUEBELLS IN WOODLAND

This is a favourite image of Oliver's fans and is often ordered as a large print. Oliver specifically went out one evening with his father Mike to get a shot with both the sun going down, and some lovely bluebells in it.

RED CAMPION, BUTTERCUPS, NETTLES AND GRASSES

Oliver and his mum were driving around the Quantock Hills of Somerset on a warm summer's day when Oliver shouted *"Stop!"* (as he often does when he spots something!) His eye had been drawn by this patch of colour at the side of the road. He hopped out, took this picture, hopped back into the car again and said, "Look at this mum – I got all the pink and yellow together." This clump of wild flowers, grasses and nettles is featured on a large canvas and is another of Oliver's mother's all-time favourites.

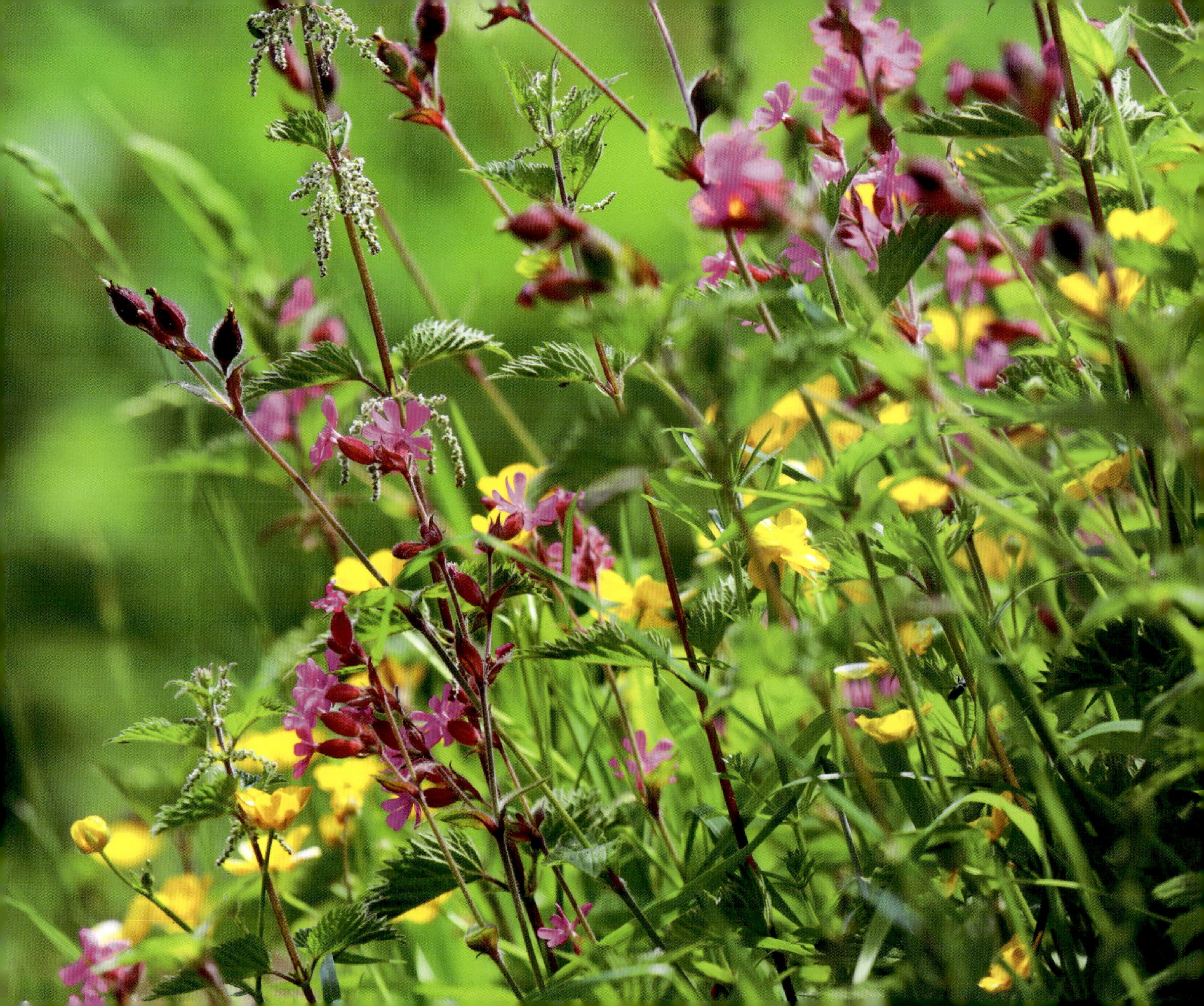

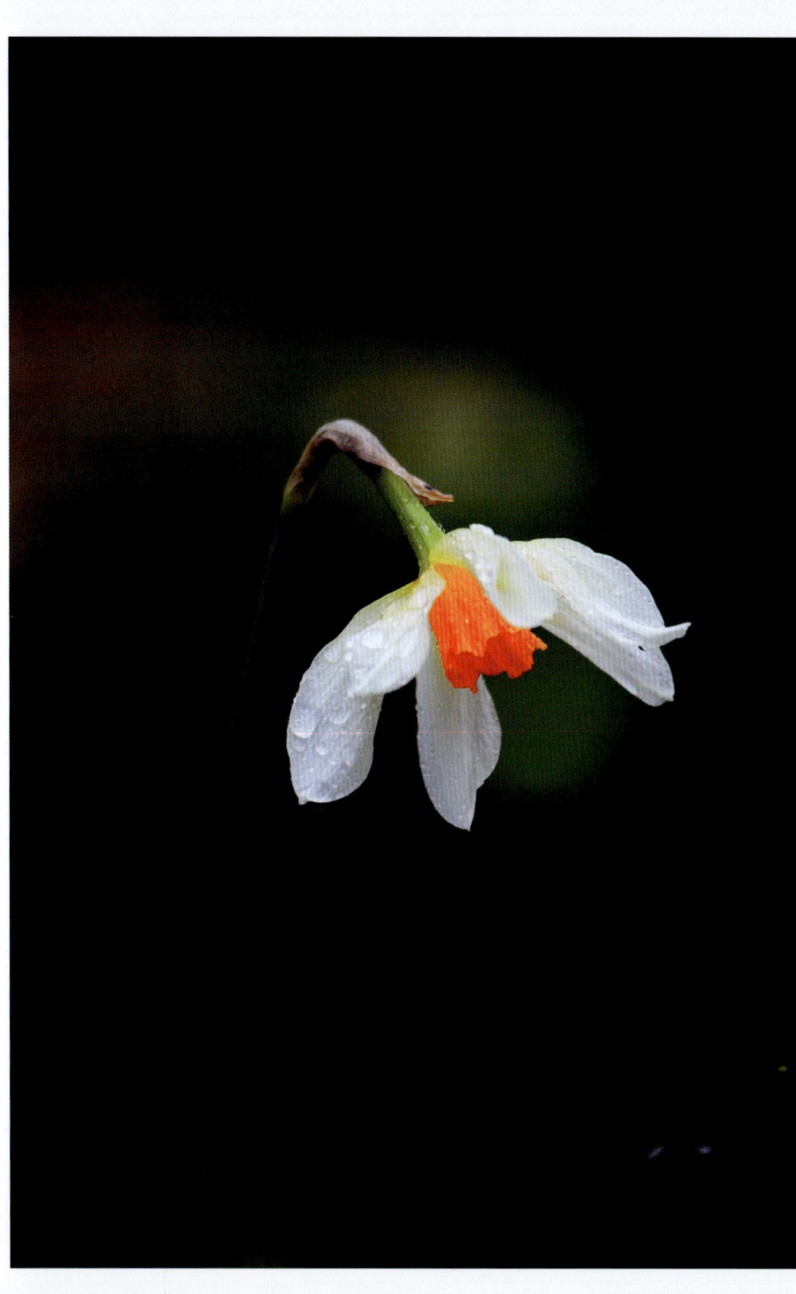

DELICATE DAFFODIL GROWING WILD
Oliver's favourite

"I like the detail in this one – you can see the droplets on the petals. The white petals really stand out on the dark green background, don't they? I like that."

ROCK DAISIES

A cottage garden staple.

COMMON DAISIES

Oliver likes to lie down or put his camera on the ground to capture daisies. He was pleased with this image because he liked the way one daisy was taller than the rest and looked like it was reaching up. It is one of his mother's favourite images. She says it reminds her of Oliver and the expression 'why fit in when you were born to stand out?'

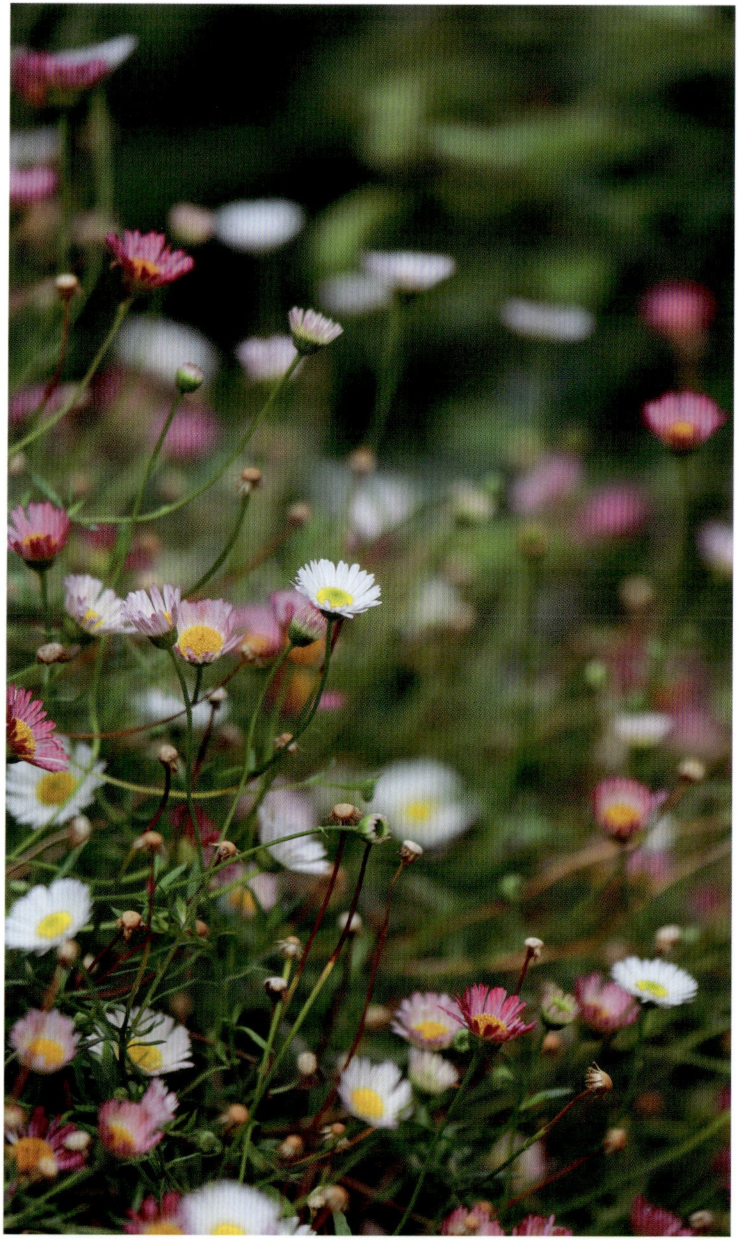

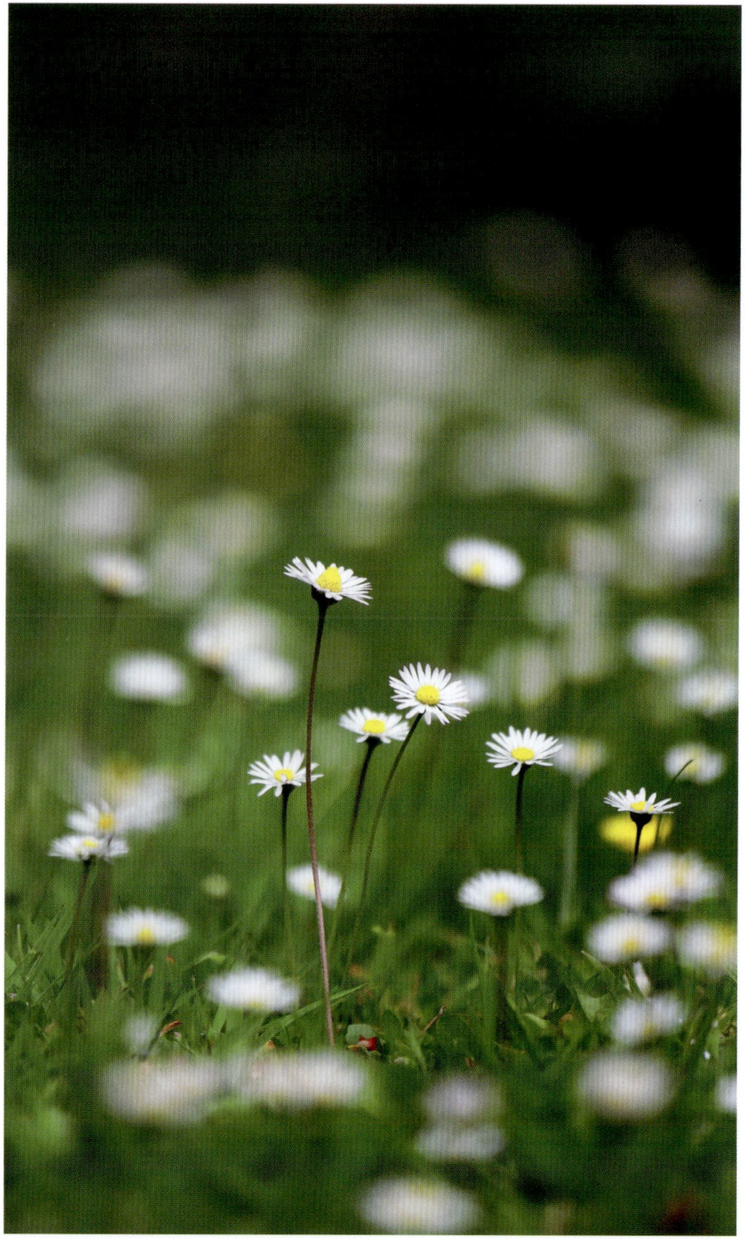

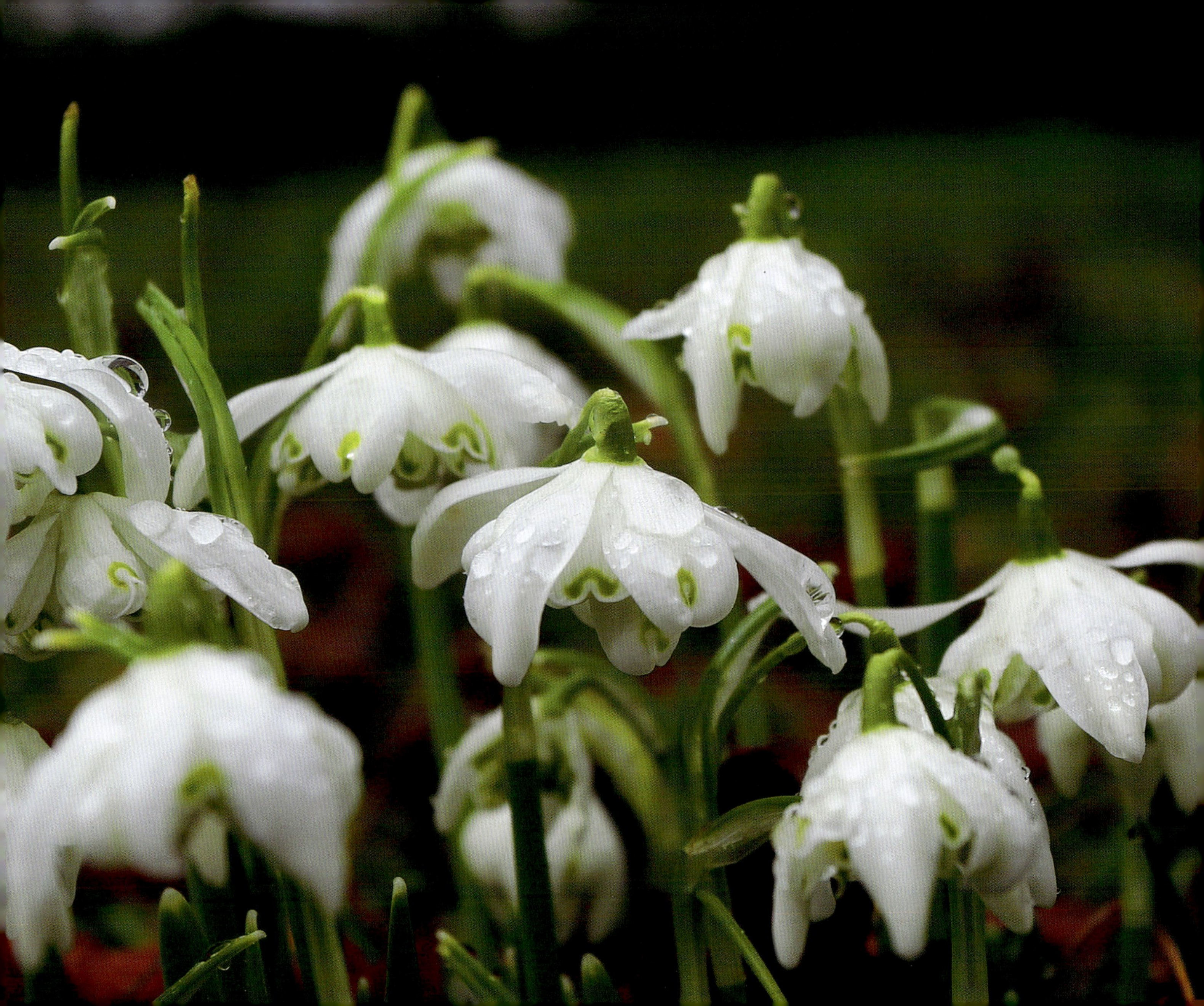

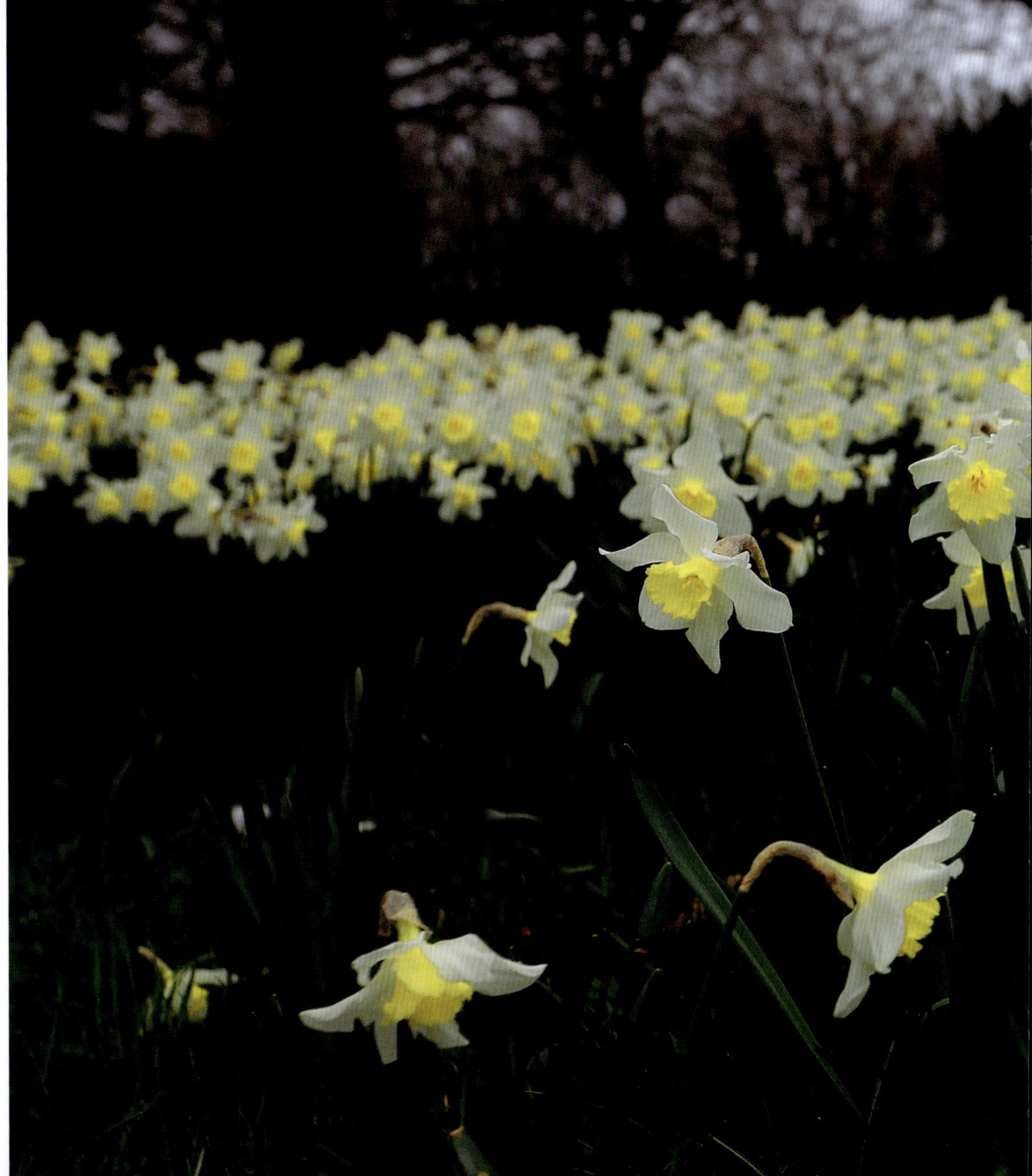

Oliver's favourite

"I chose this one because the daffodils really stand out. They are so bright and there's lots of them. The day was quite dark but the daffodils were bright."

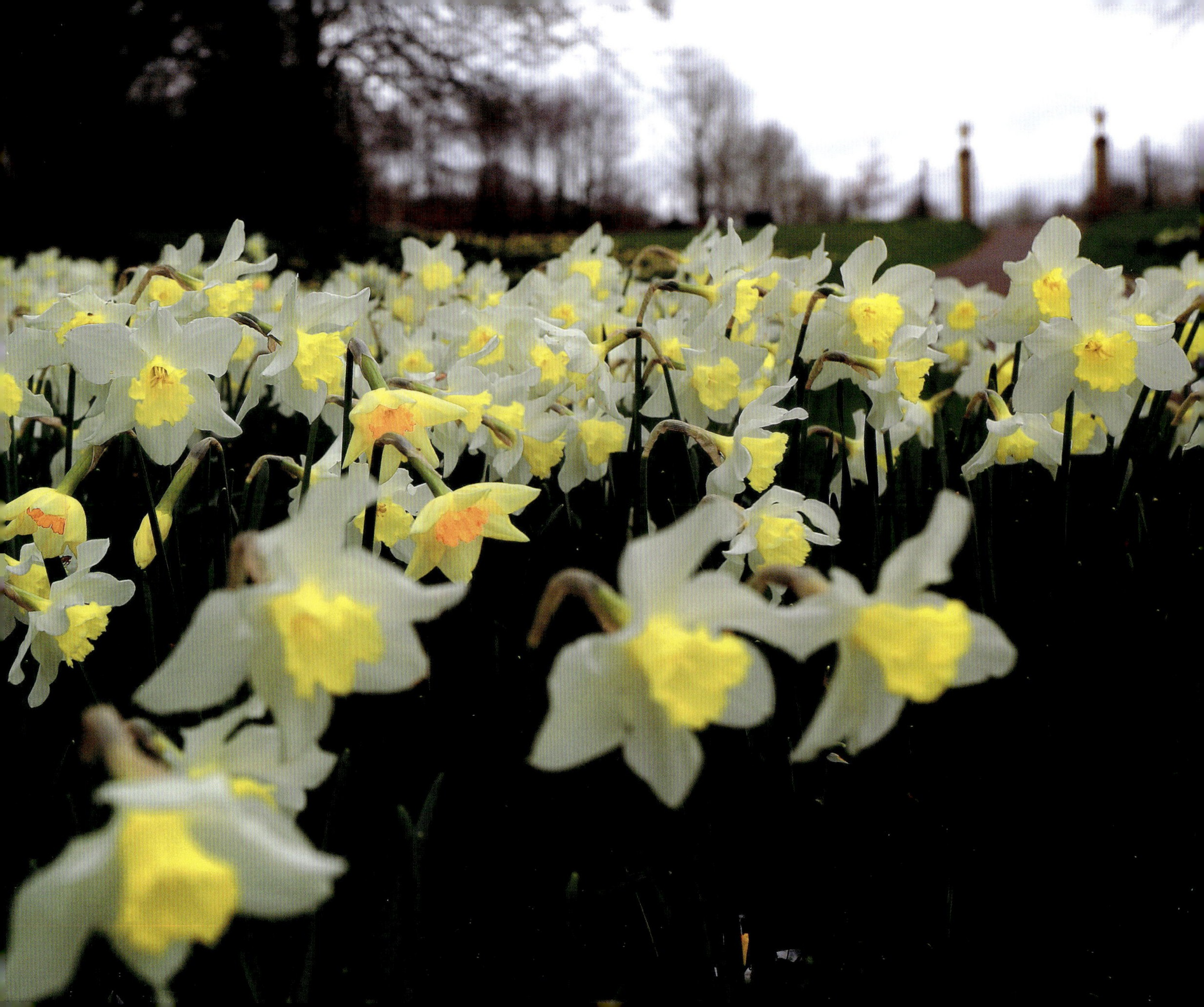

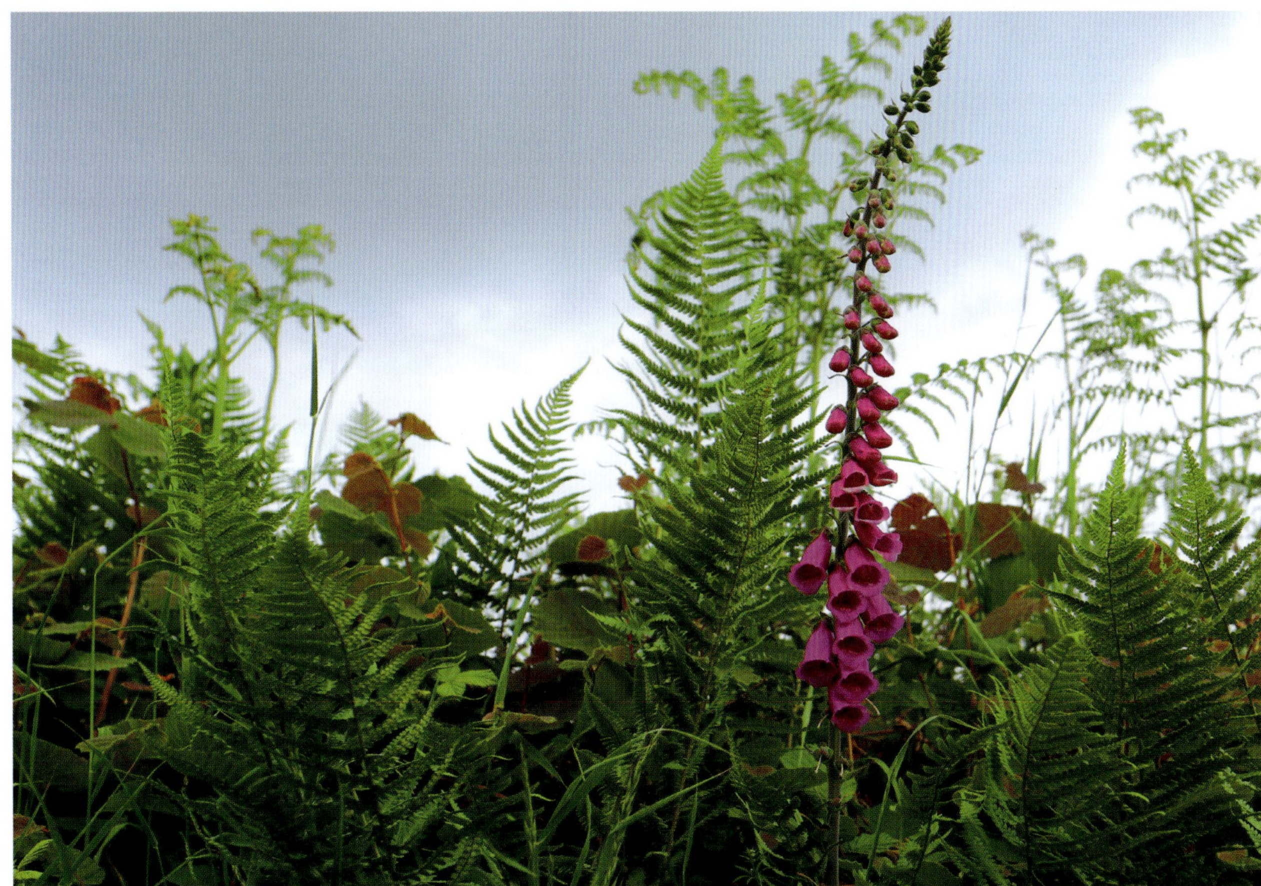

ROADSIDE FOXGLOVE AND FERNS

This is a very typical roadside view found along so many of our country lanes. Foxglove spikes and frondy ferns wave in the breeze and bring bolts of colour to the edges of our fields and paths.

ROADSIDE POPPIES
Oliver's favourite

"When we were having a drive-around together, me and my mum, I shouted 'Stop!' because I saw these bright red little poppies and I thought 'Oooh, they would look good'. I really like the bright red and the dark green behind. There was a big canvas of this at my exhibition and a lady from Wales bought it."

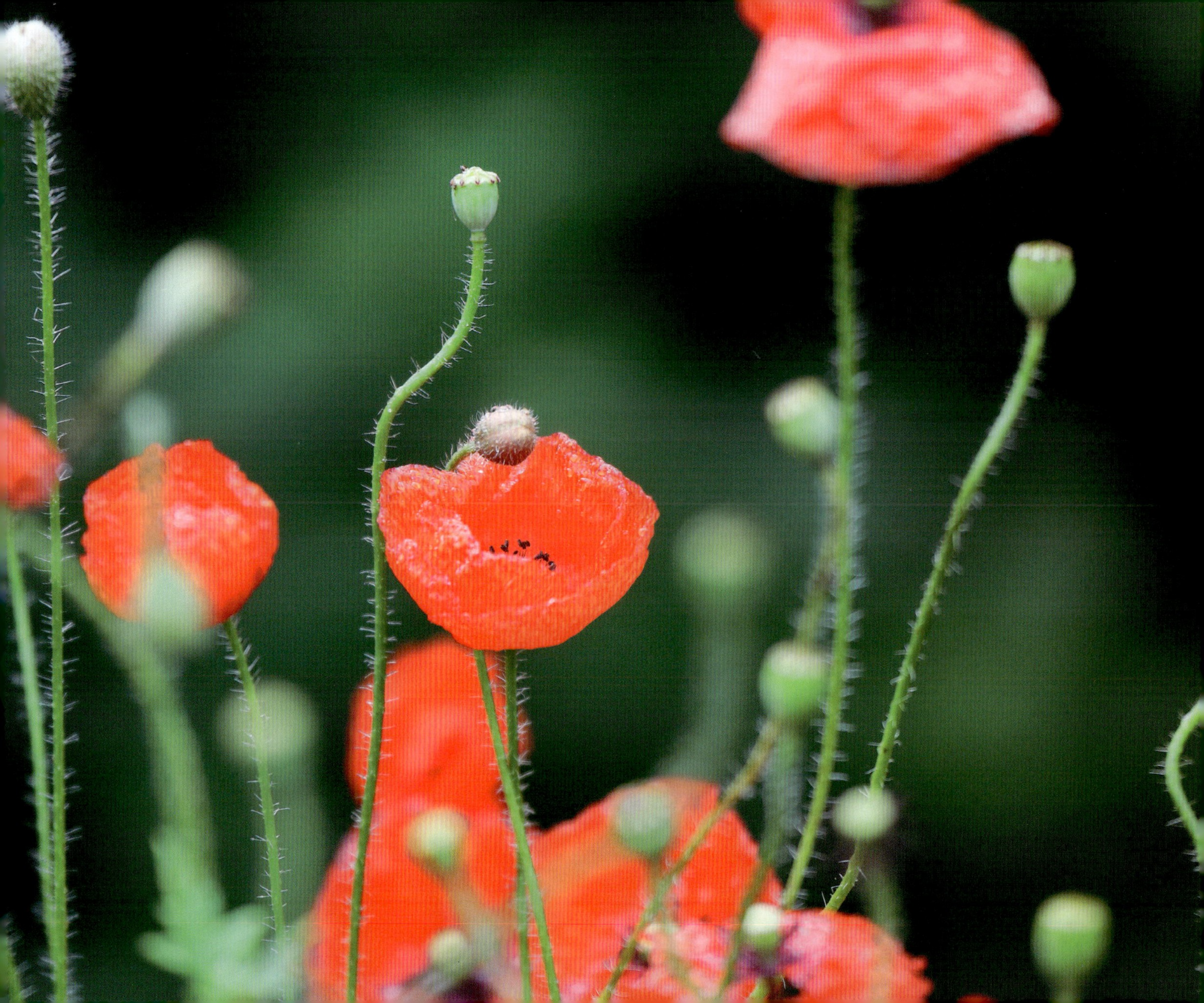

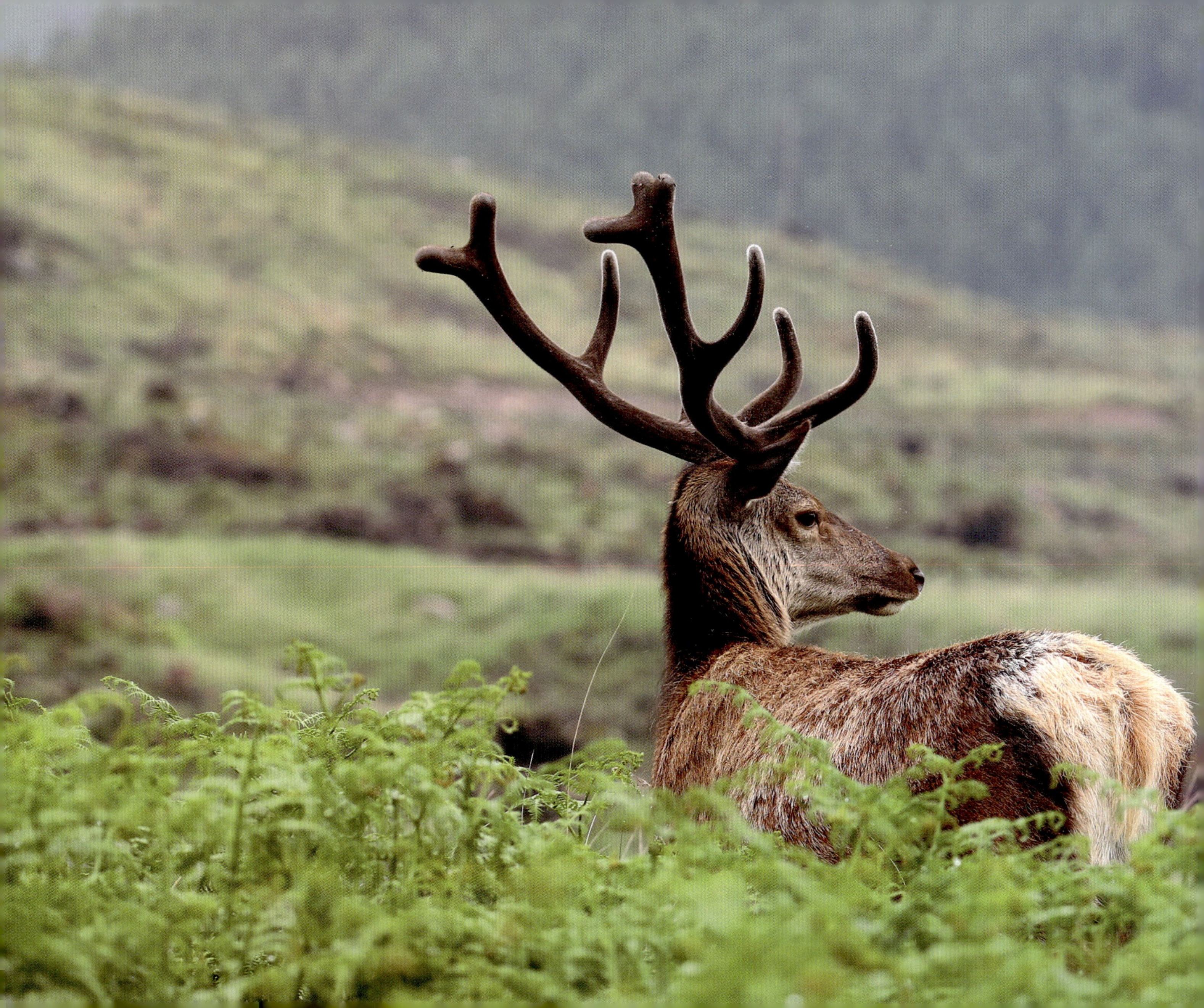

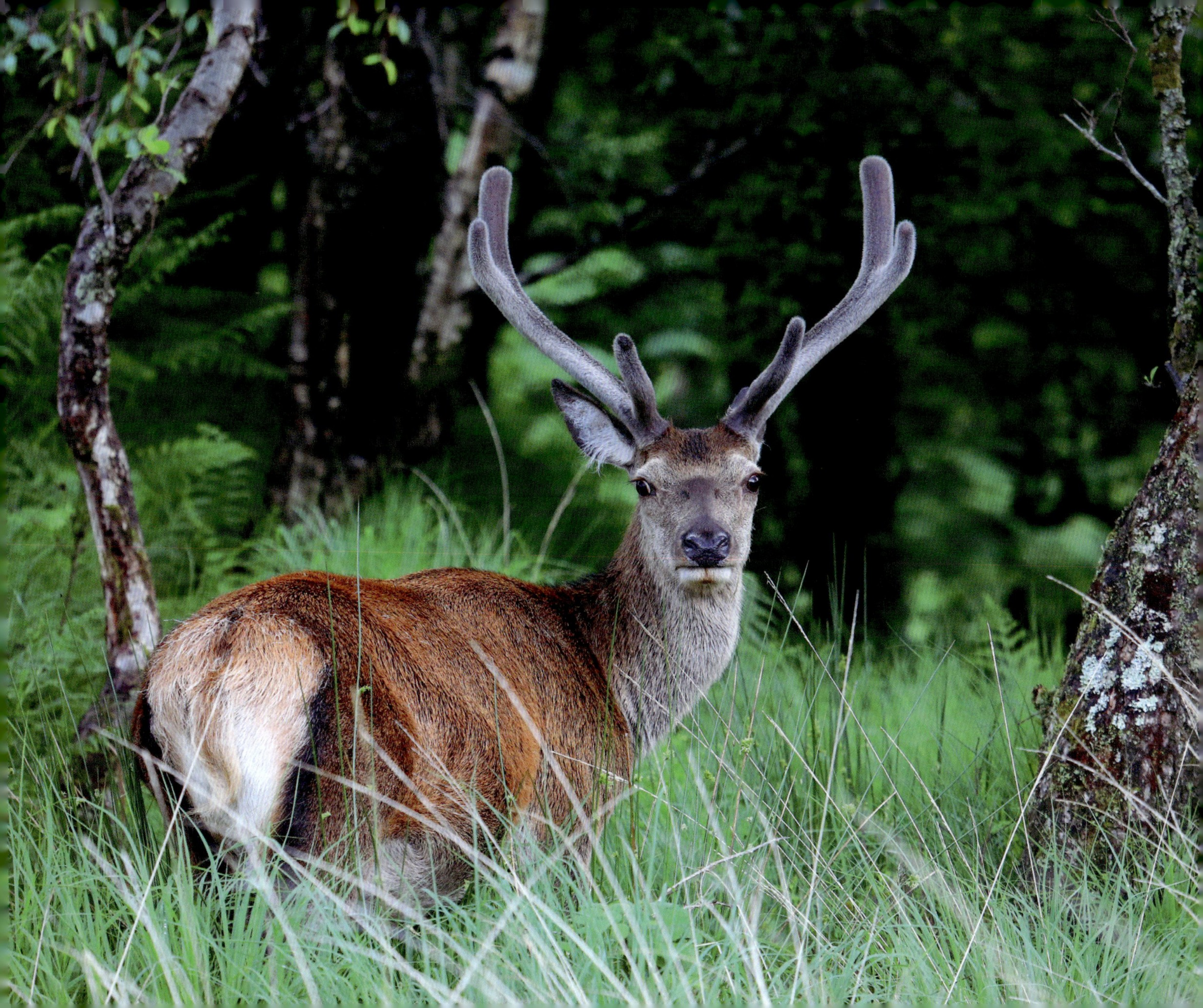

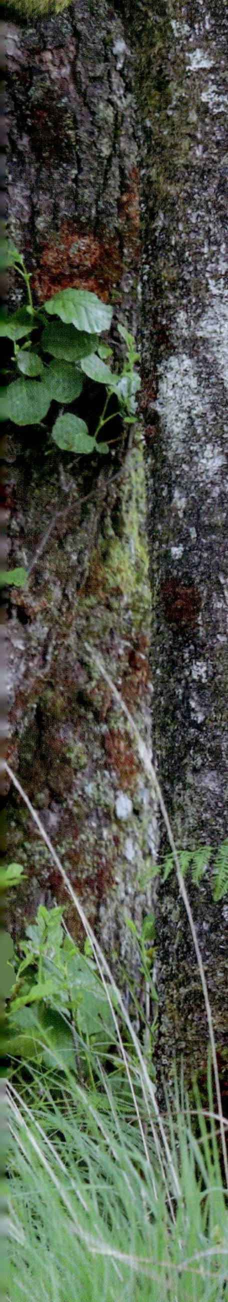

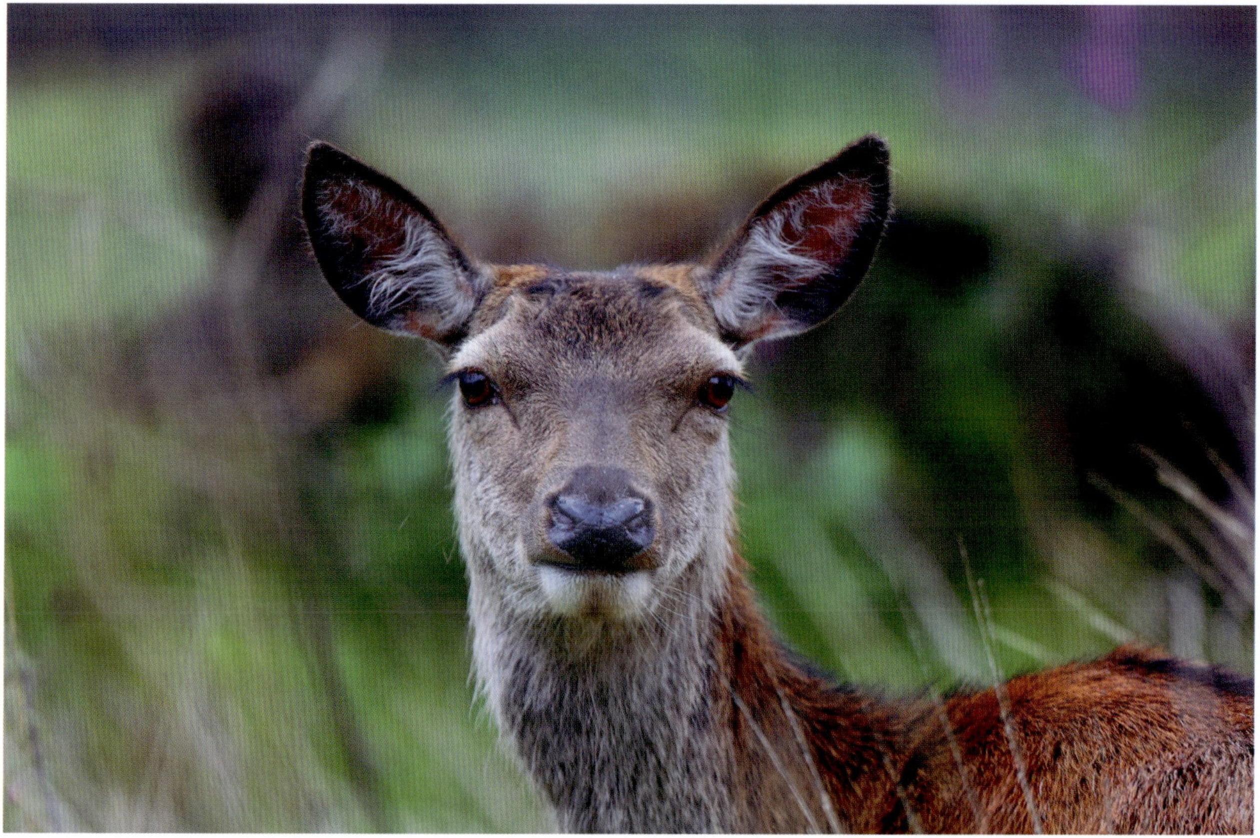

RED DEER STAG
Oliver's favourite

"I like the detail of the stag, and the colours on the tree. He's right in the middle of my picture and I got him perfect! I got lots of pictures of red deer when we were in Scotland."

RED DEER – DOE IN THE BRACKEN

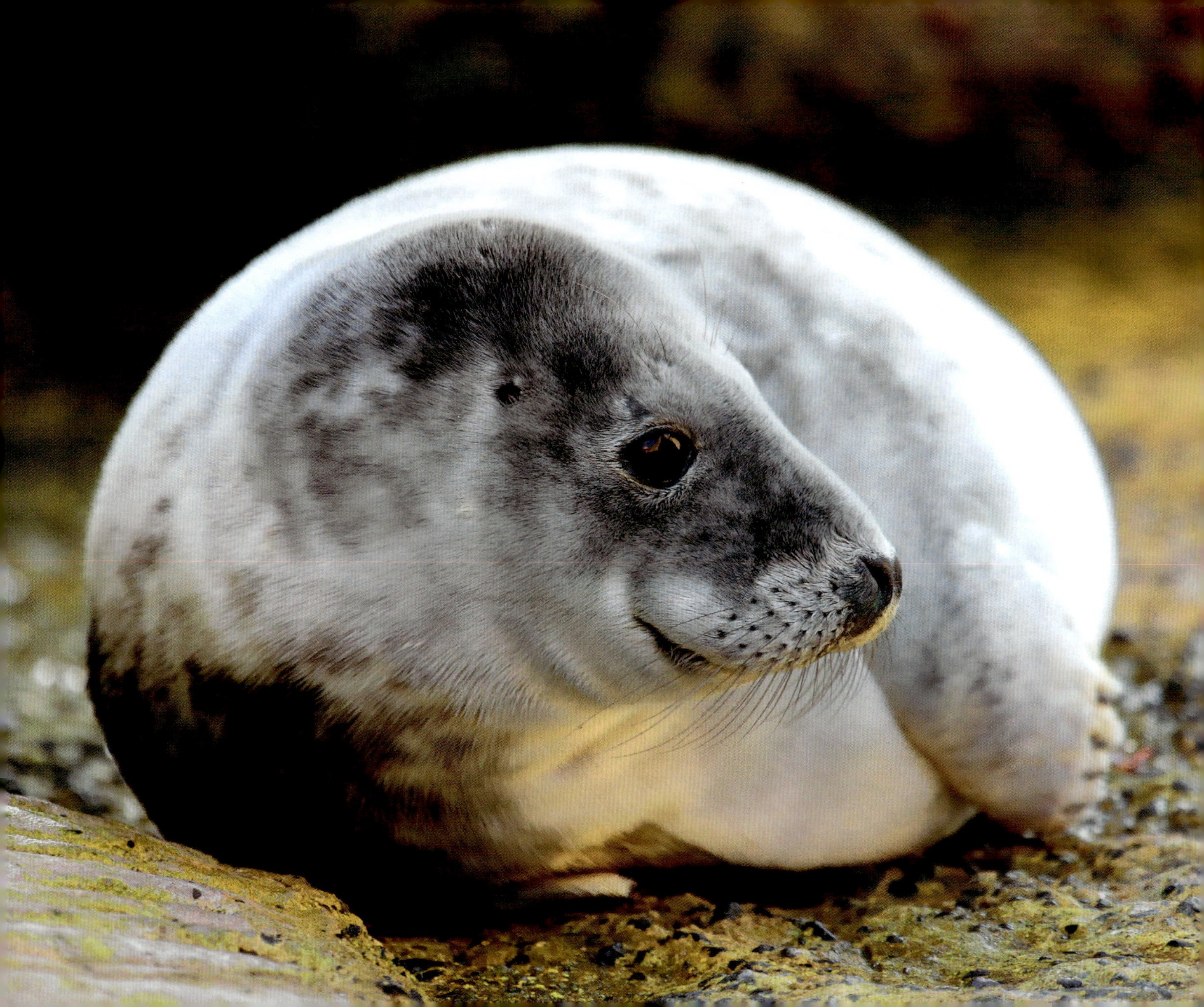

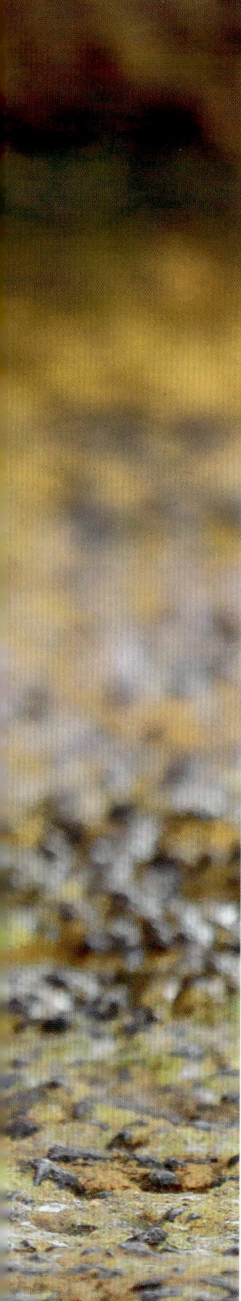

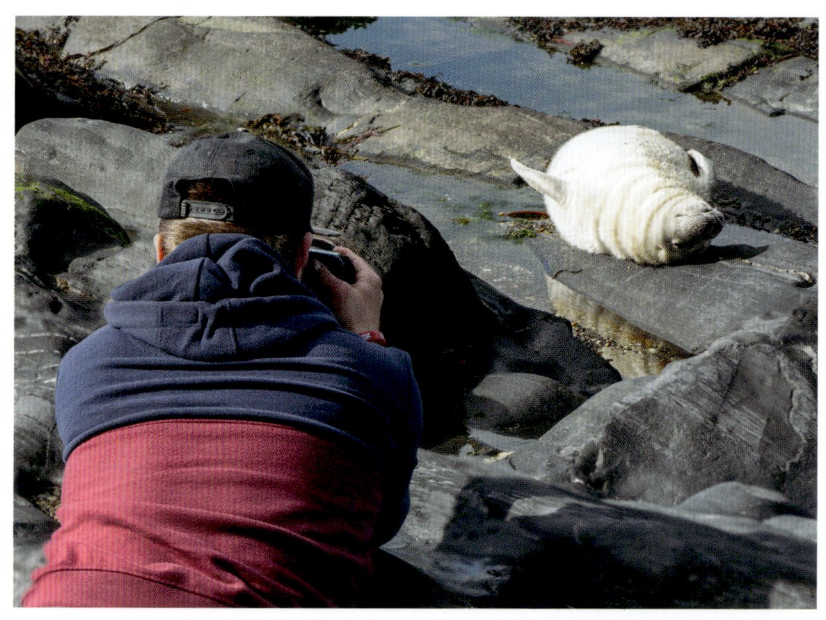

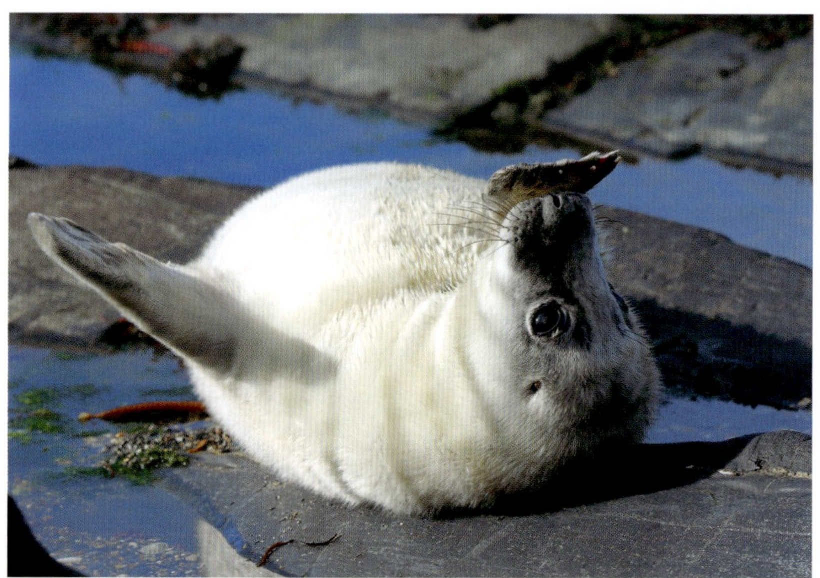

Oliver was very quiet and
patient when he took these seal
pup pictures.

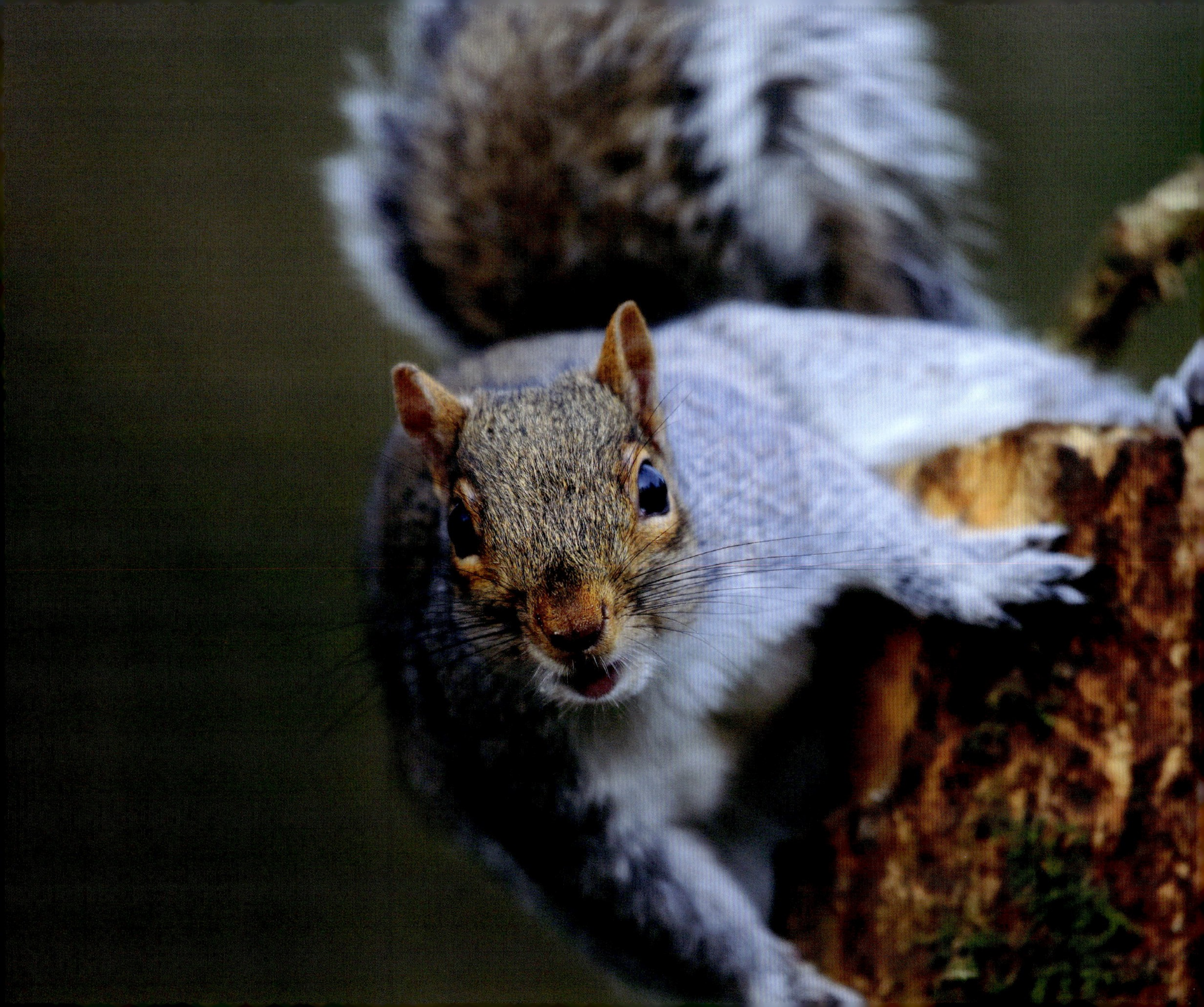

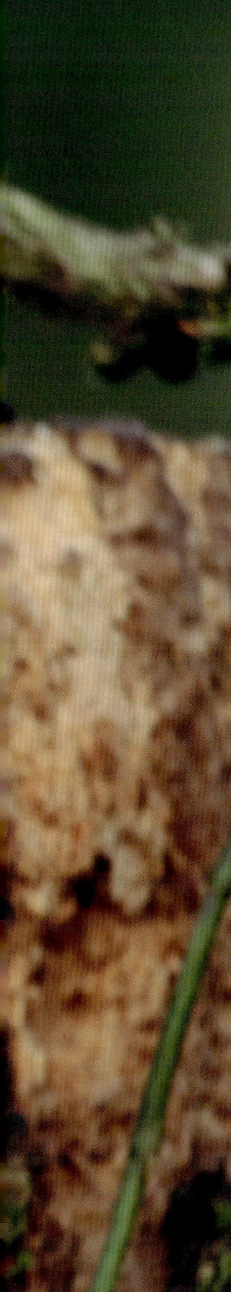

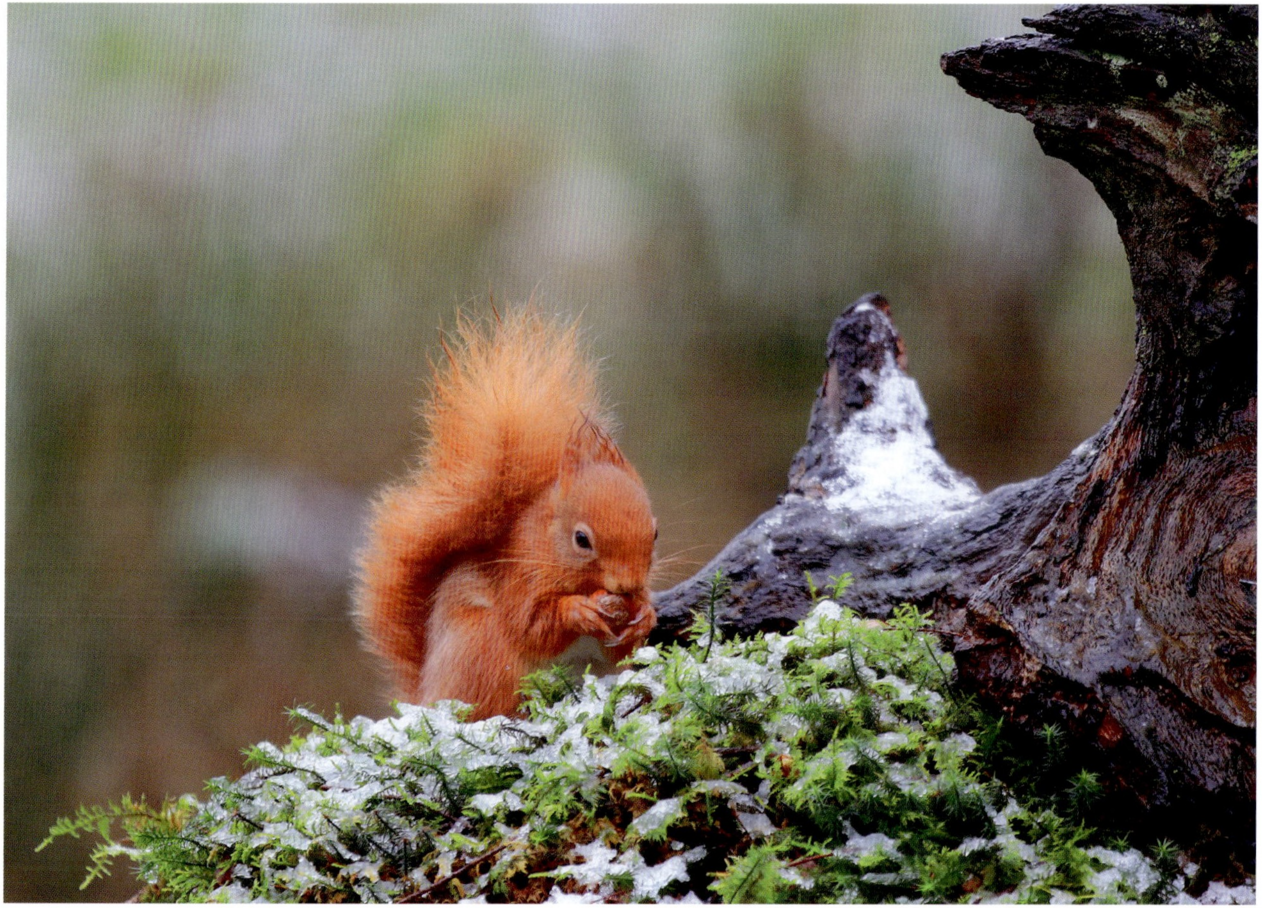

RED SQUIRREL ON A FROSTY MORNING

Another great image captured from one of Alan McFadyen's hides.

NOTE from IOLO WILLIAMS

Oliver Hellowell is a very talented individual with a rare eye for photography. His first book, *Oliver's Birds,* is a wonderful collection of avian photographs, but this one is even better. Here, Ollie combines nature with landscape and travels further afield for his subjects.

Ollie sees photographs where us mere mortals just see shades of light and dark. Even more impressive is his ability to transform what he sees into a stunning photograph. That Ollie has Down Syndrome is completely immaterial; he is just an outstanding photographer.

These days, Ollie is also a celebrity, having been featured in numerous magazine and newspaper articles, travelled to America, and appeared on TV far more often than I have. I'm delighted to say that all this attention has not changed him one bit. He is still the same witty and kind individual I first met nearly a decade ago. All I ask is that I can hang on to his coat-tails as he deservedly makes his way to superstardom – and I'll even promise to buy the bacon butties!

Please buy this book. I can guarantee that you will not be disappointed.

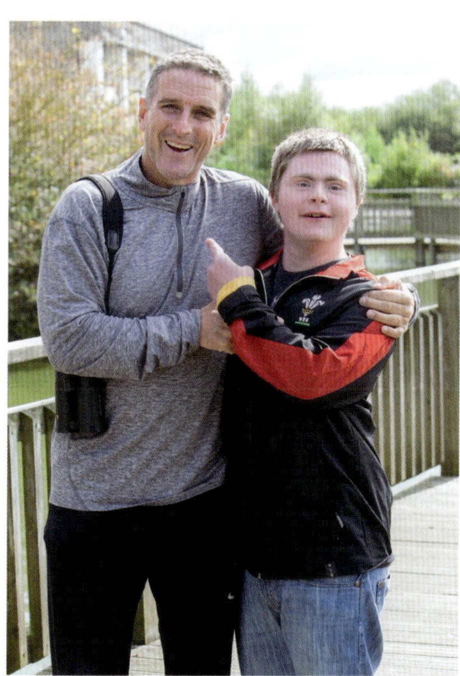

Iolo Williams
Welsh naturalist and wildlife presenter

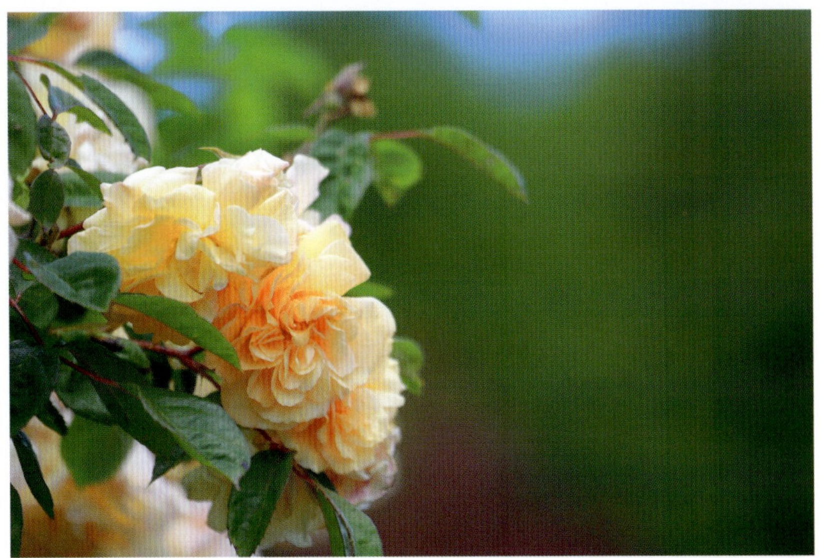

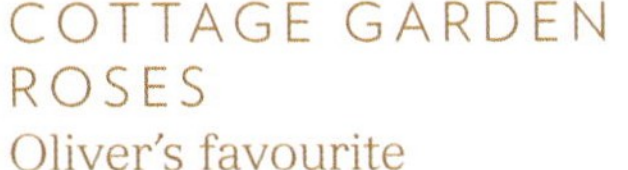

COTTAGE GARDEN ROSES
Oliver's favourite

"In the spring and the summer, me and my mum do 'flower drive-arounds' and we look for lovely flowers for me to take pictures of. I like the composition of this one with the roses on the left. I like the blurry background and the green space in it, and that peachy colour of the roses."

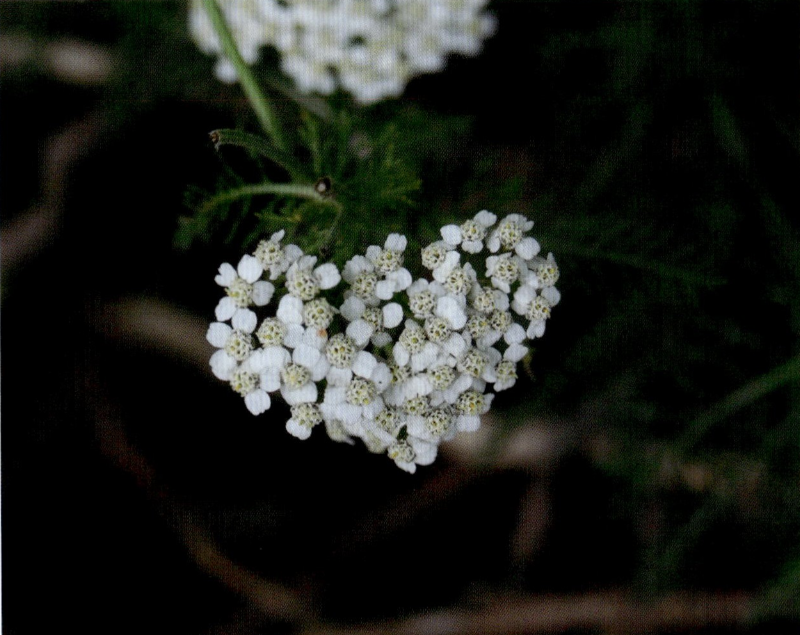

HEART-SHAPED WILD YARROW (ARCHILLEA)

Whilst wandering around Skenfrith Castle by the river, Oliver spotted this heart-shaped wild yarrow and knowing how much his mum likes hearts, he took the picture for her.

SNOWDROPS – THE FIRST SIGN OF SPRING

Oliver put his camera on the ground to capture this beautiful clump of snowdrops and was very pleased that he got some of the big dew droplets on the petals, nice and sharp and in focus.

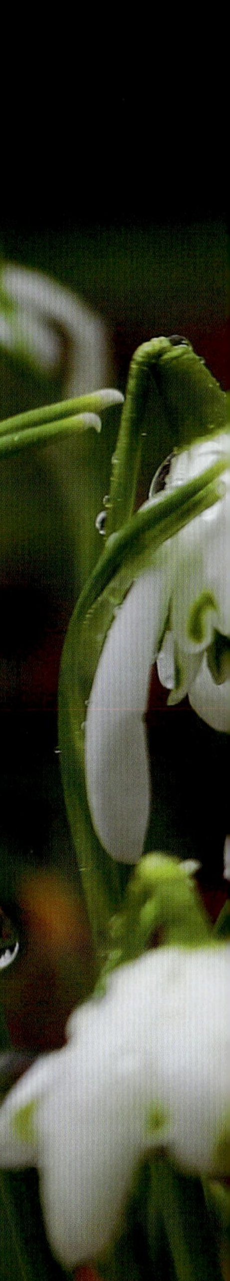

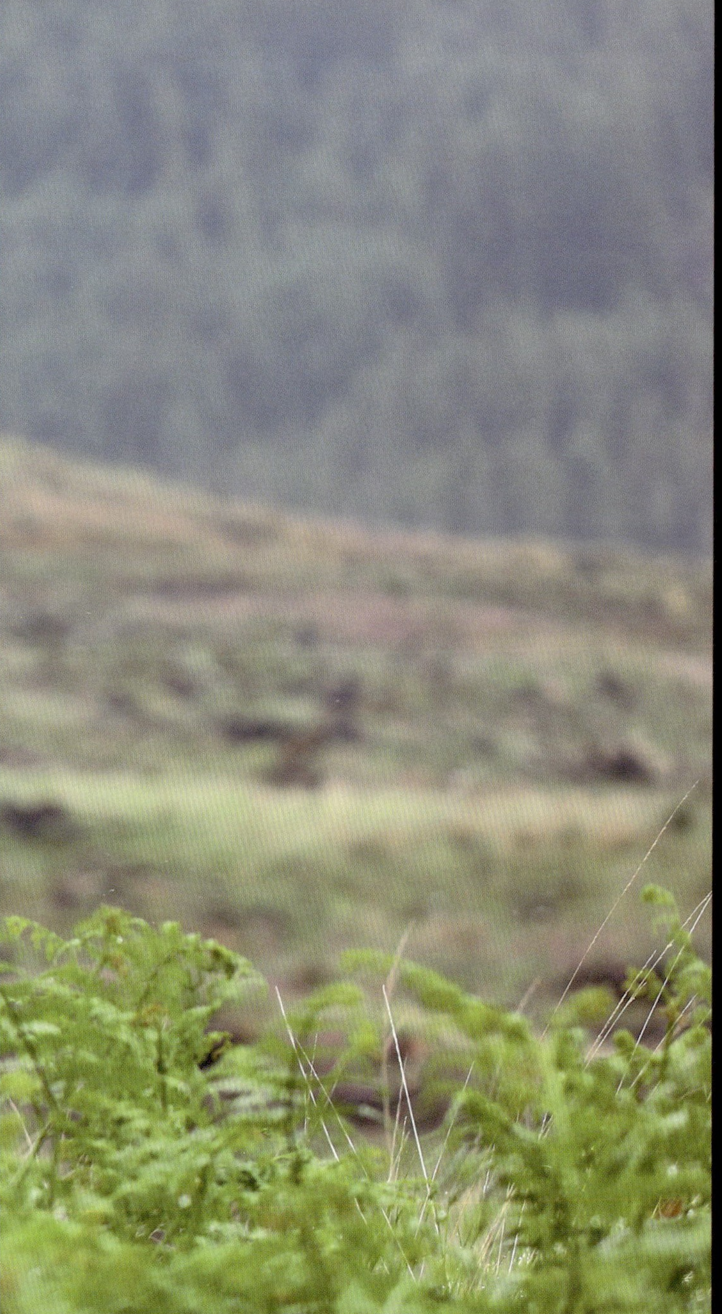

WILDLIFE

Oliver found it very difficult to narrow down his 'wildlife' images for this chapter, but hopes that this small selection still provides you with a taste of the wonderful variation of wildlife we are fortunate enough to enjoy. There is *so* much missing, there will need to be another book!

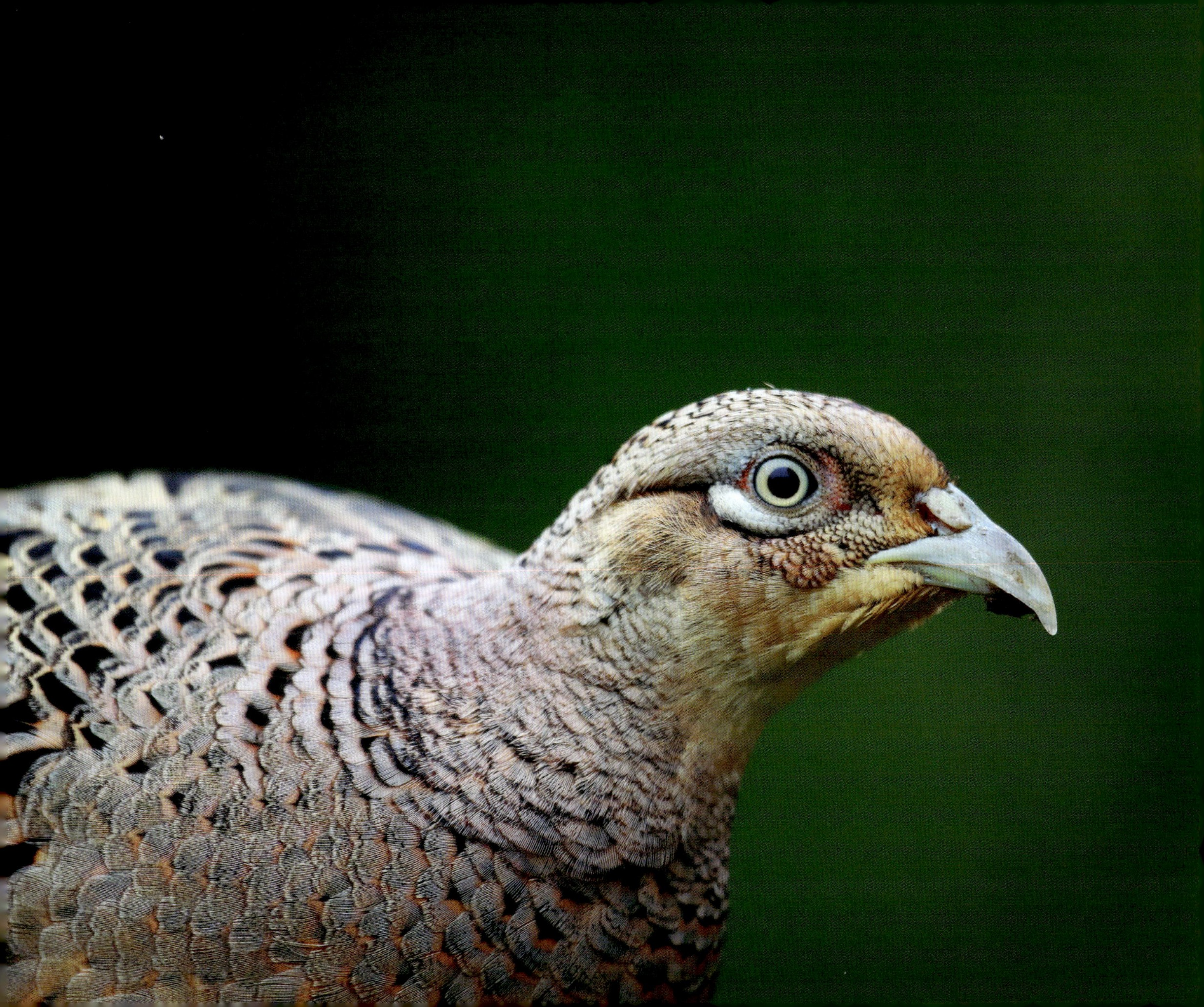

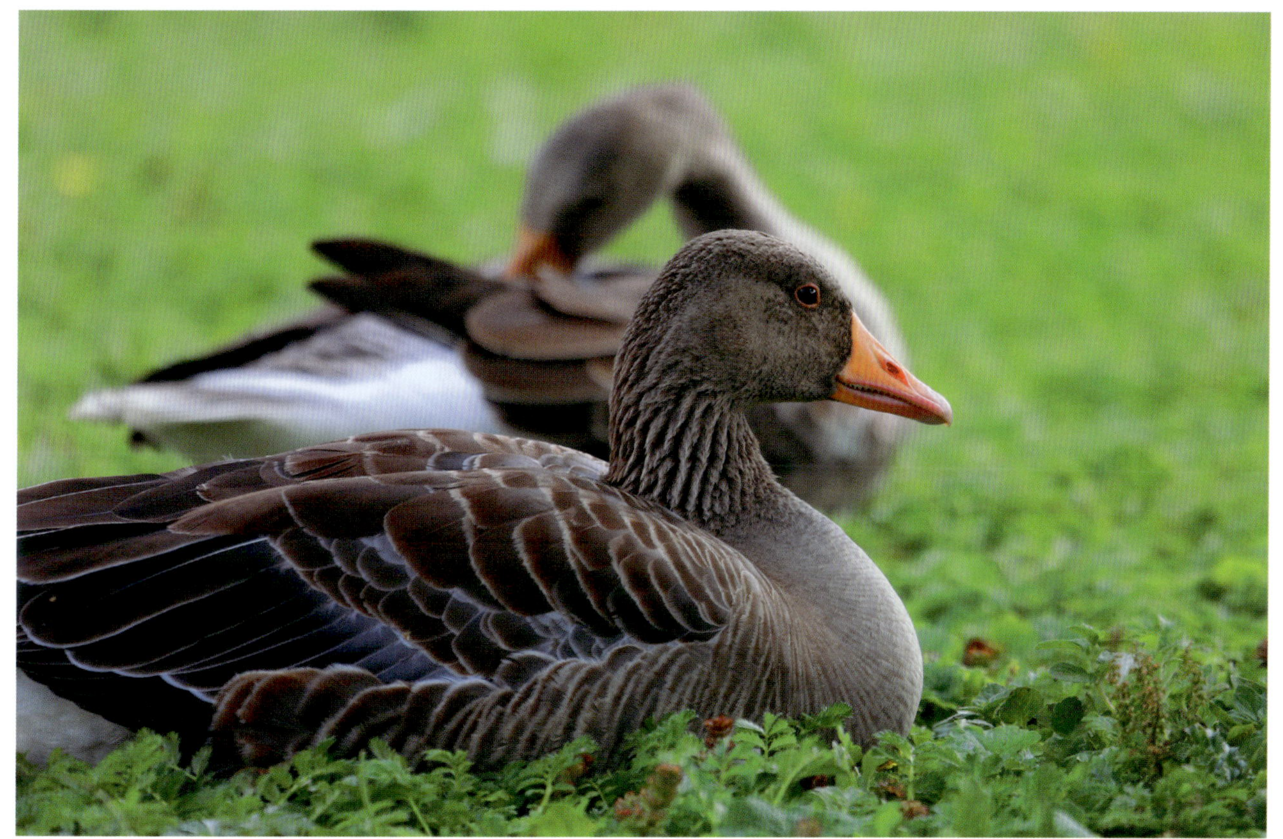

FEMALE PHEASANT
Oliver's favourite

"Female pheasants aren't just brown; they're really colourful actually! I like the detail of the eye and the beak here. And I like the dark green background."

GREYLAG GOOSE
Oliver's favourite

"I like the feathers in this picture, and the beak and the colours. I like the goose at the front in focus with all the detail and the background behind out of focus."

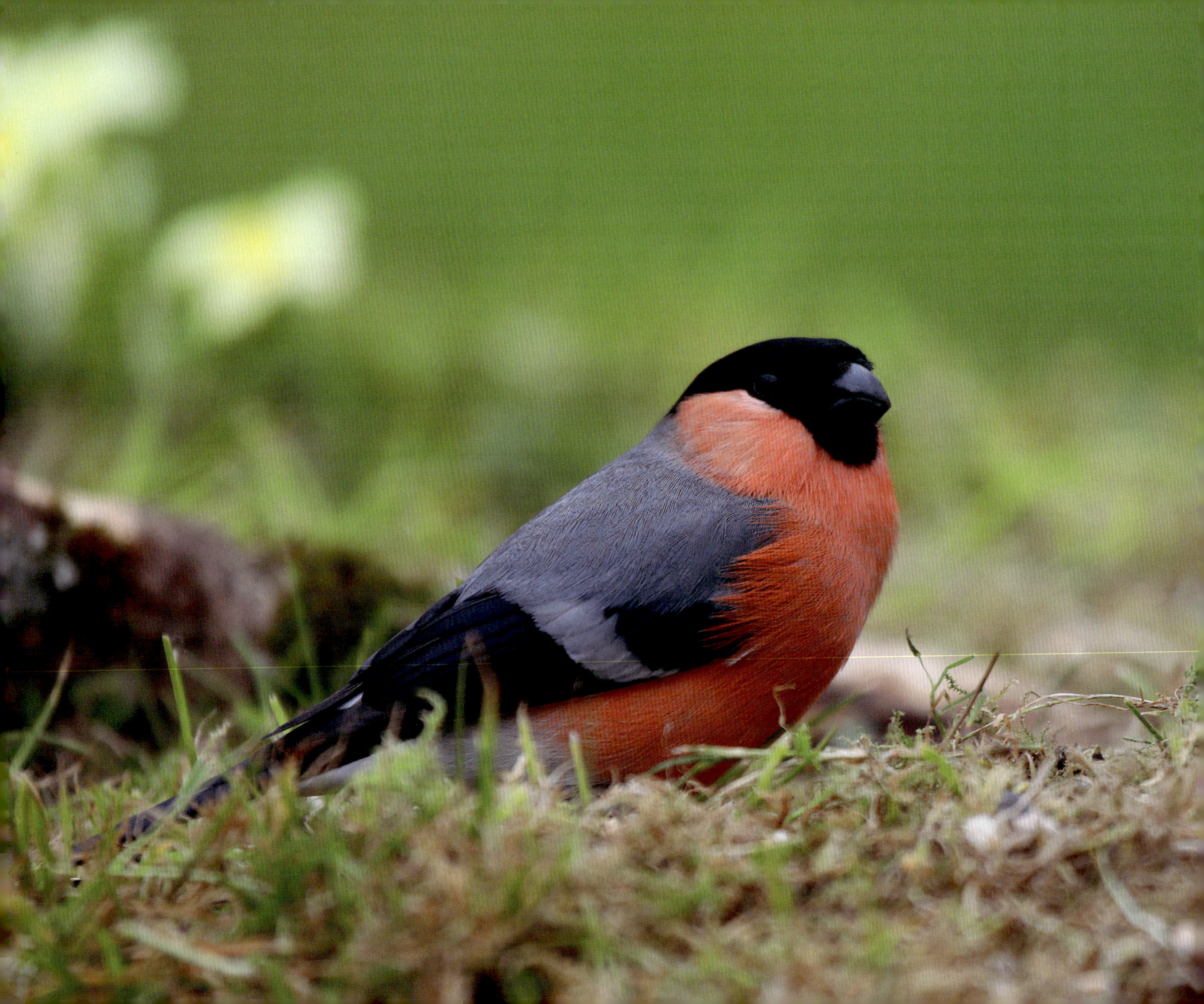

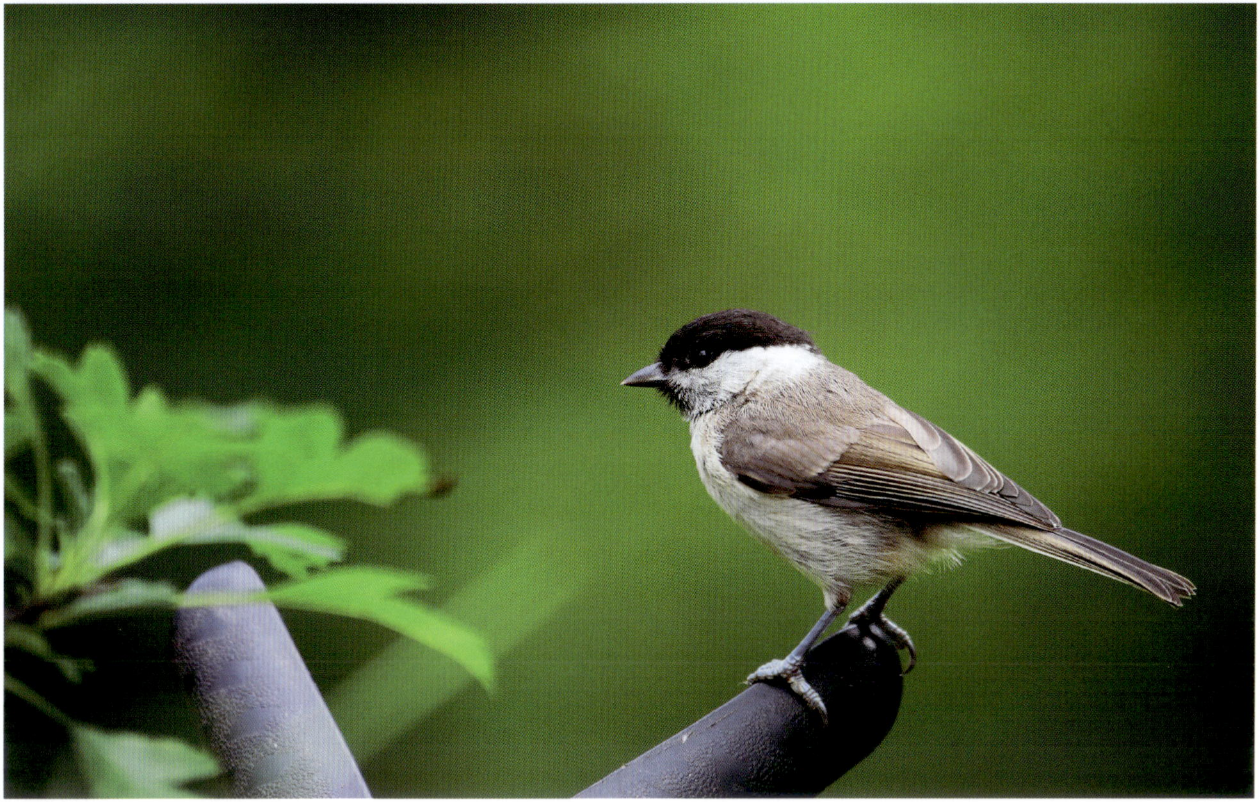

MALE BULLFINCH
Oliver's favourite

"It was Mother's Day, and I got my first ever bullfinch picture. My mum said it was the best present! It was after my book of birds was published so it didn't get into that book."

MARSH TIT
Oliver's favourite

"They're one of my favourite birds, and they're quite striking. It's really difficult to tell the difference between a marsh tit and a willow tit. They're almost identical."

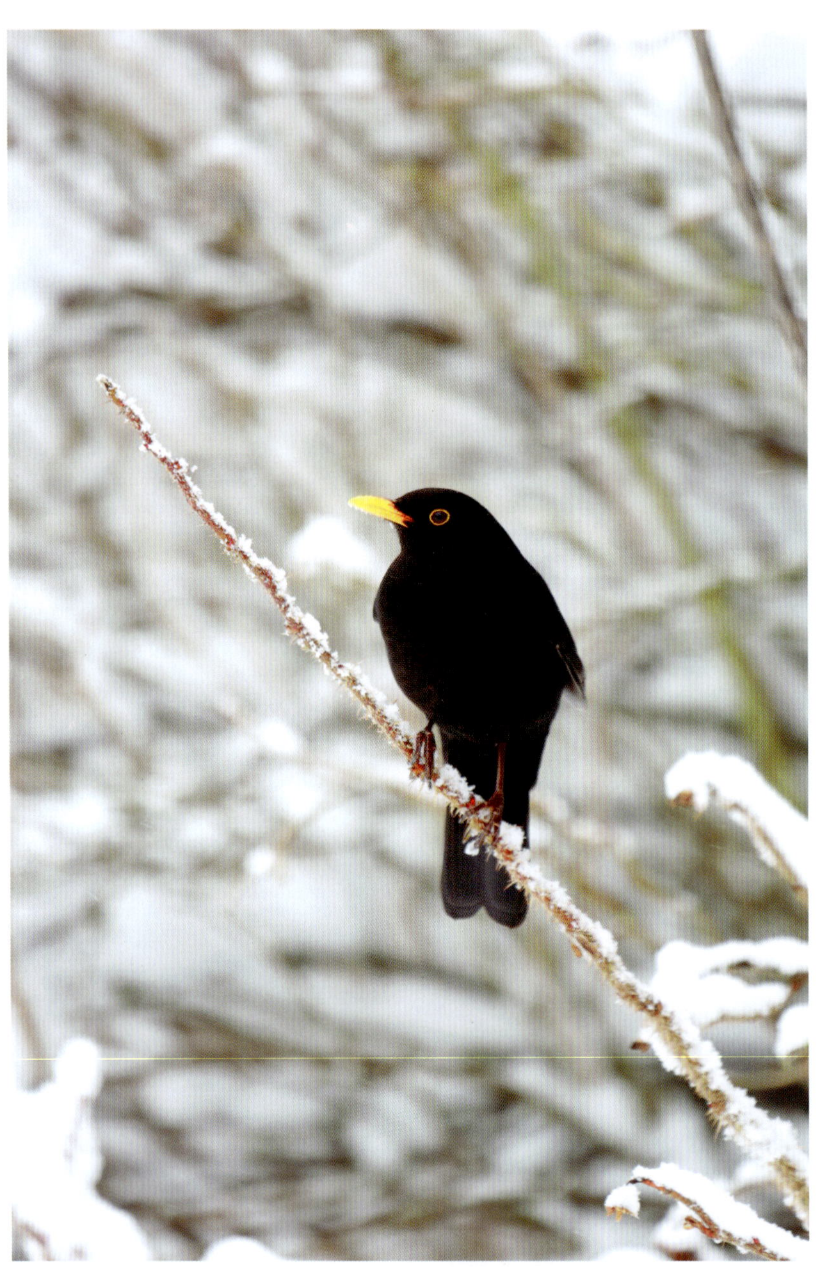

MALE BLACKBIRD IN THE SNOWY BRANCHES
Oliver's favourite

"I love blackbirds, and they are very common everywhere. I take lots of pictures of blackbirds with their bright orange beak."

KINGFISHER
Oliver's favourite

"You can see kingfishers near water because that's where they go fishing. I see them when I go fishing but they are very fast. It's really difficult to get a picture. A lovely man called Alan McFadyen invited me up to Scotland into one of his hides to get this picture and I was very pleased."

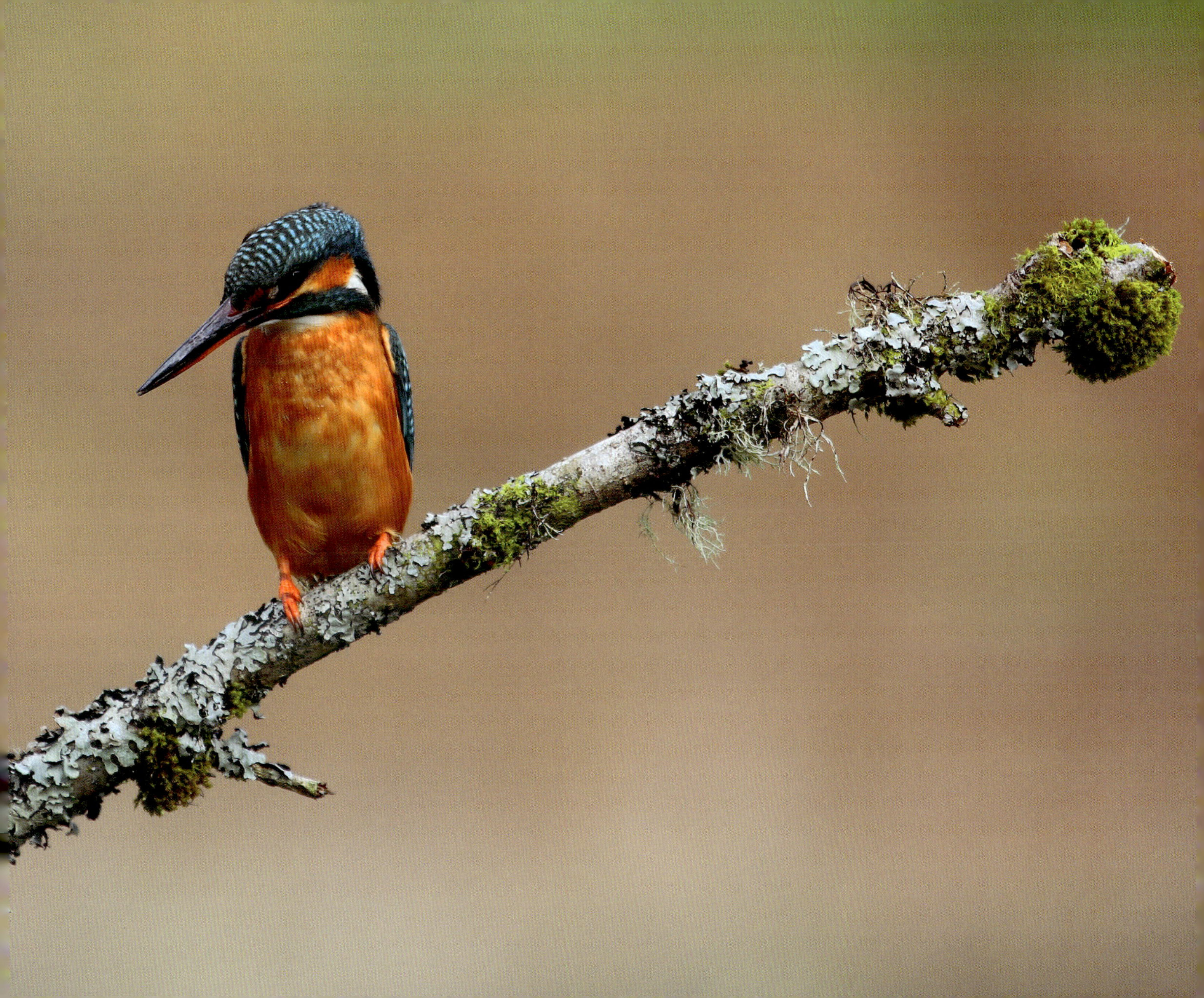

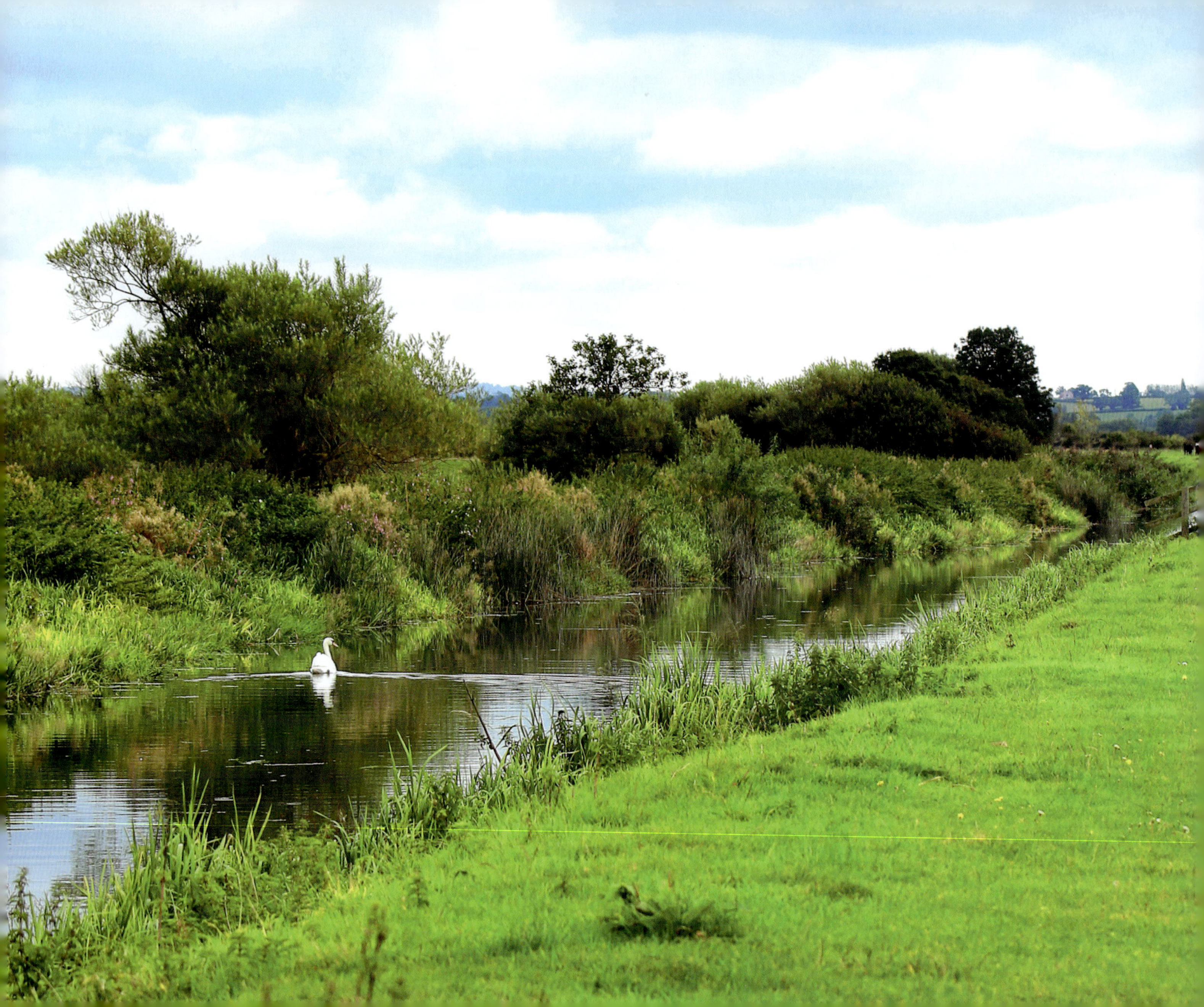

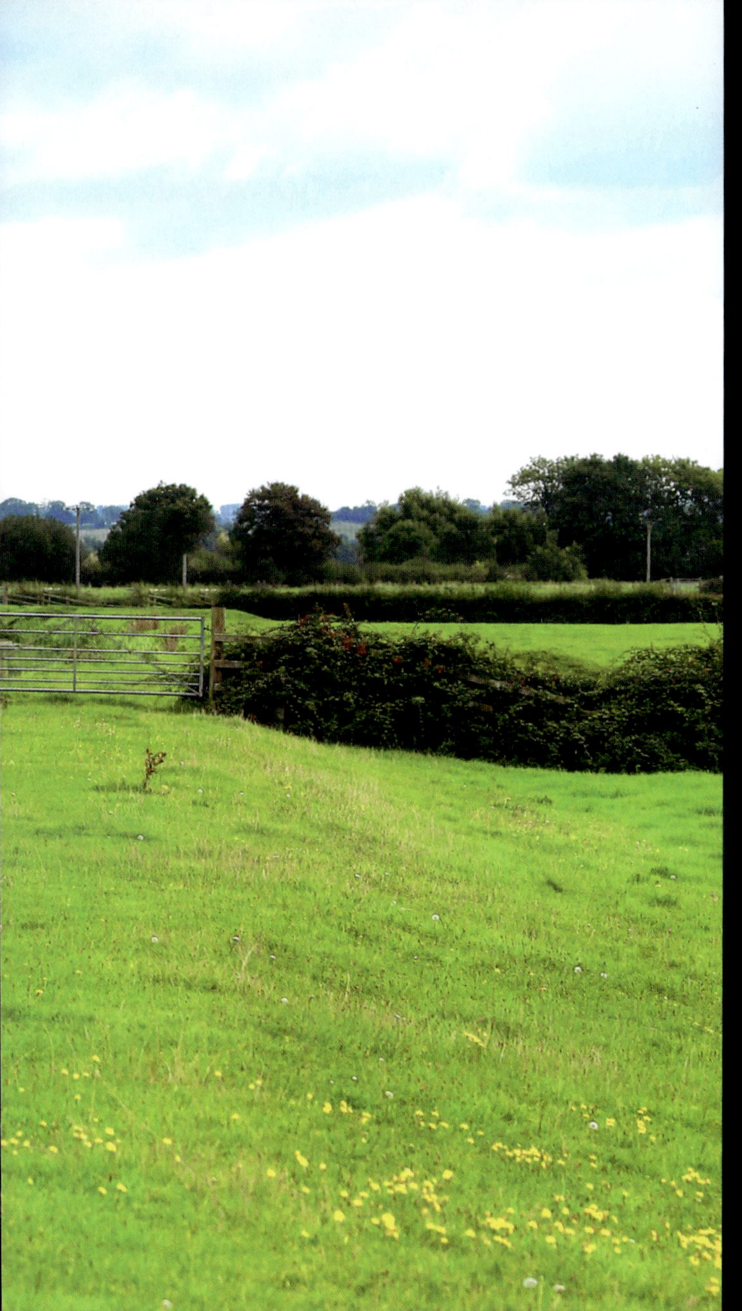

GONE FISHING

Fishing is a very popular pastime across Britain and Oliver goes fishing at least twice a month with his father Mike. He hasn't mastered fly fishing on rivers but thoroughly enjoys coarse fishing with a rod or pole on lakes and still water. He always takes his camera and usually leaves Mike to keep an eye on the fishing while he wanders off – sometimes for hours at a time – capturing countless images of the water, reflections, trees, flowers, landscape, birds, etc. Oliver considers a day out fishing and wandering with his camera in the gentle, quiet British countryside a day well spent; it's possibly one of his best and most favourite ways to spend time.

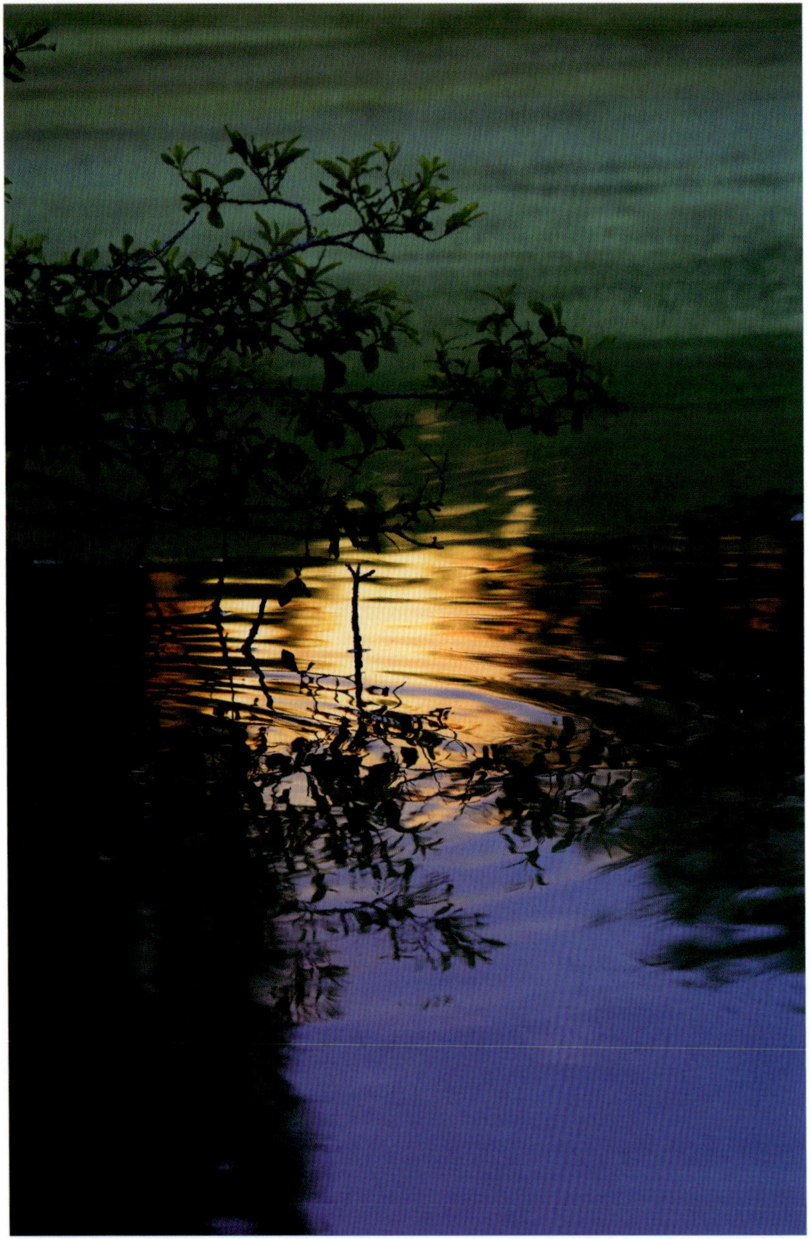

PAVYOTTS MILL – SUNSET ON THE WATER
Oliver's favourite

"I went overnight fishing for my birthday at a place called Pavyotts Mill in Somerset. I took this in the evening as the sun was going down. My fans love this picture and my mum likes it too. I like the mood of this picture and the colours in the evening light."

EVENING SUNLIGHT

This image is so typical of the paths around the many lakes Oliver likes to fish on towards the end of a day. It portrays so beautifully the simple and gentle scenes that Oliver feels so at home in and loves to capture. He loved the golden light in this one.

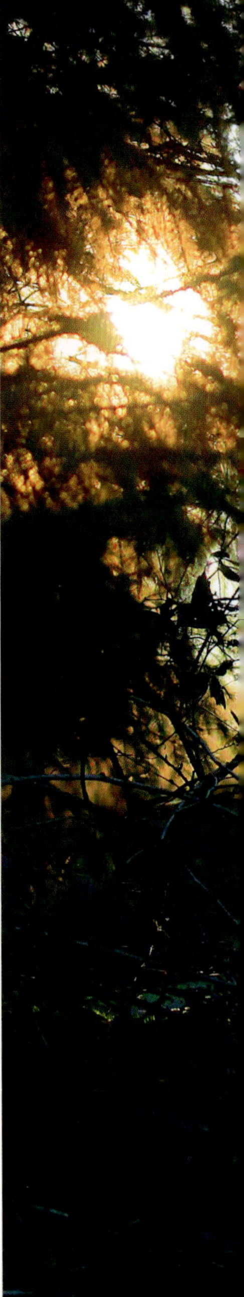

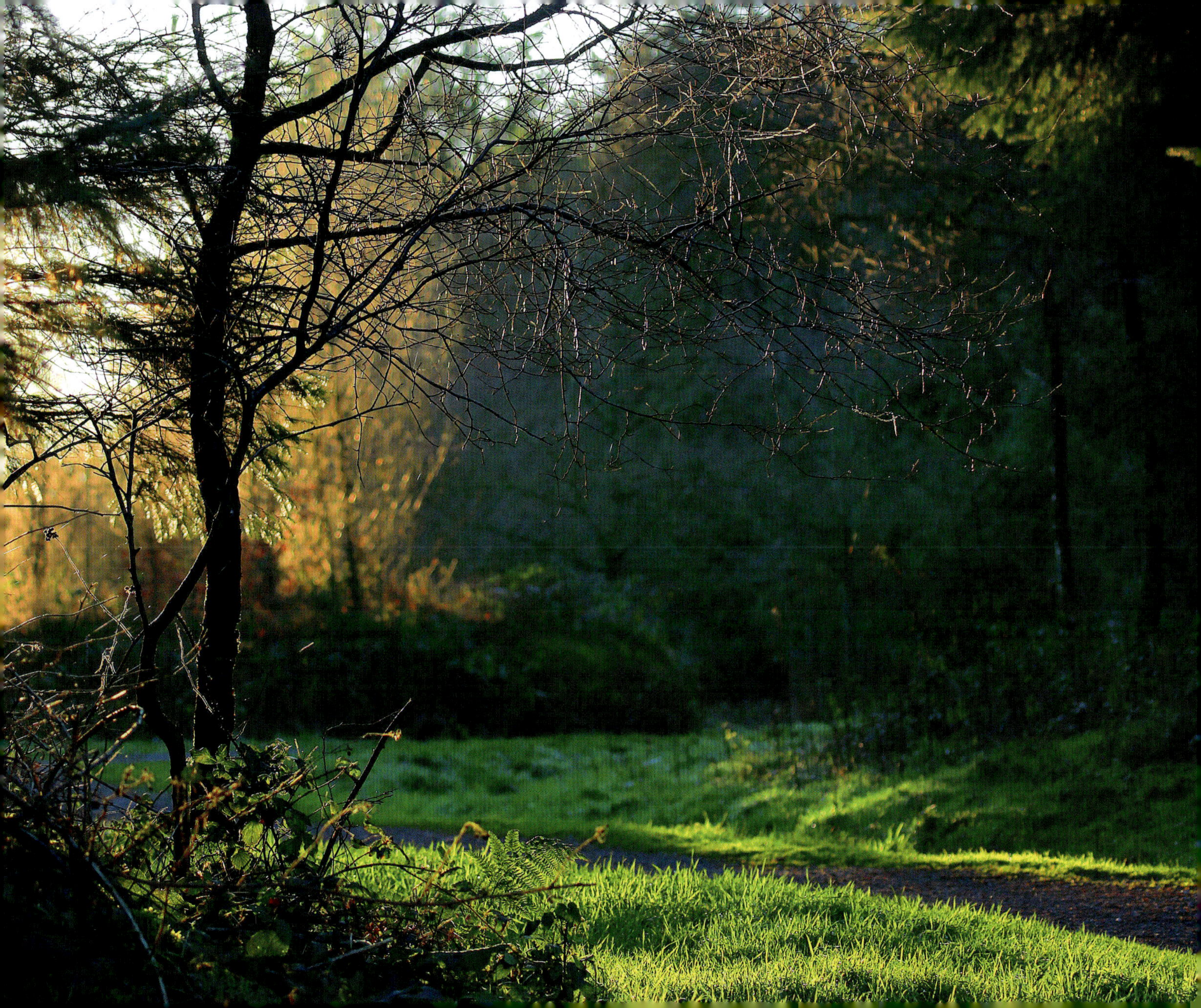

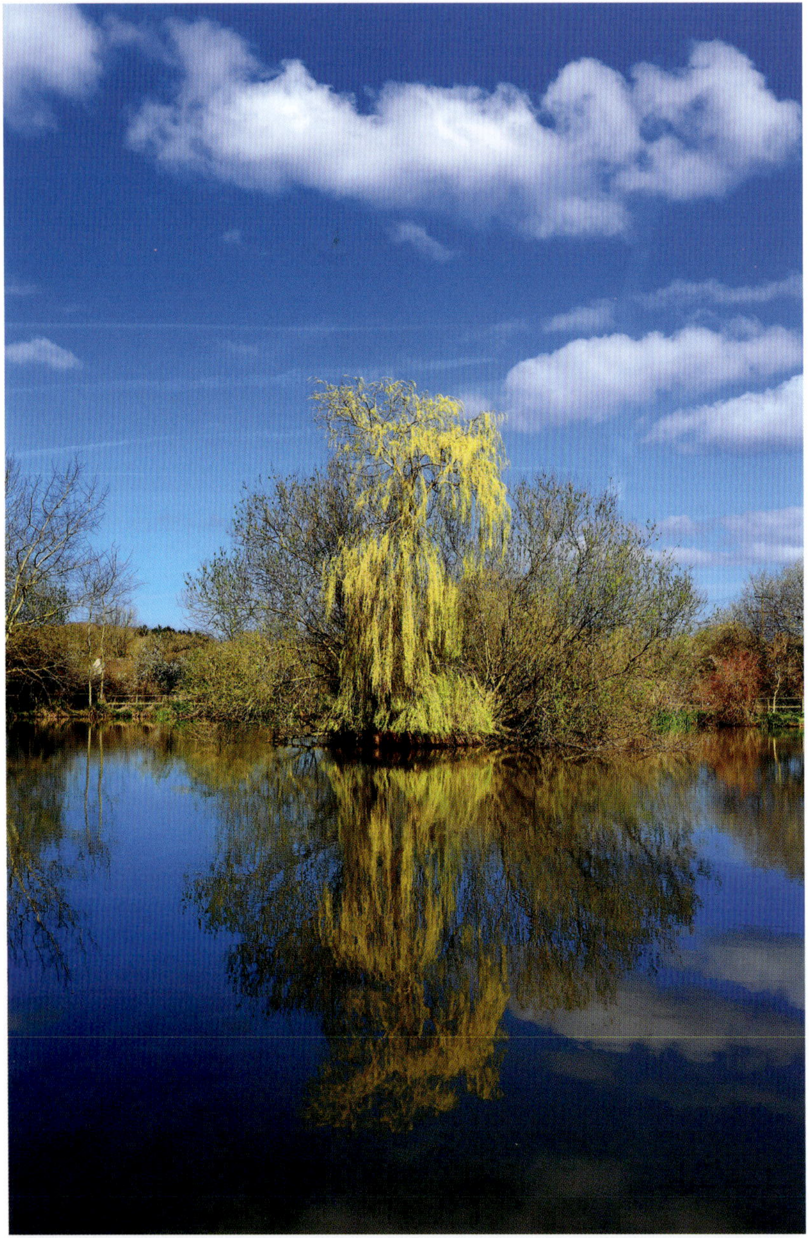

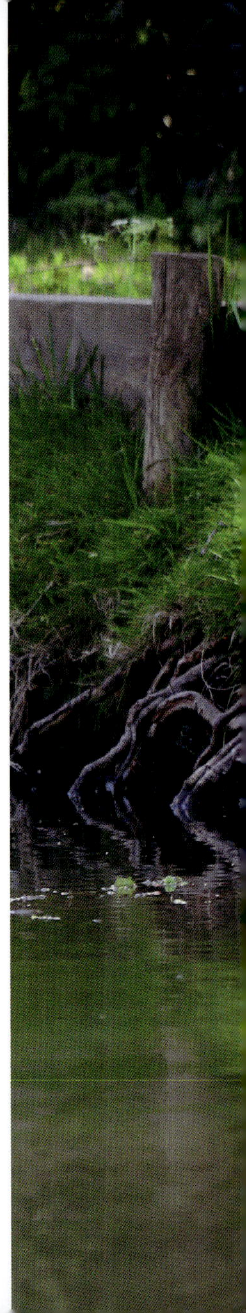

GOODIFORD MILL, SOMERSET

Oliver caught this stupendous and colourful reflection and loved that one of his Facebook followers said it looked like fireworks exploding.

HERON FISHING
Oliver's favourite

"Herons are one of my favourite birds and they are big. I like the detail of his face. His beak looks really sharp. Herons are *very* good at catching fish."

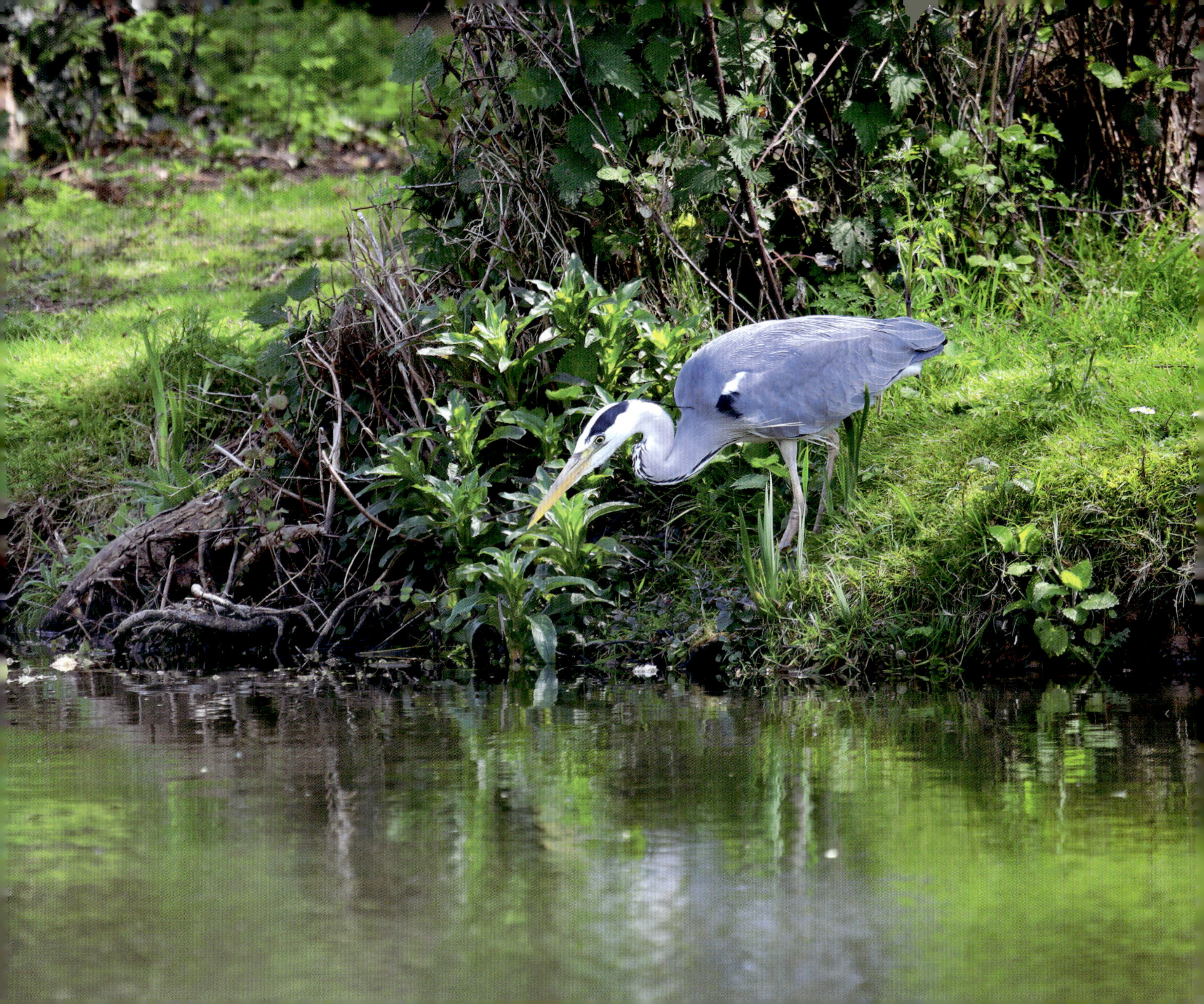

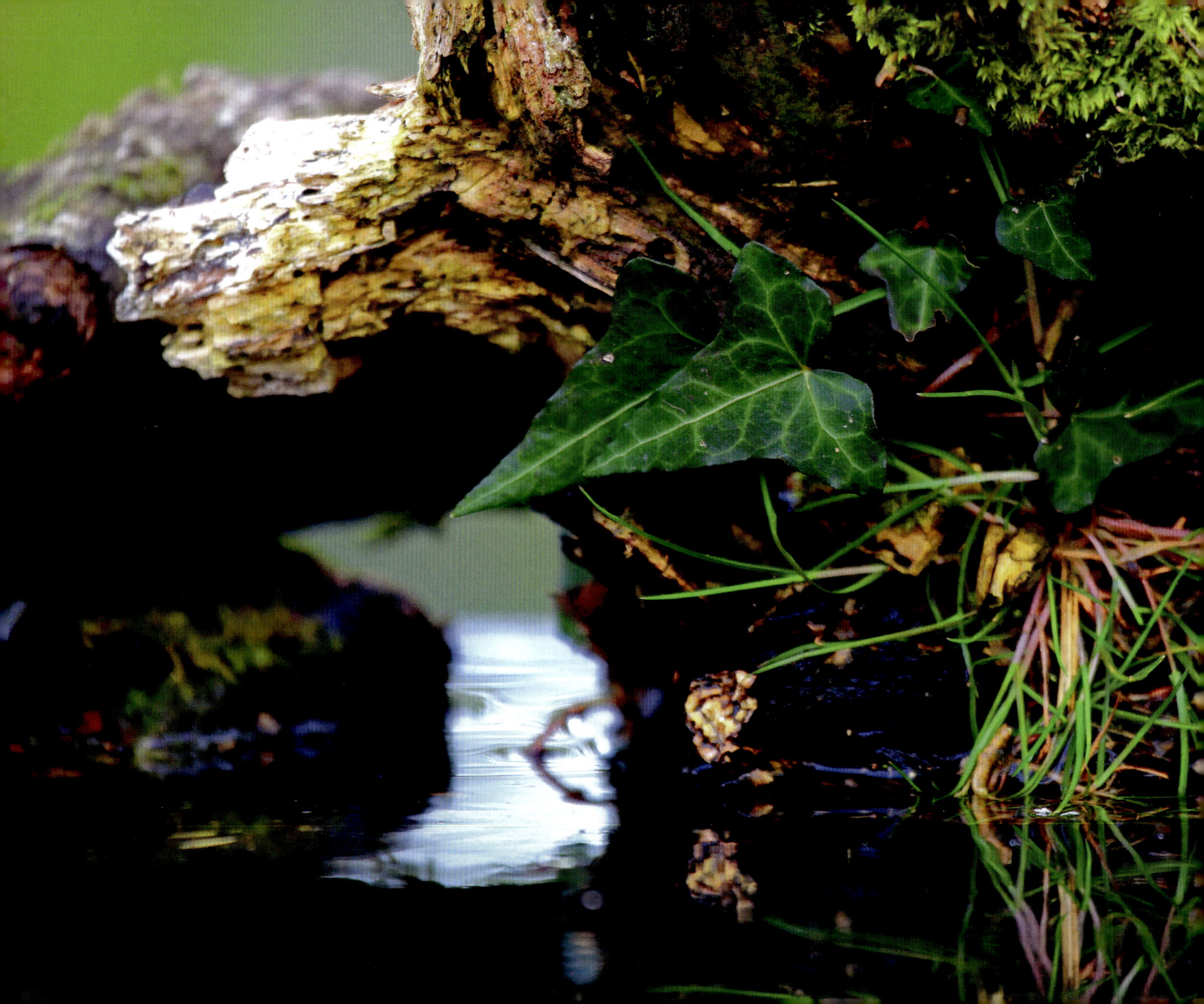

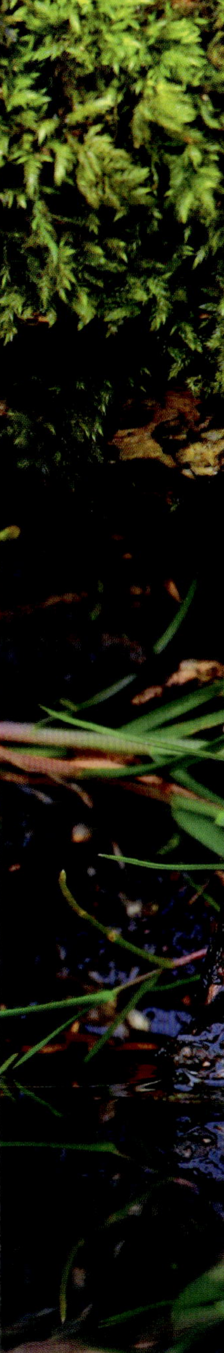

IT'S ALL IN THE DETAIL

This image has been included to represent the many thousands of images not shown, where Oliver concentrates on the finest detail, or smallest part of the scene around him. He often ignores what others might think of as a truly majestic vista because his attention has been taken by some small detail that many people would consider insignificant. But everything has its beauty – especially to Oliver – and so this tiny fragment of wood, water, moss and ivy has earned its place here.

WATER LILY AT TRINITY WATERS

Oliver's favourite

"I love going fishing with my father. We sometimes go to a place called Trinity Waters and I got this great water lily picture there. I like the colour of the flower; I got the right exposure and I wanted the flower in the middle and the water behind blurred so I could get the flower sharp and a good reflection."

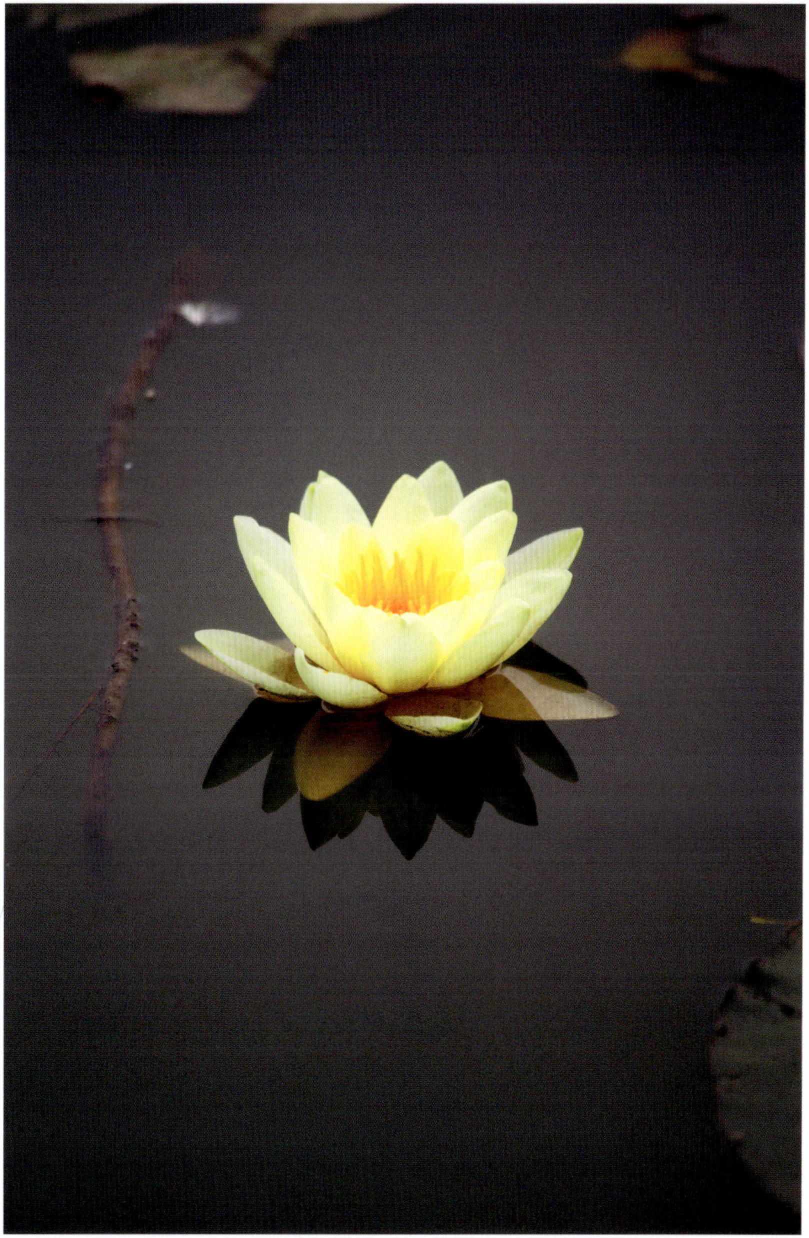

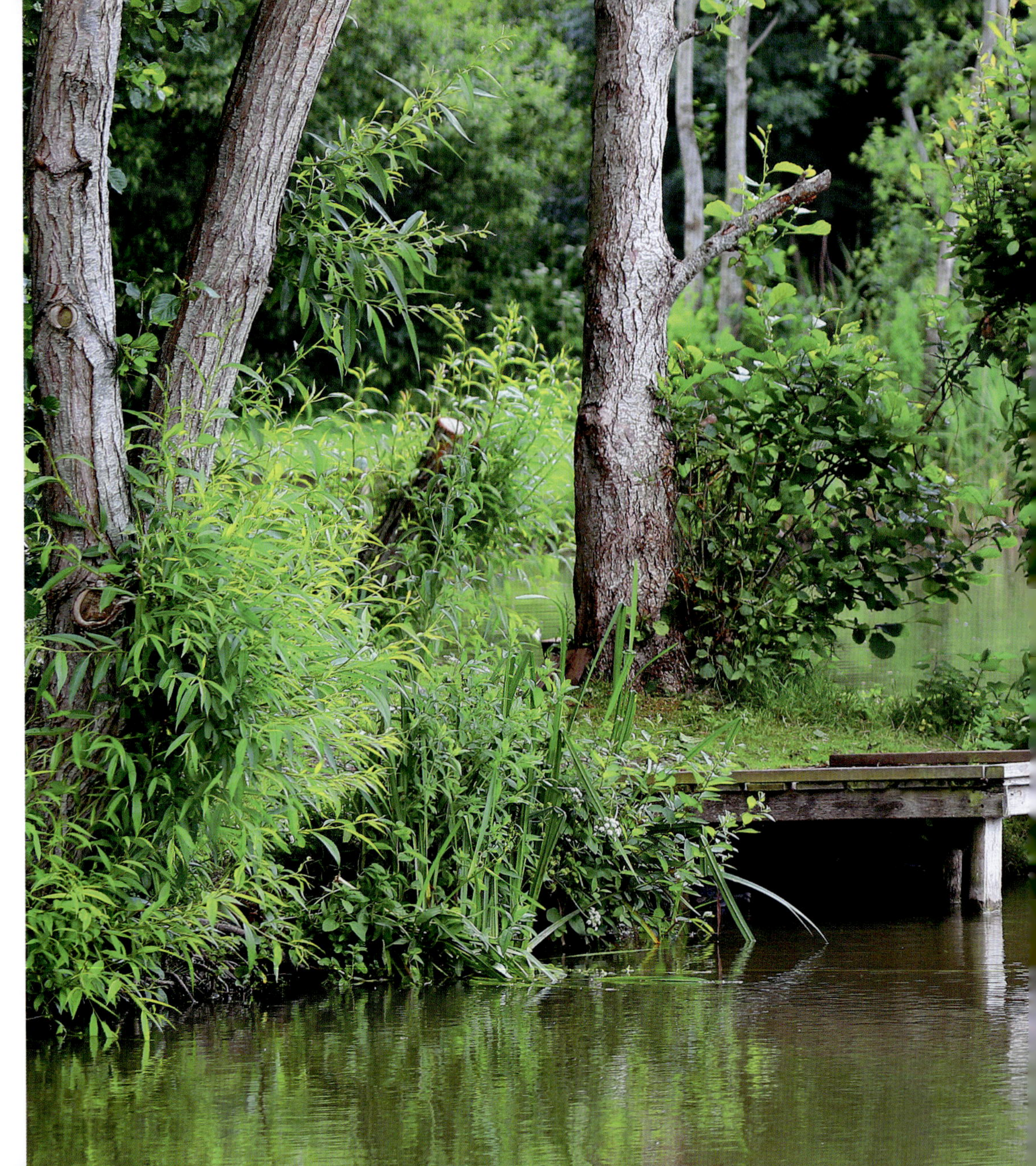

A 'fishing peg' at one of Oliver's favourite fishing haunts. Very typical of carp fishing lakes all over the country.

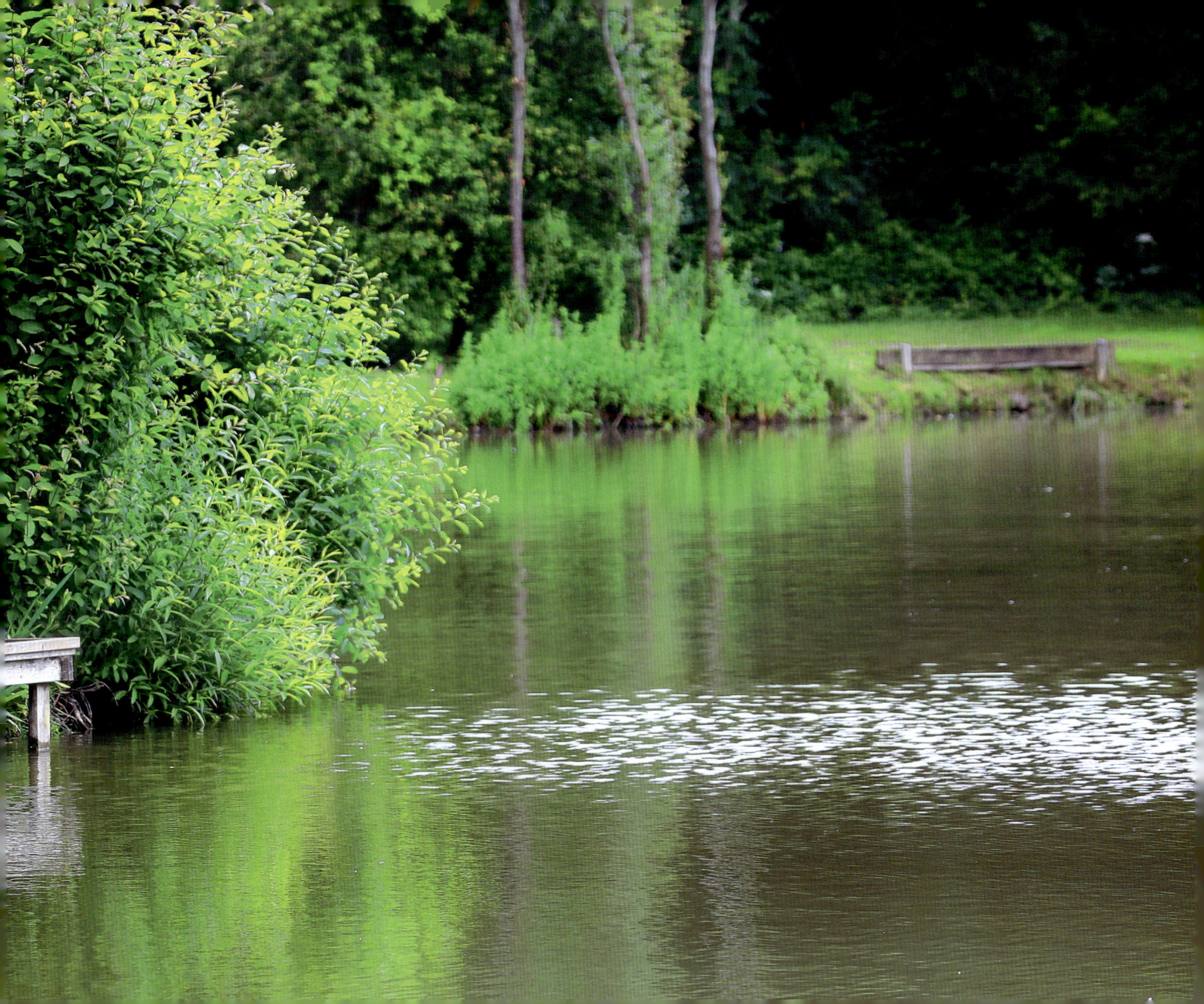

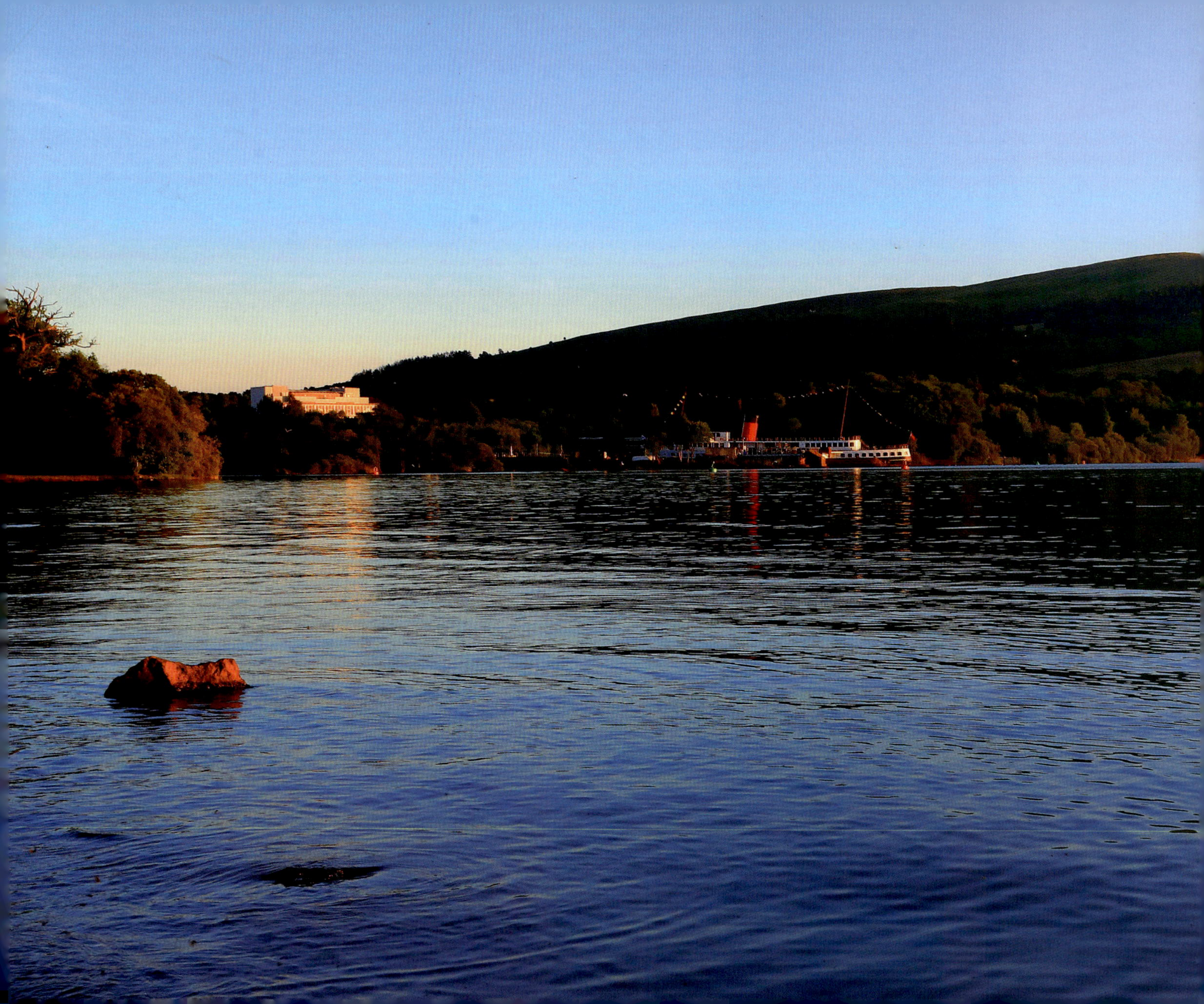

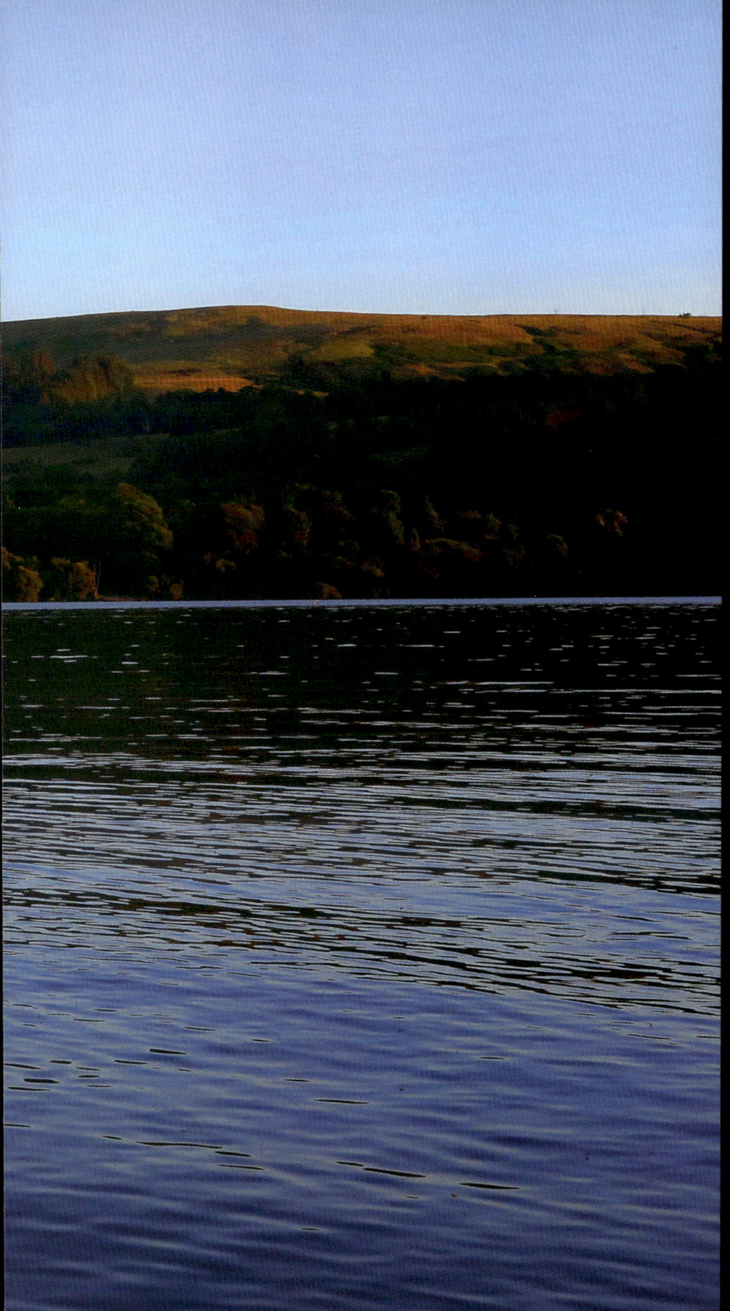

LAKES, LOCHS, RIVERS and WATERFALLS

Water has always been a favourite subject of Oliver's. Britain, being a nation that enjoys plenty of rain, is able to provide him with thousands of wonderful watery photographic opportunities! He will often sit beside a river, lake or waterfall and take hundreds of images. He even loves the individual splashes produced by tumbling rivers and waterfalls, and tries to capture those as well as the larger picture. It took a *very* long time to narrow down Oliver's many *thousands* of wondrous water images to a few that would fit in this chapter, so a book of *Oliver's Love of Water* will *have* to be produced one day!

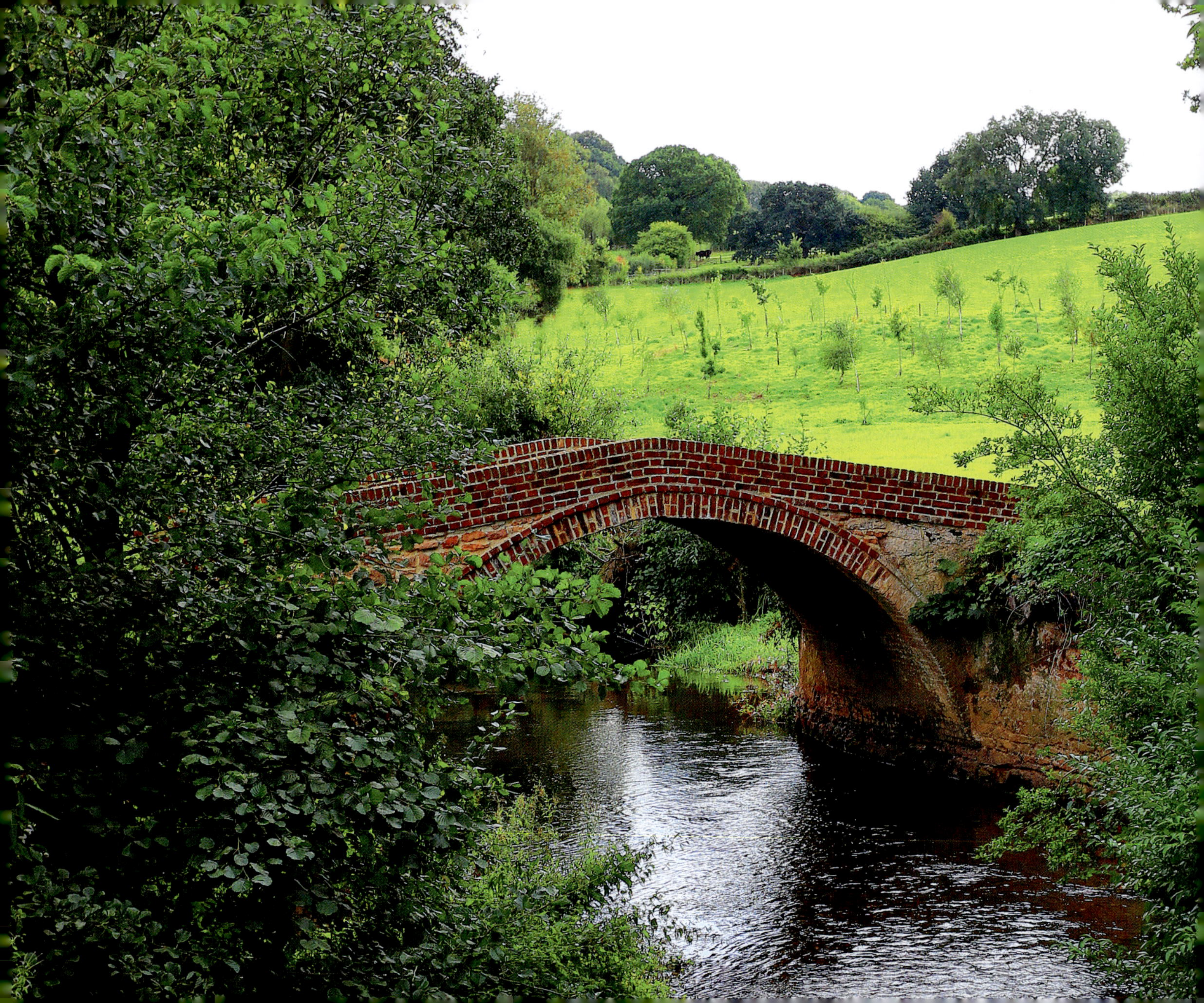

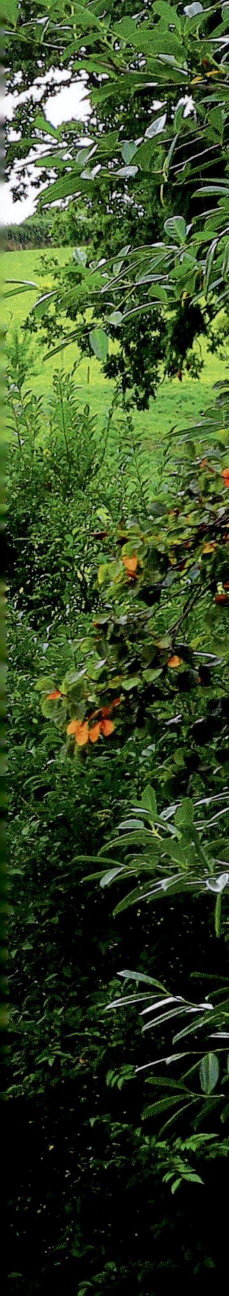

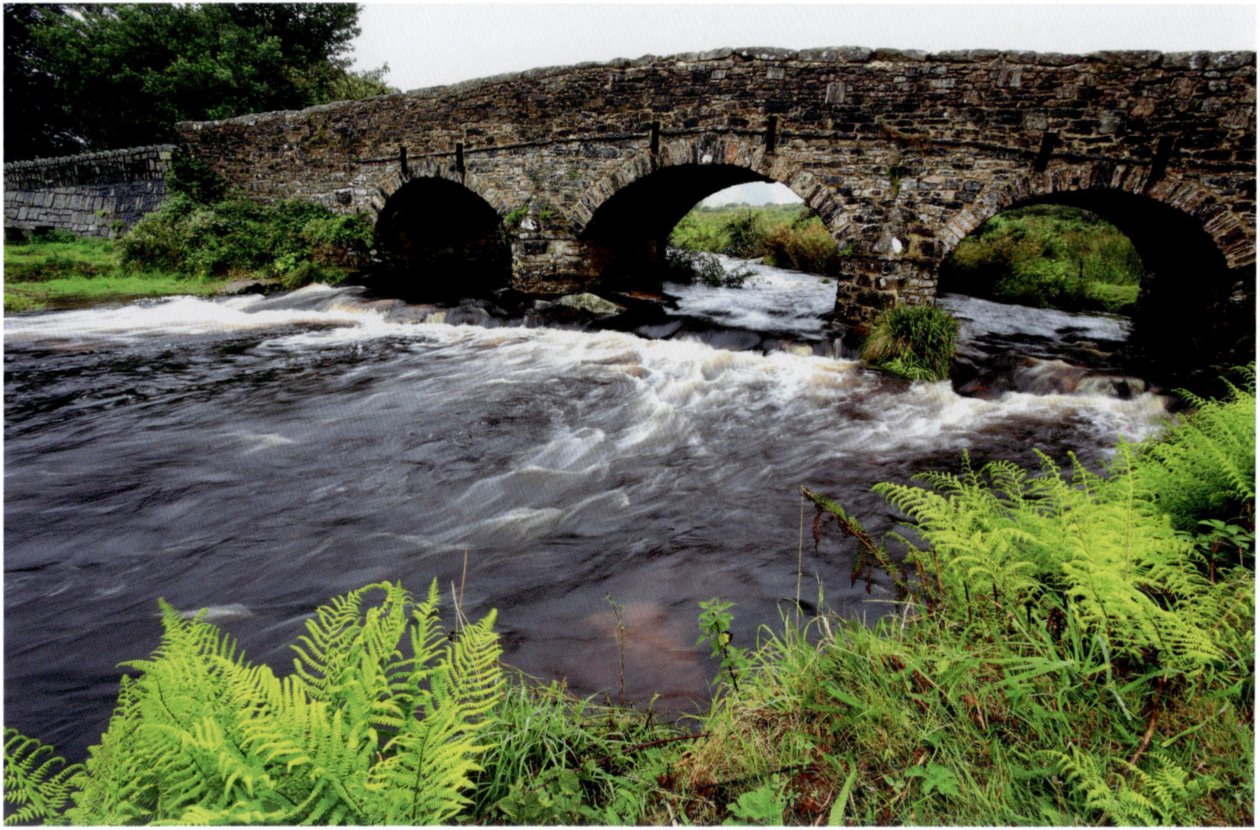

THE LITTLE RED BRICK BRIDGE
Oliver's favourite

"I like the colour of the bridge and I like the scenery and the water is crystal clear. The bricks on the bridge are vibrant and they stand out, and there is bright, bright green behind it."

GRANITE BRIDGE BUILT IN THE 1700s – POSTBRIDGE, DEVON

A stone bridge and rushing water – always a photo opportunity for Oliver.

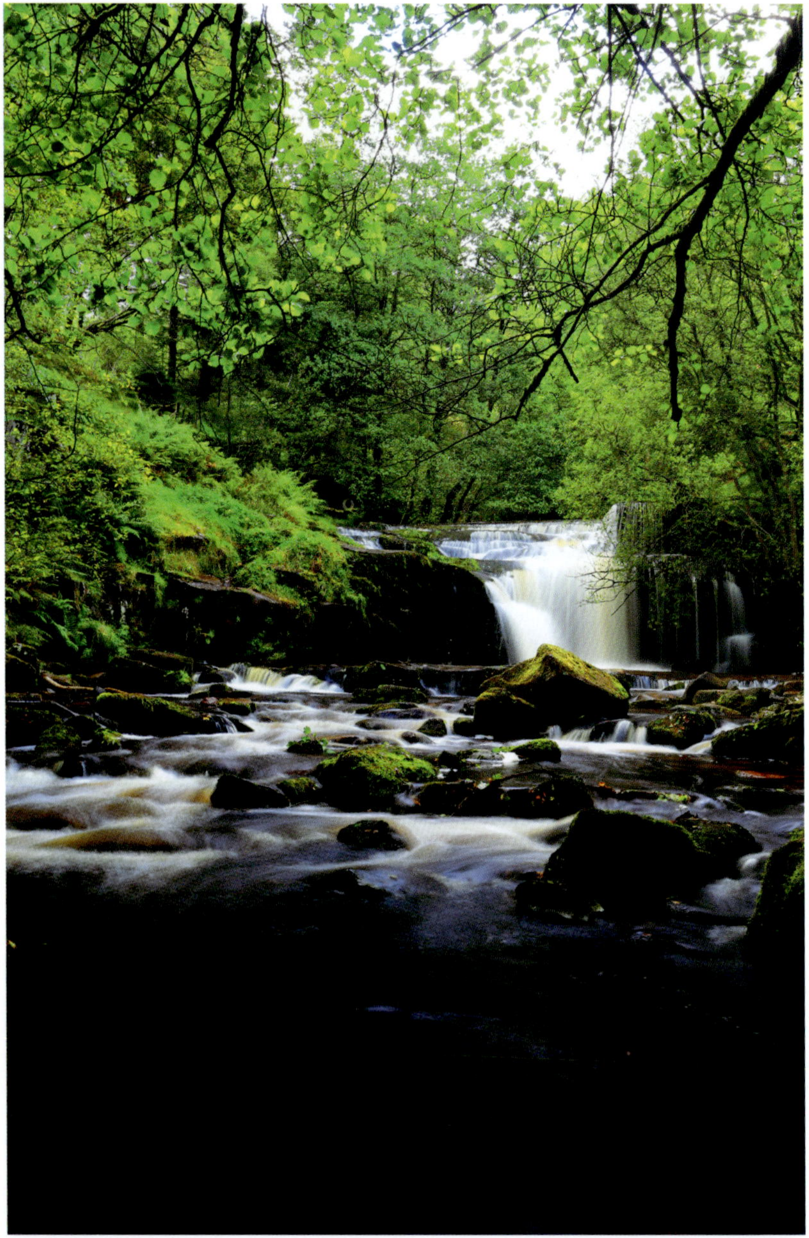

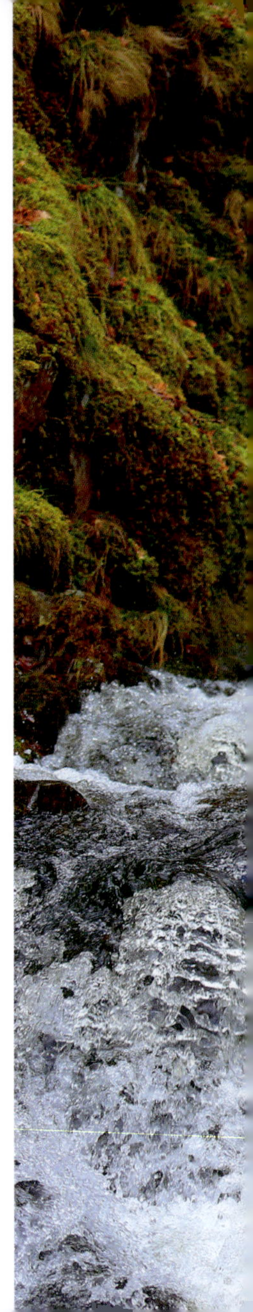

WATERFALL IN THE BRECON BEACONS

WELSH MOUNTAIN STREAM

A typical trickling, tumbling mountain stream. Just the kind Oliver enjoys having a picnic beside!

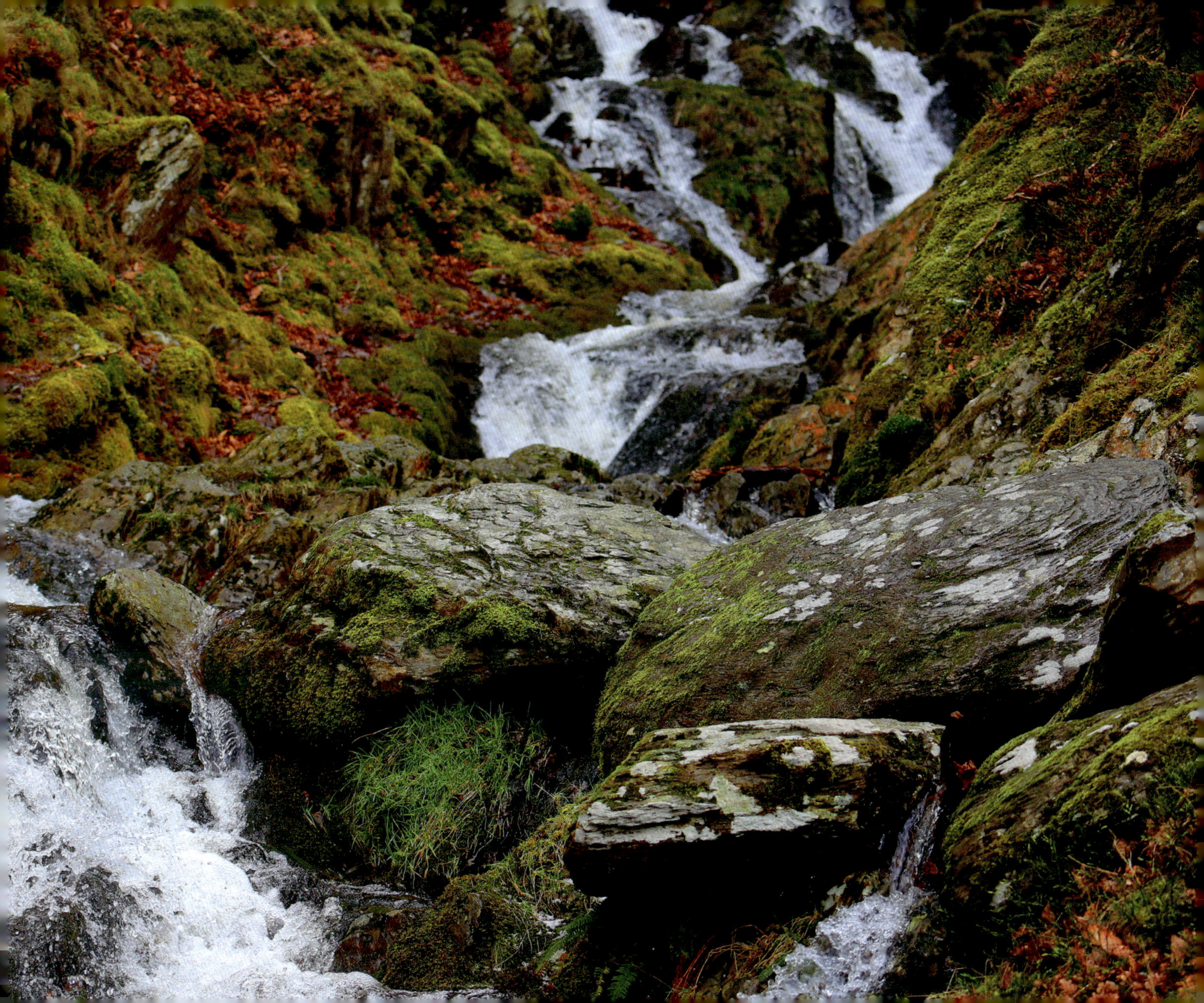

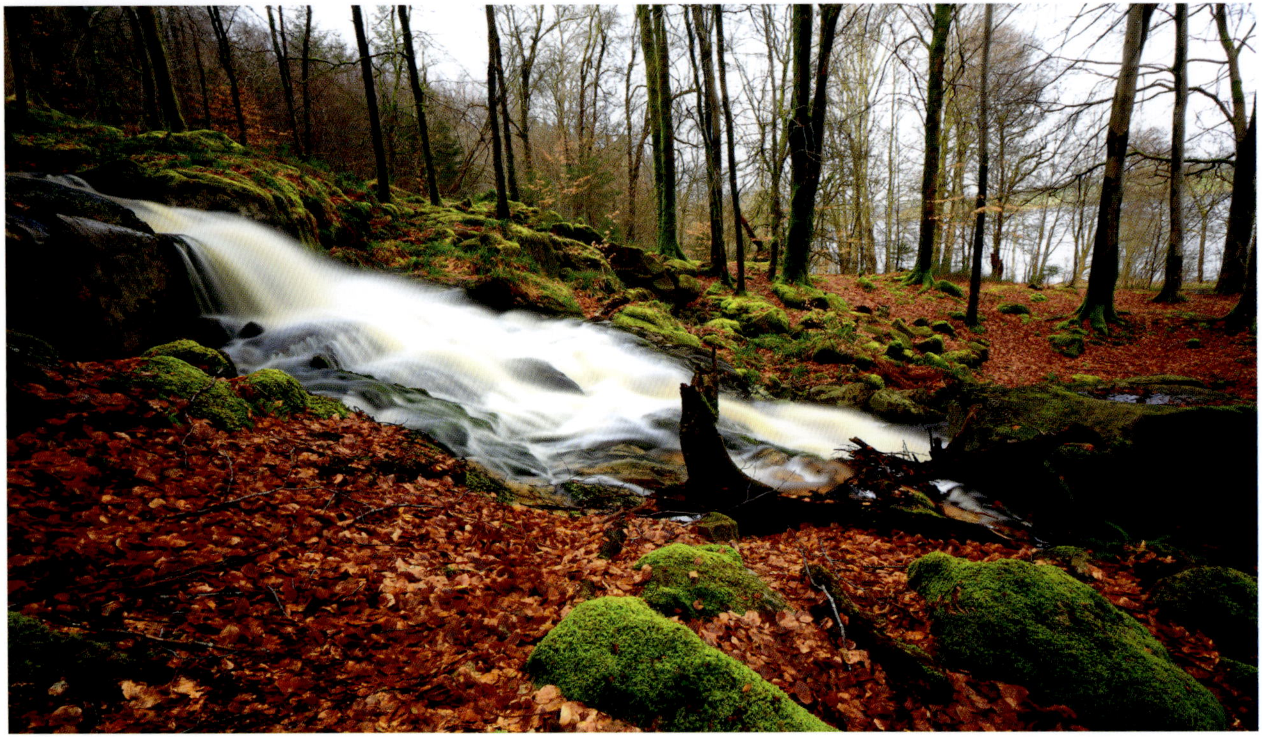

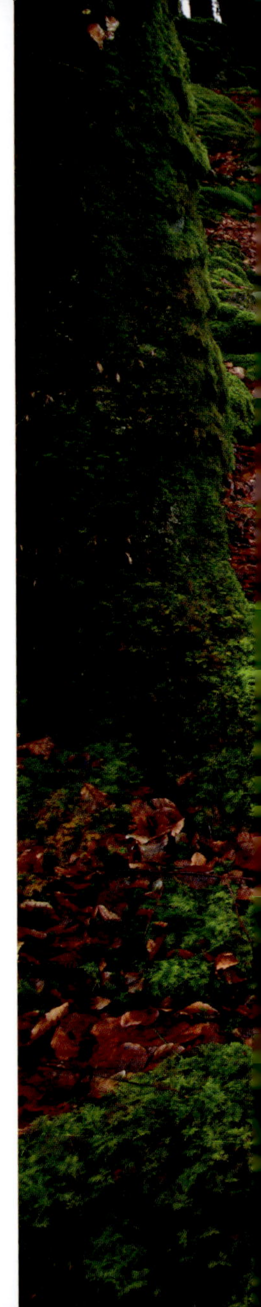

LOWRAN BURN, SCOTLAND

Oliver's favourite

"I took this picture in Scotland. I used my tripod and did a long shutter speed to get the movement of the water. I really love the colour of the leaves and the moss and the white water. This is one of my favourites."

LOWRAN BURN FALLS, SCOTLAND

Oliver was very pleased with this image when he took it. It took centre stage as the cover for his 2020 calendar.

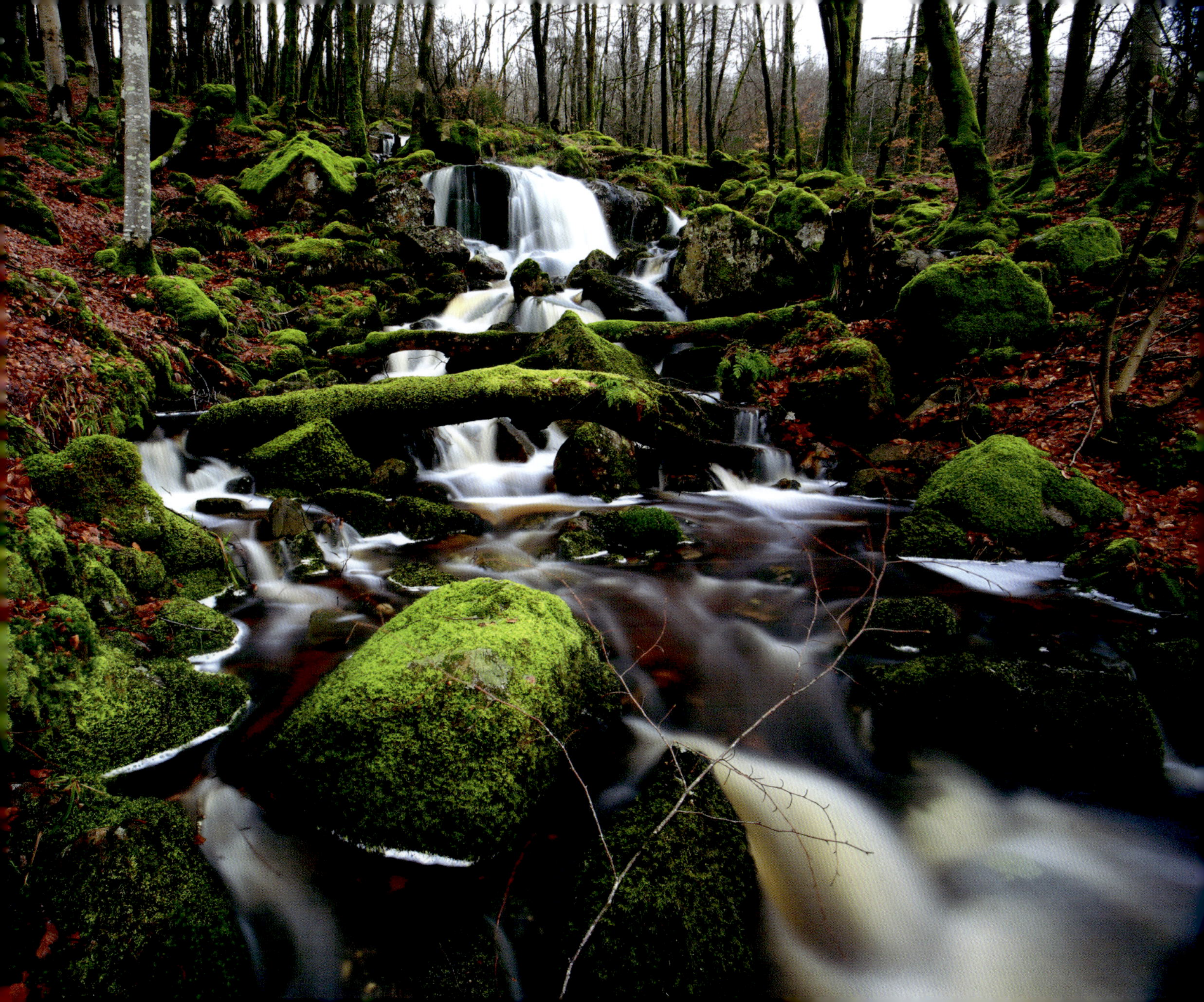

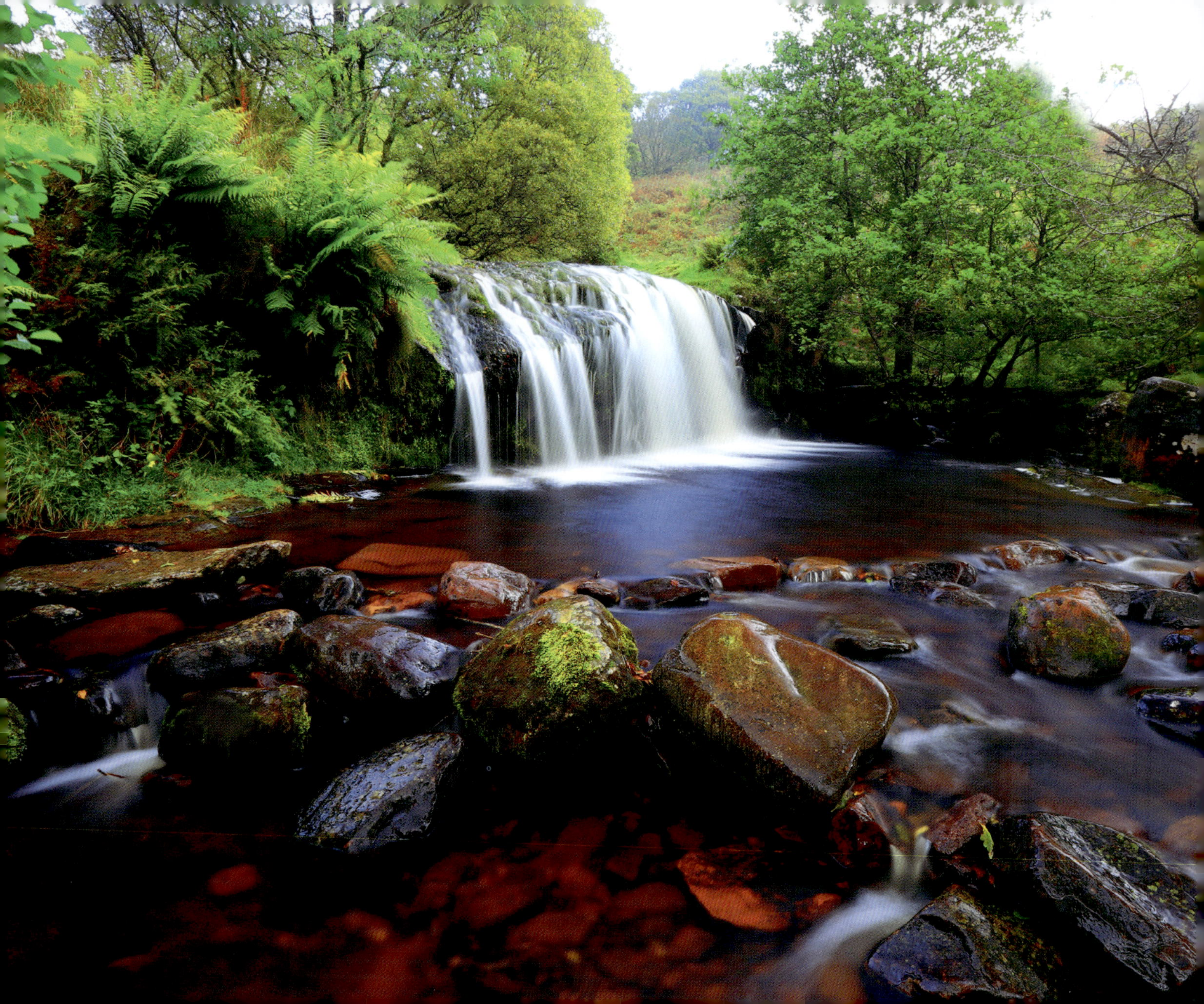

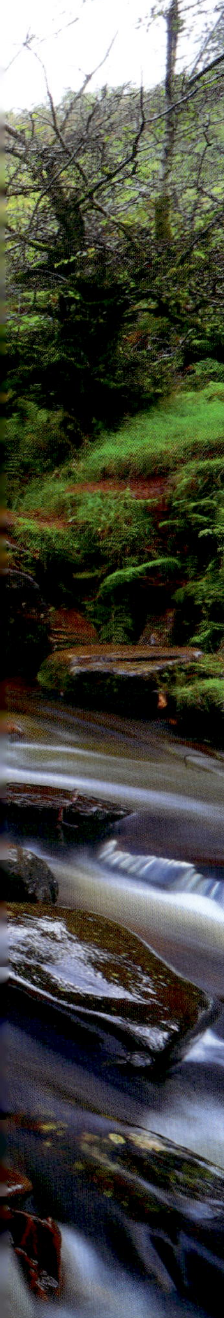

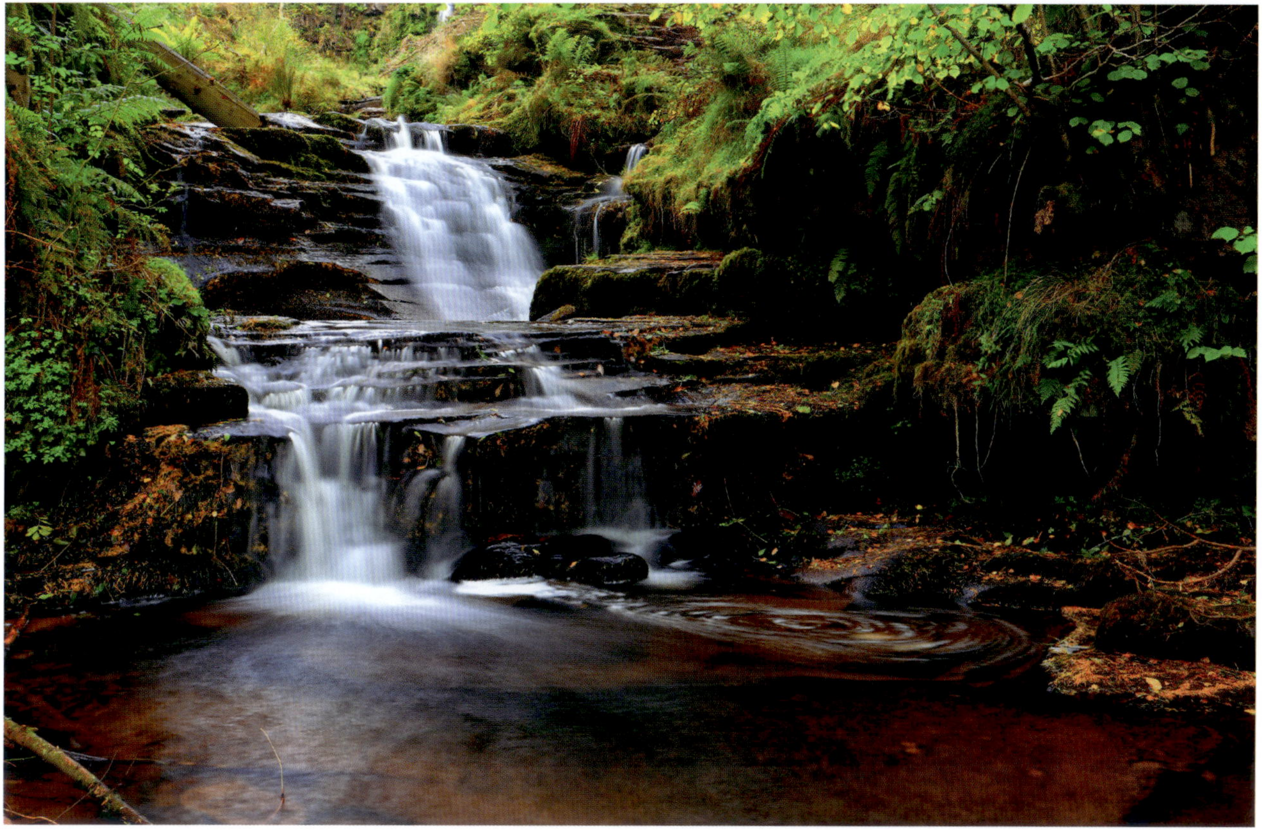

BLAEN-Y-GLYN WATERFALL WALK, WALES – 1

Oliver's favourite

"I like the red colour in the water in the foreground. I did a long shutter speed to get the water milky and smooth."

BLAEN-Y-GLYN WATERFALL WALK, WALES – 2

Oliver's favourite waterfall walk is in the Brecon Beacons, Wales, not far from Talybont reservoir. The circular walk is not too long and seems to present a new waterfall every few steps! Oliver has taken countless pictures here in all weathers and seasons.

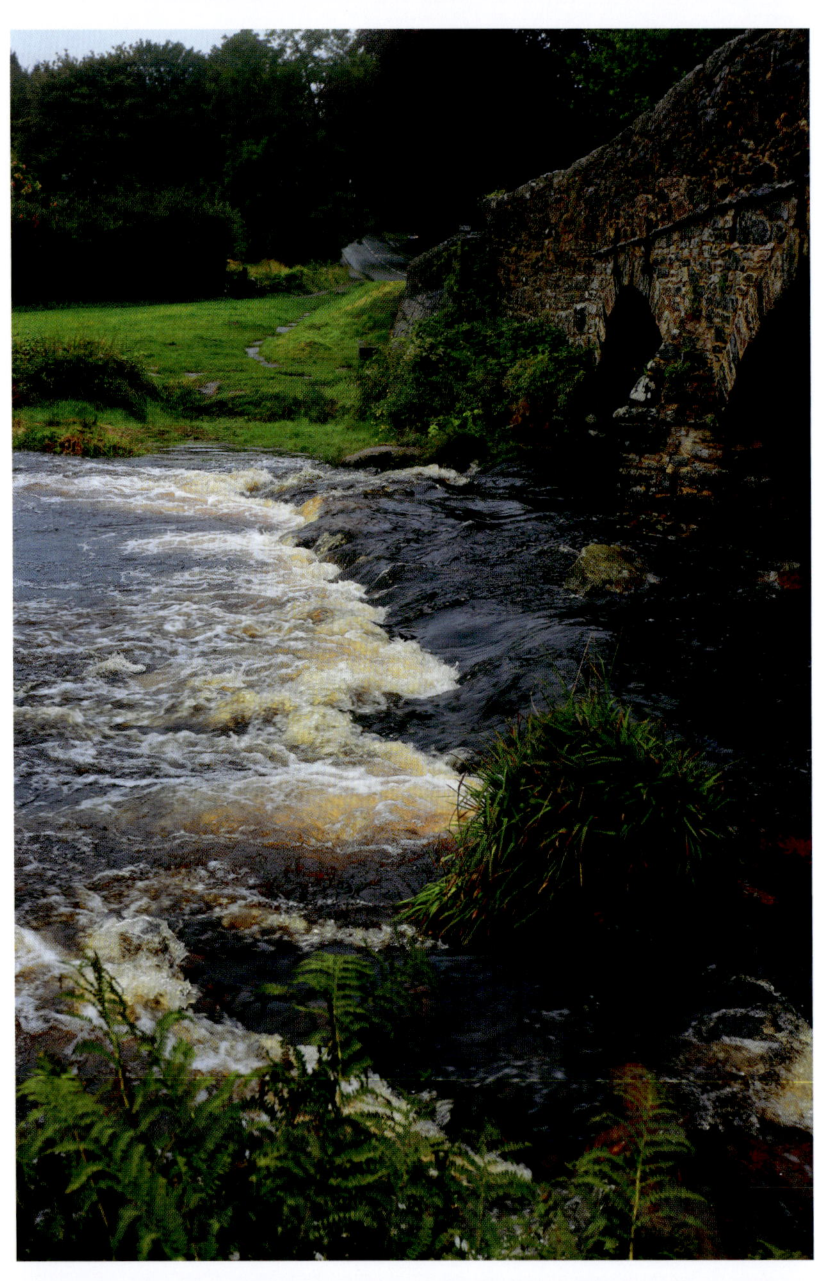

"I went to Dartmoor to get some pictures of the rivers. I love rivers. I like taking pictures of water. In this picture I like the view of the bridge from the side and the water flowing out fast. It looks like rapids. And I wanted to get the little path on the other side in the picture too."

MOUNTAIN FALLS, NEAR GLENCOE, SCOTLAND

OLIVER LOVES WATERFALLS

Even though you can't see Oliver's face in this picture you can somehow tell he is sitting there smiling, completely happy and in his element.

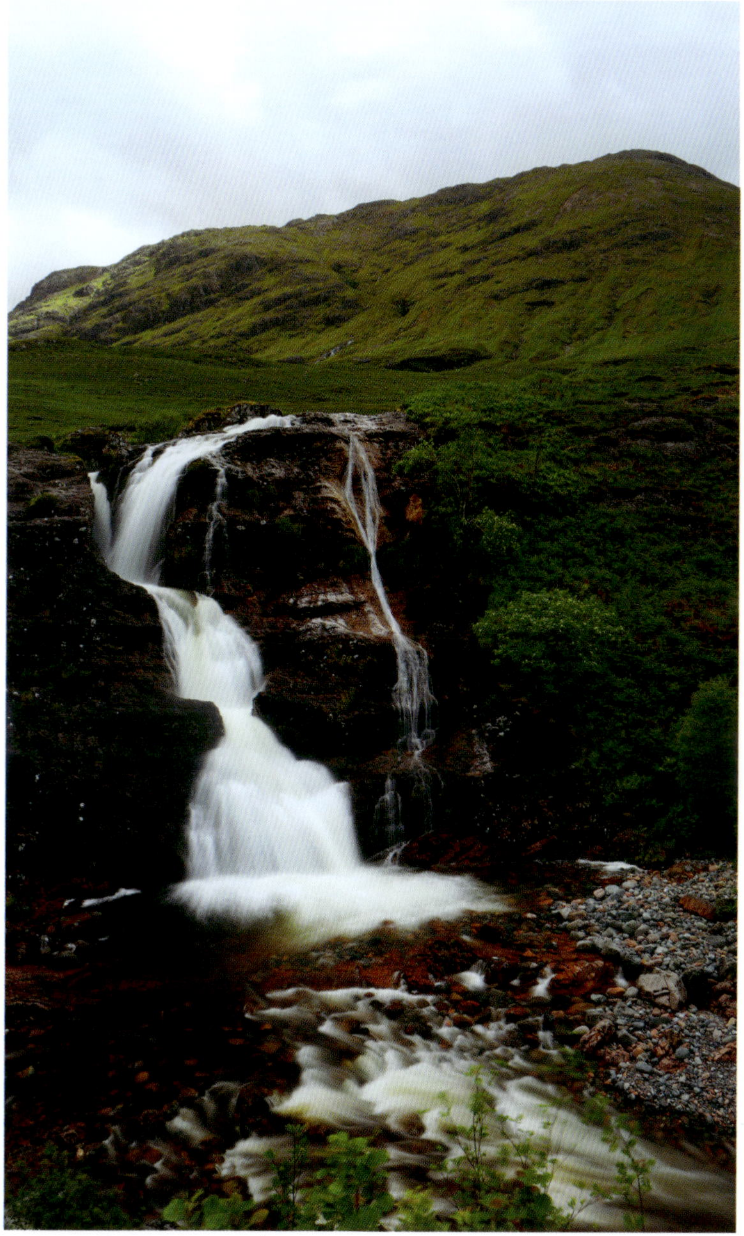

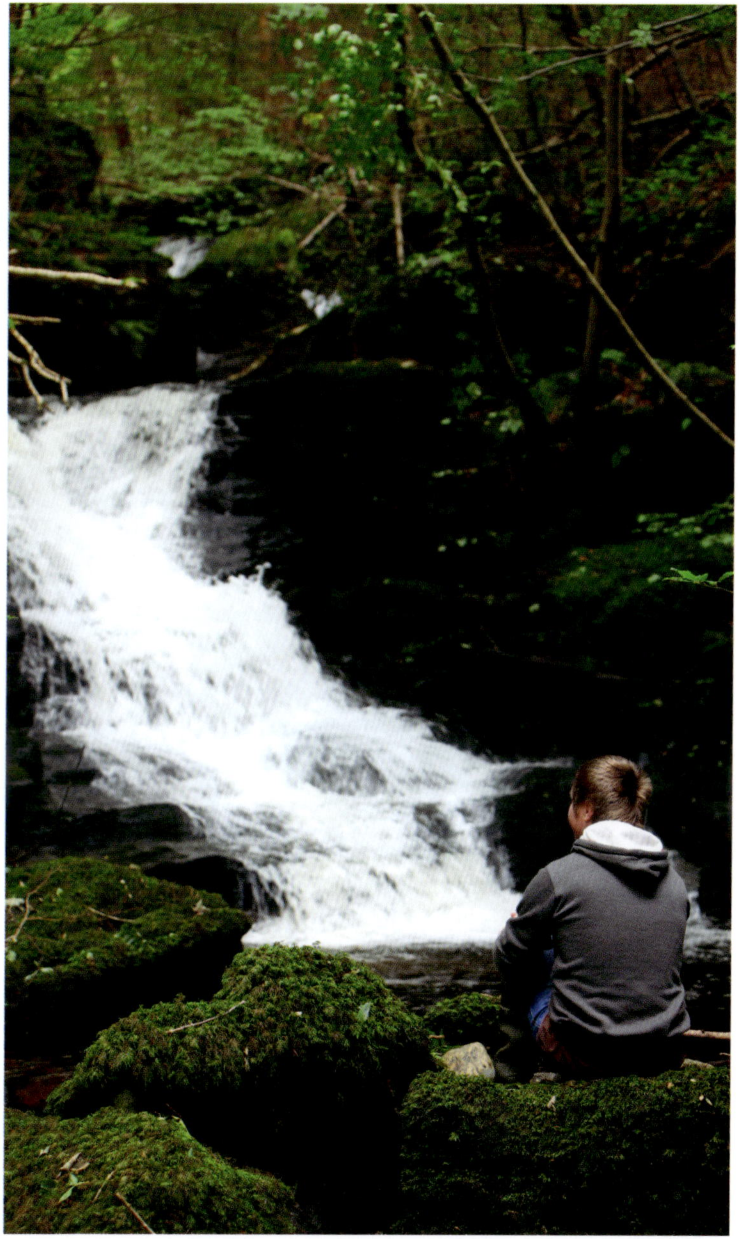

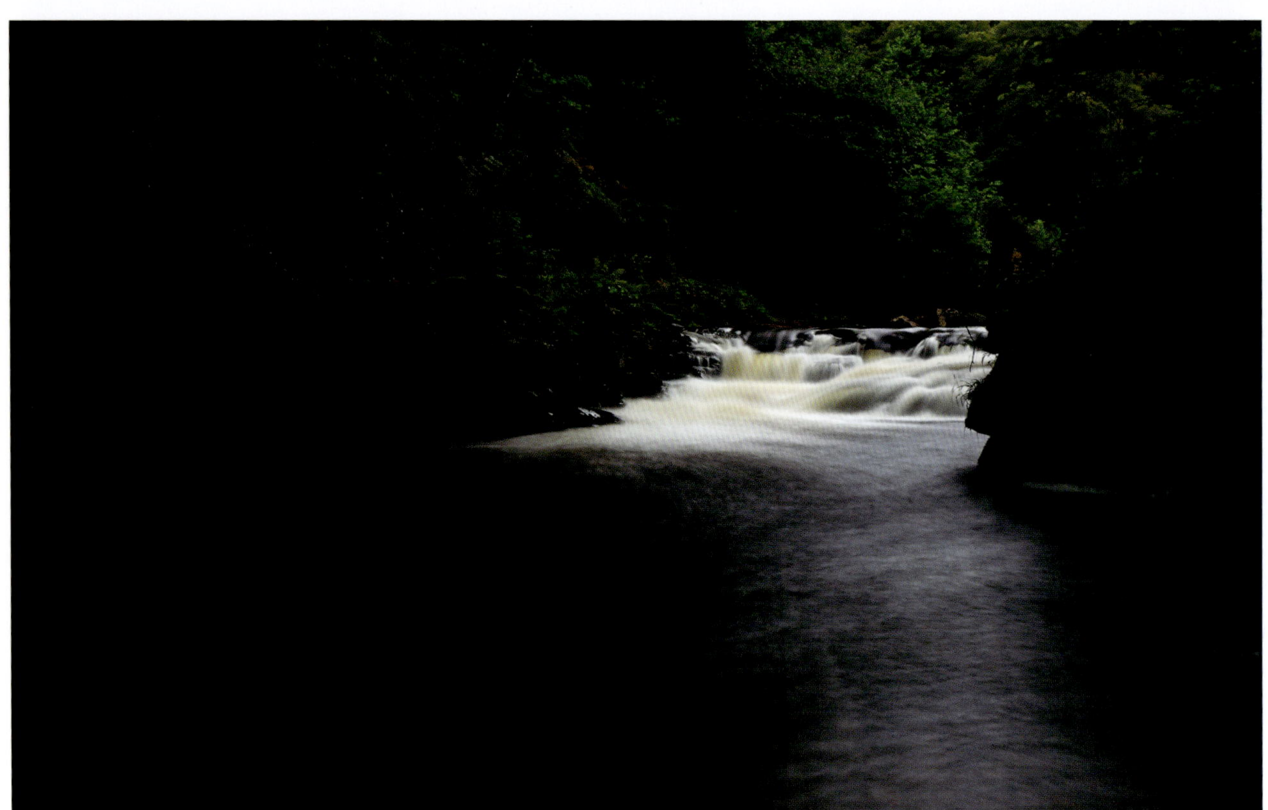

WATERSMEET, DEVON – 1
Oliver's favourite

"I like the long exposure on this one;
the water looks like a carpet of silk. I
like the colour of the trees behind the
waterfall. The waterfall really stands
out from all the dark."

WATERSMEET, DEVON – 2
Oliver's favourite

"In this one I like the background and
I like the rocks in the foreground. The
colours at the sides are vibrant."

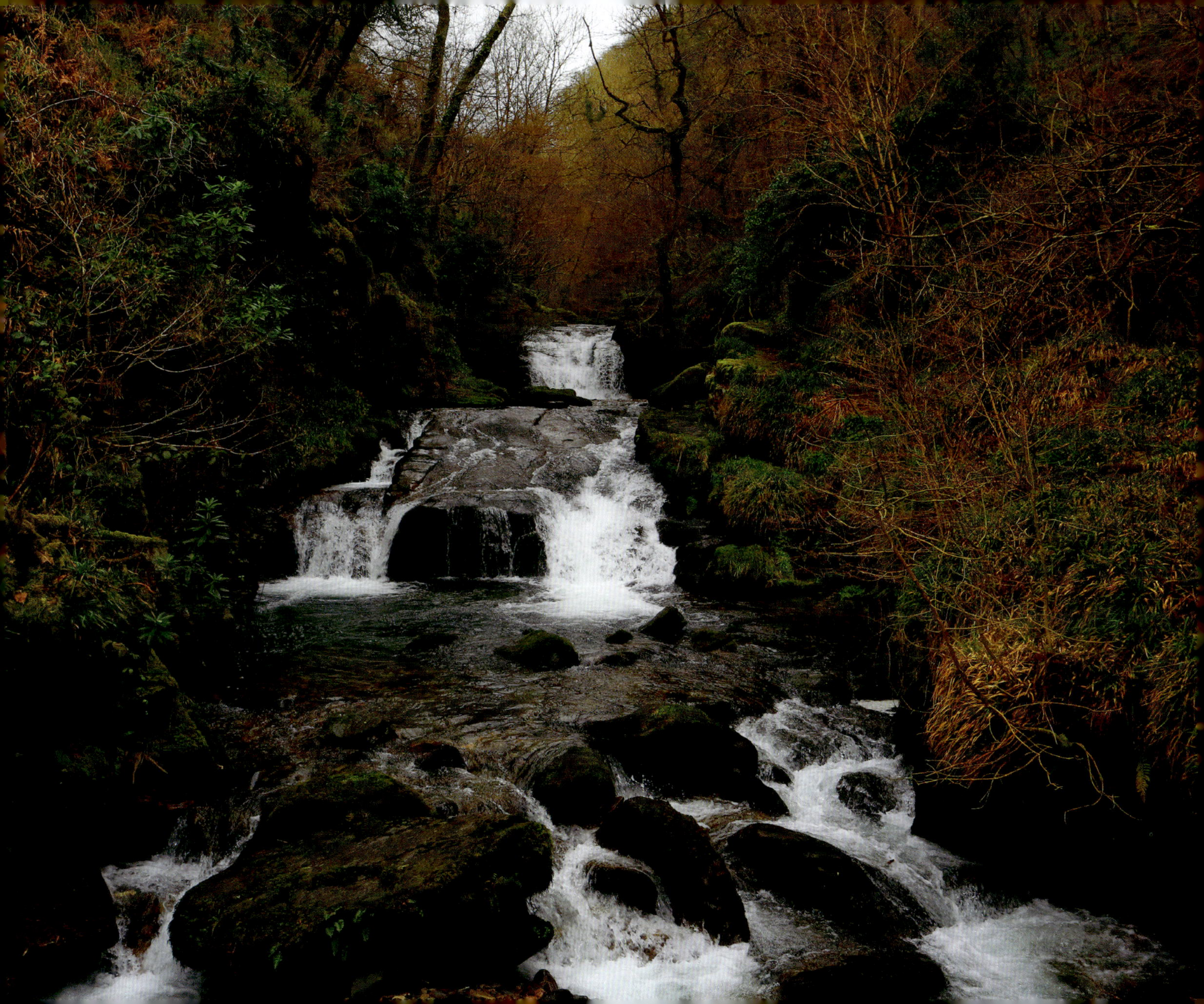

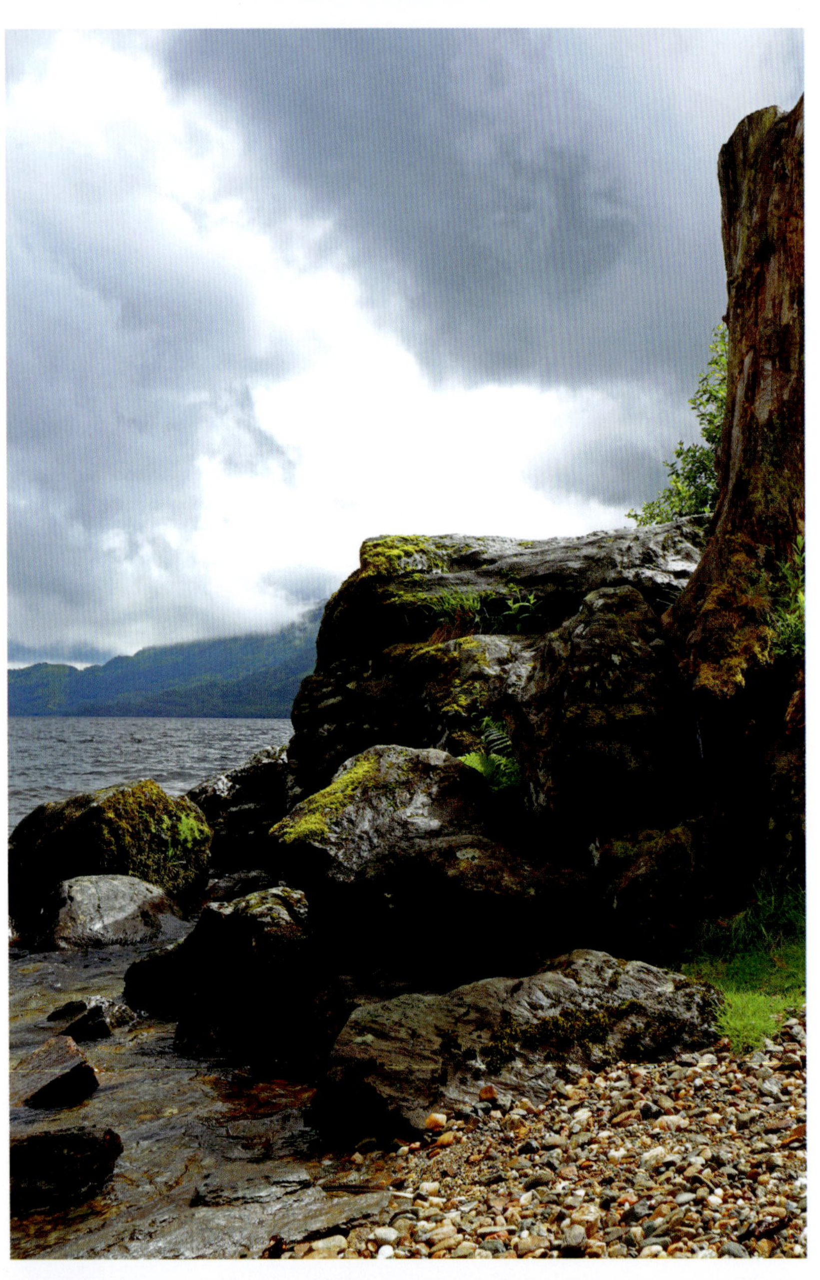

LOCH LOMOND, SCOTLAND – ROCKY OUTCROP

Taken on a cool cloudy day. Oliver spent over an hour sitting beside the loch and getting pictures, using the rocky outcrop to frame the view and form the focus of the images rather than the loch. From this location he didn't take any pictures looking straight out across the loch at all.

WINDING WATER IN SCOTLAND

Oliver remarked on the fenceposts gradually disappearing into the water as he captured this shot of a watery tree-lined Scottish landscape.

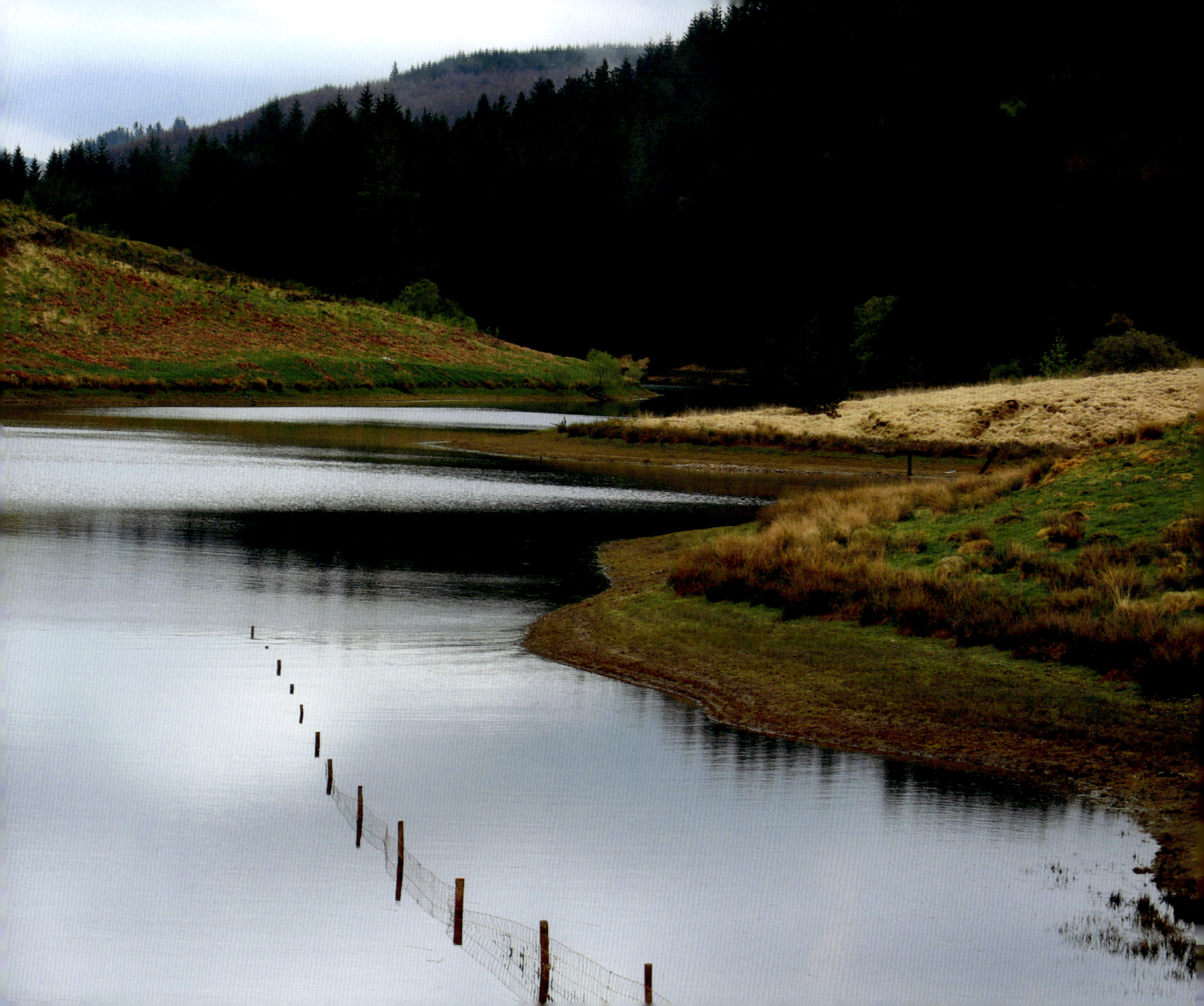

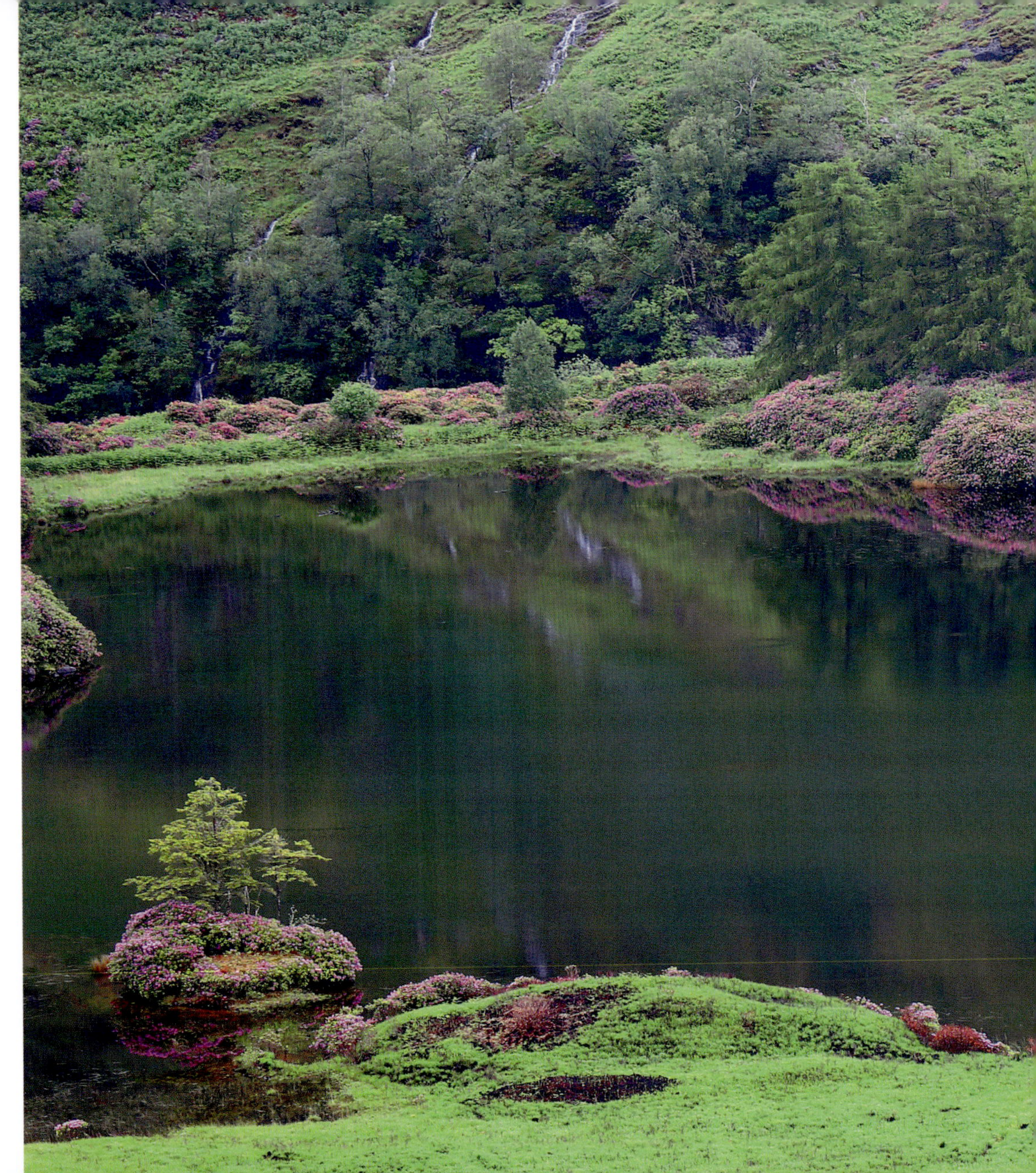

SMALL LOCH IN GLEN ETIVE, SCOTLAND

Oliver's favourite

"We called this 'the pink lake'. We were on holiday in Scotland in Glen Etive. It was beautiful. The pink in this picture is the rhododendrons. I love the colours and I really like the reflections. The pinks are so colourful."

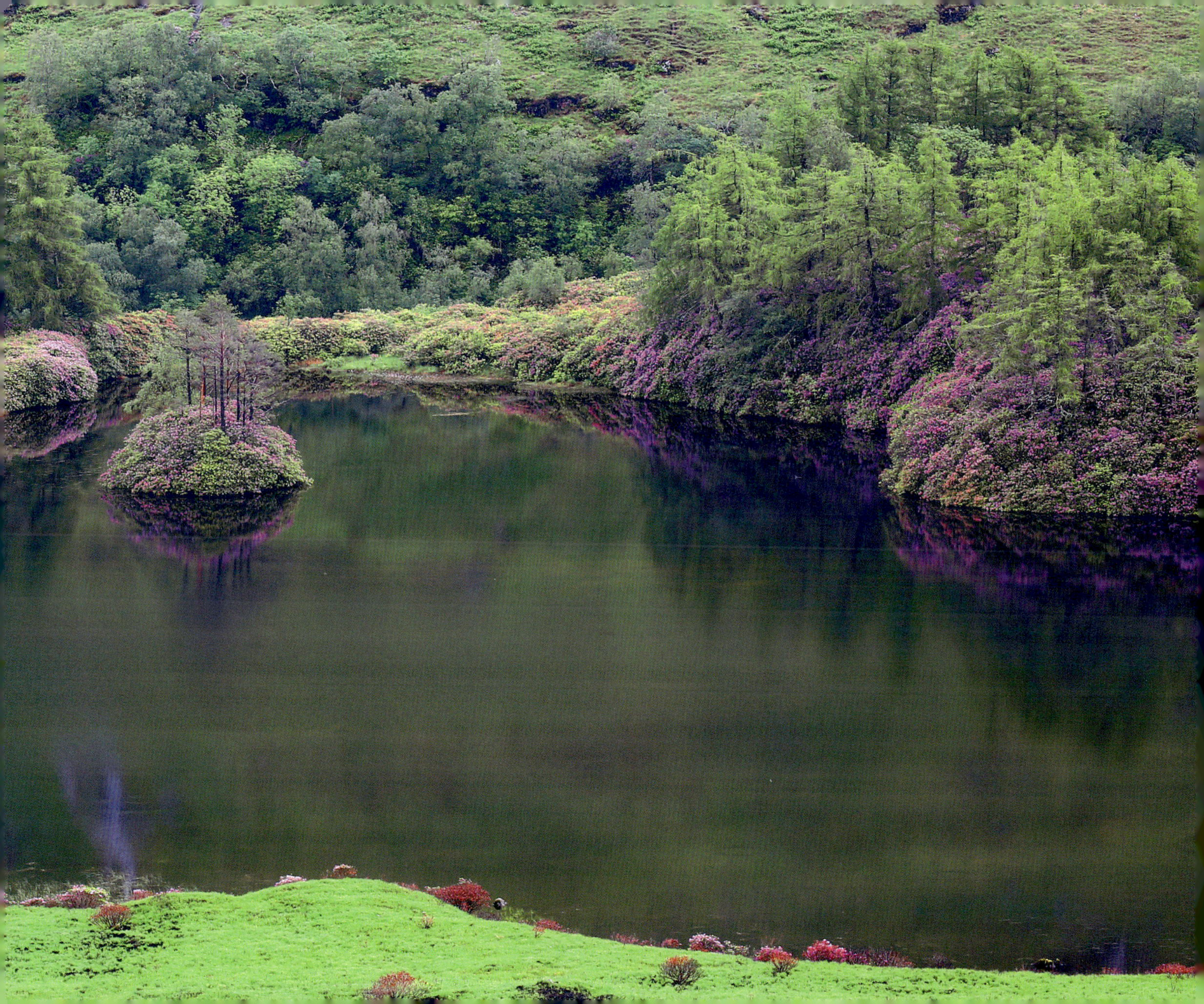

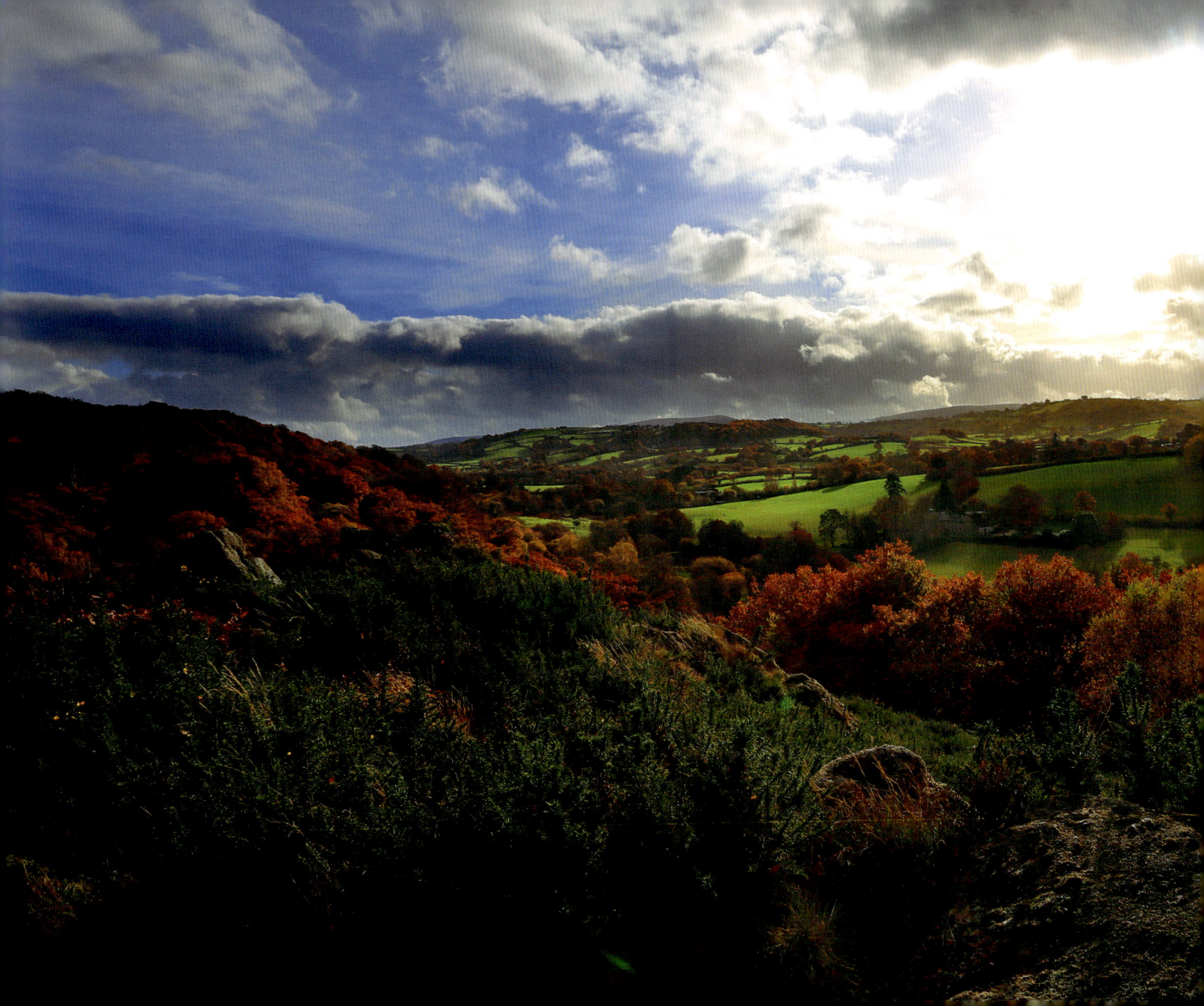

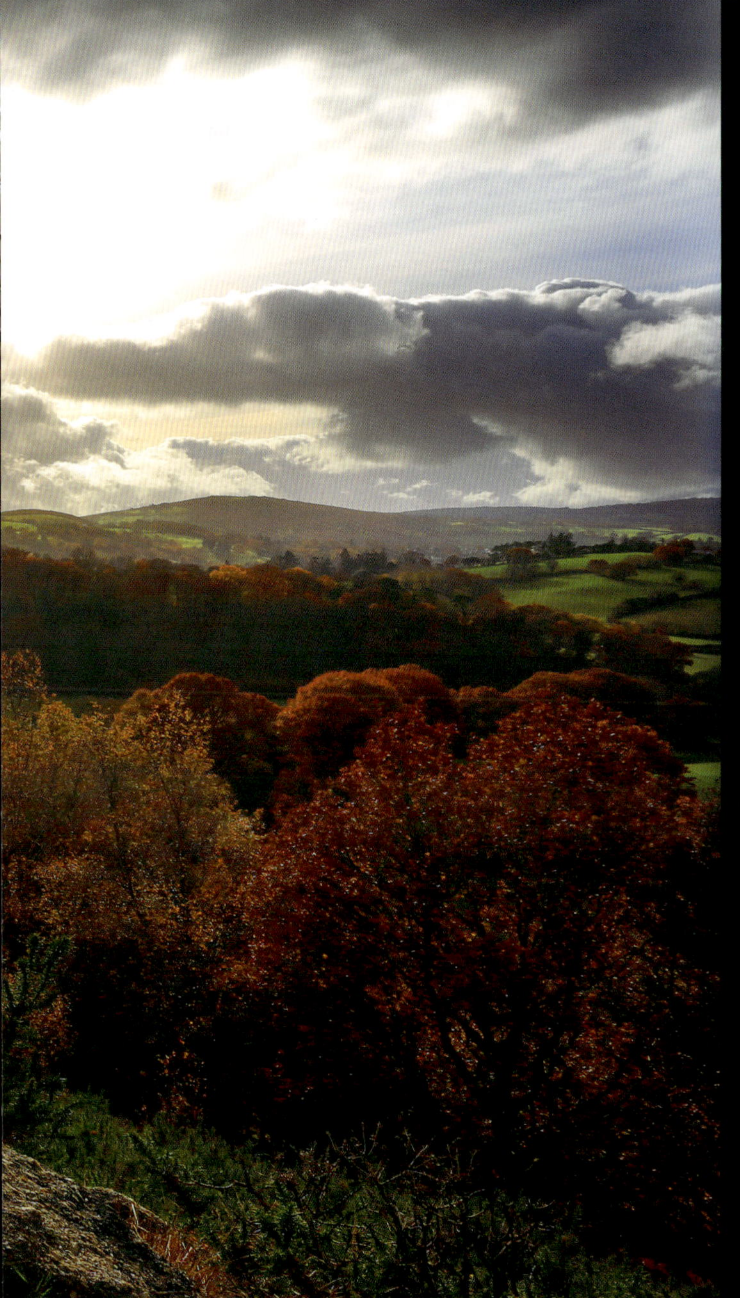

Here in Britain, Oliver is able to enjoy a wonderfully varied landscape. Whether it is mountains or moorlands, wetlands, marshes or rolling hills, canals, rivers, stony or sandy beaches and the sea, or simple fields and grassy roadsides, Oliver has enjoyed and photographed them all. His love of the great outdoors started when he was a young boy, always asking to "go out to the wild!" and his deep enjoyment of nature has never left him. Through his photographs and imagery, he is able to express his pleasure and delight in the many and varied landscapes of his homeland, and then pass that joy to others.

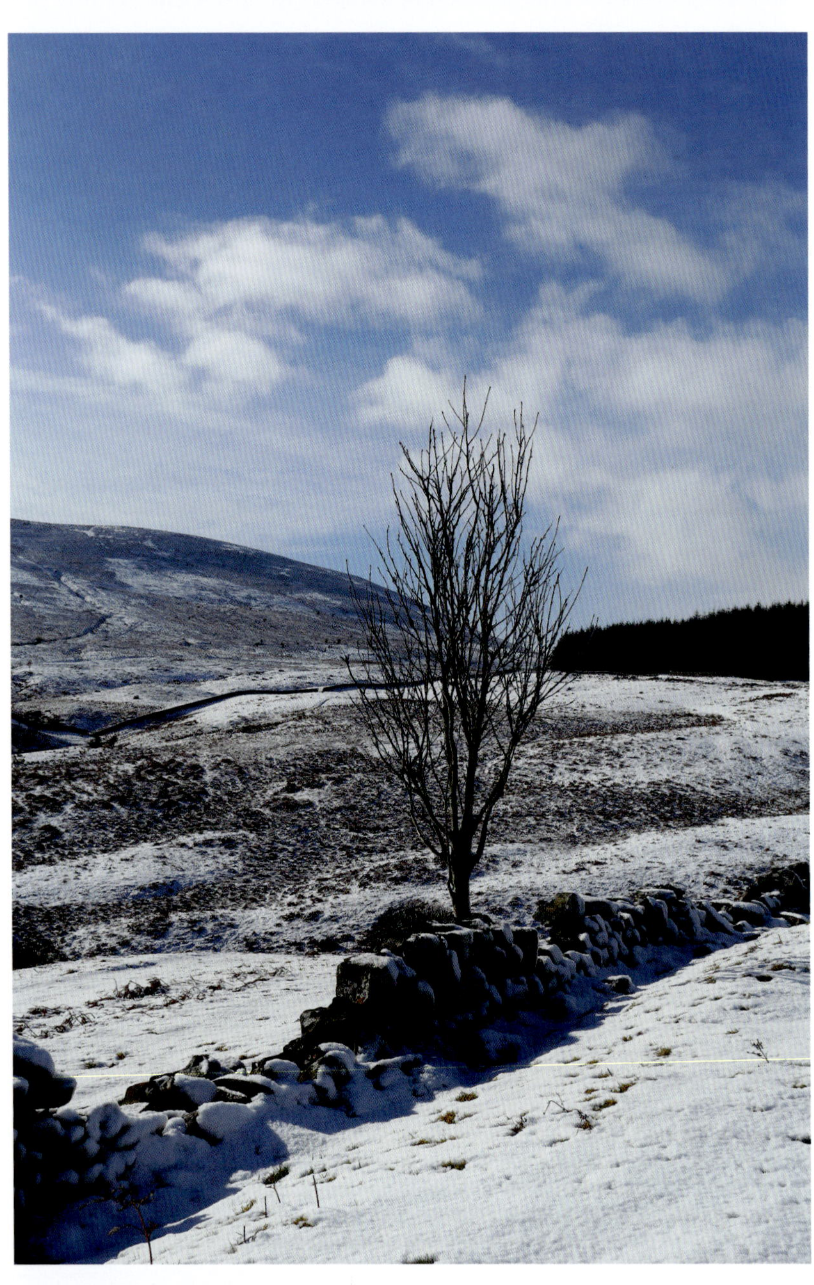

SNOWY SCOTTISH MORNING

One of the unspoken 'rules' of modern photography is not to have the focus or subject of your image in the centre of your picture. Oliver very frequently ignores this rule completely, to great effect!

THE MOOD OF THE MOUNTAINS, GLENCOE, SCOTLAND

This is an incredibly evocative and moody image of the craggy mountain tops of Glencoe, shrouded in heavy, threatening clouds that are rolling into the Glen, bringing storm and rain to the valley.

GLEN ETIVE, HIGHLANDS, SCOTLAND

The cloud cover and mist sweeping across the mountains in Glen Etive.

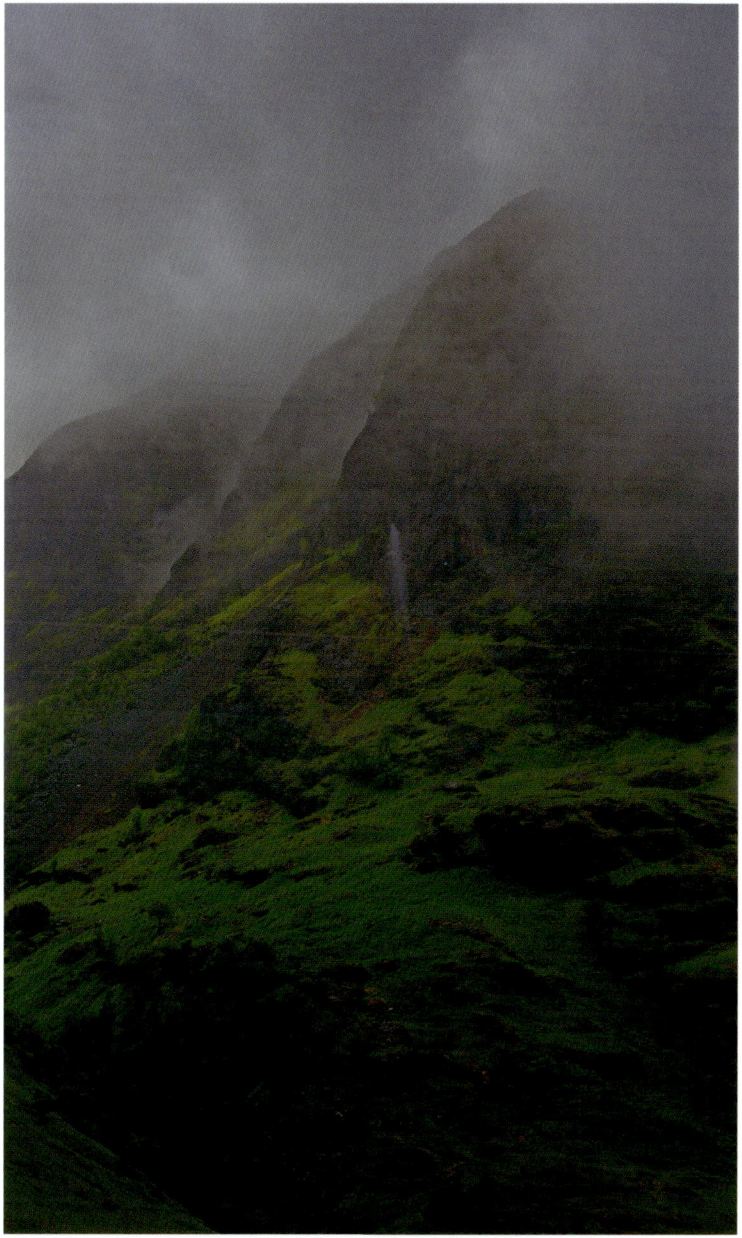

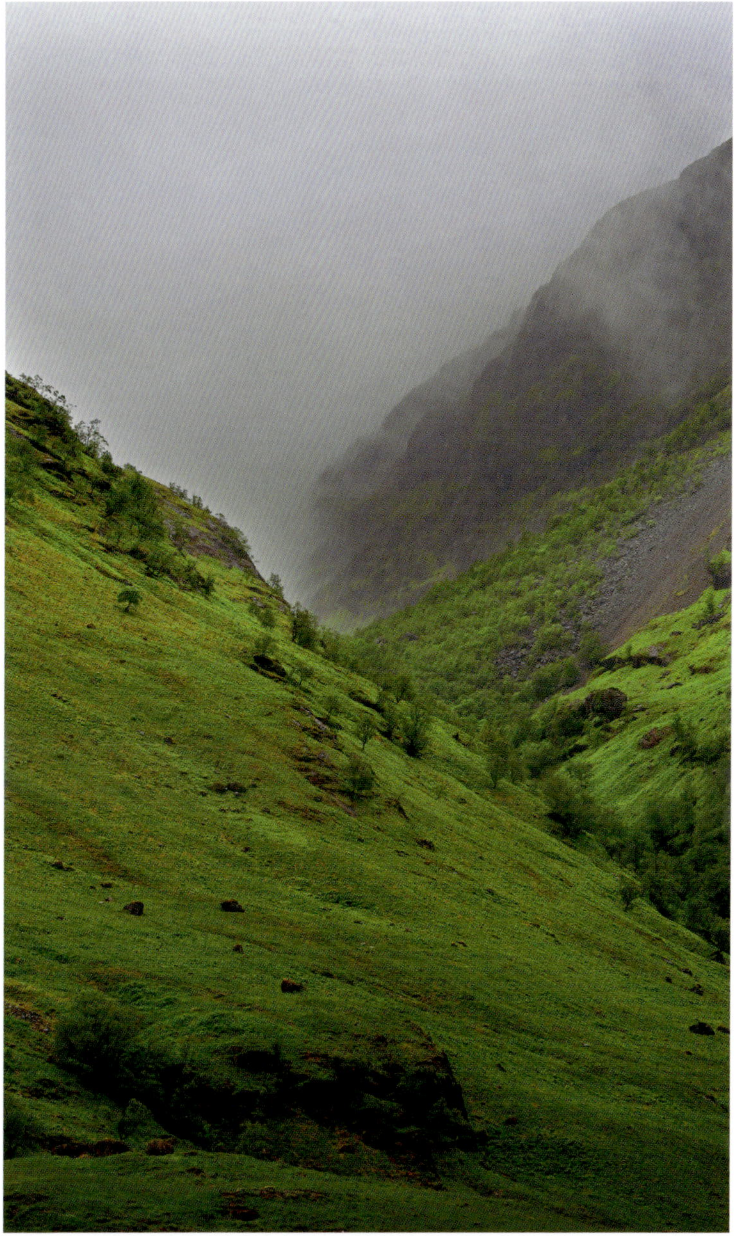

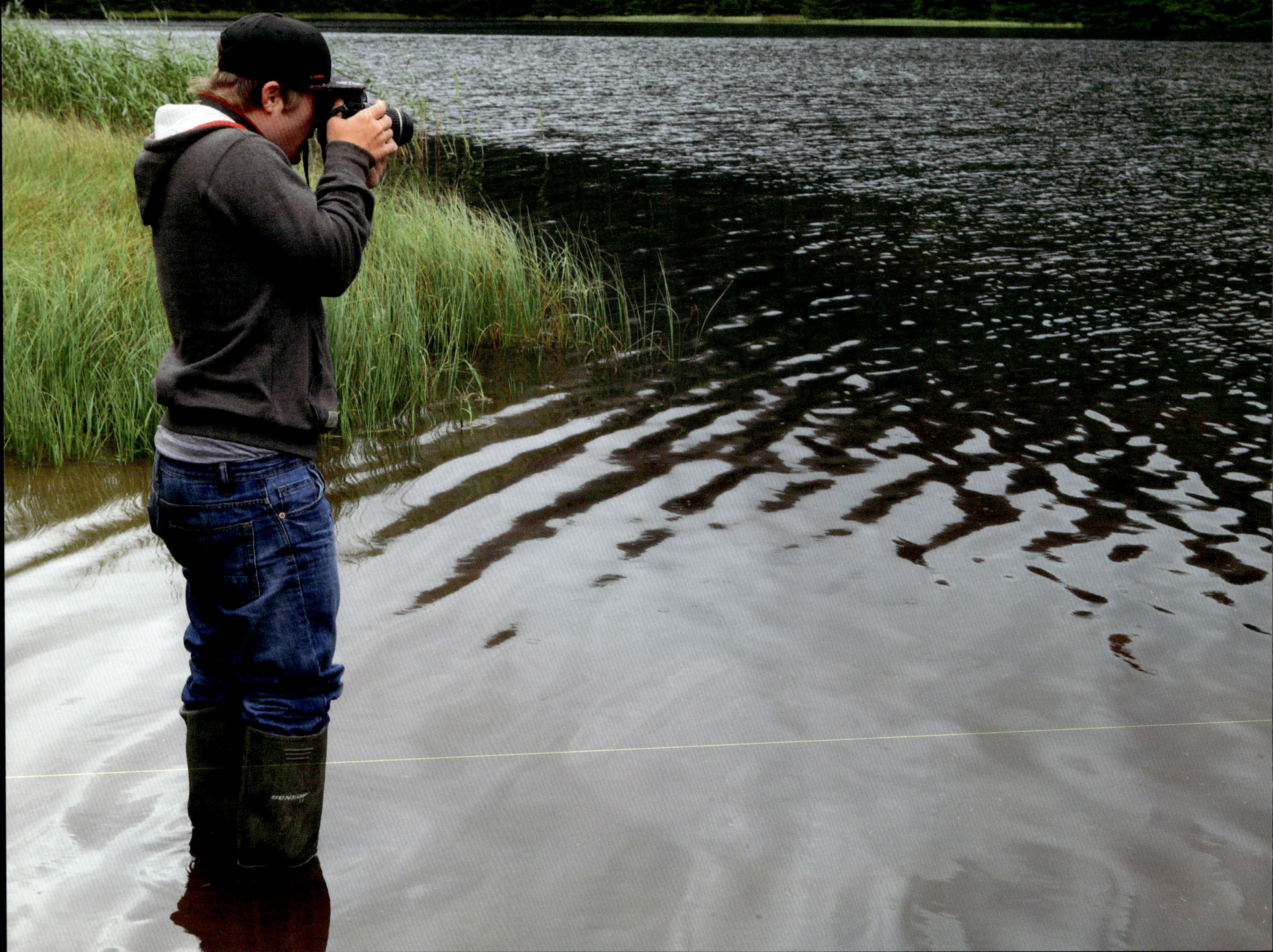

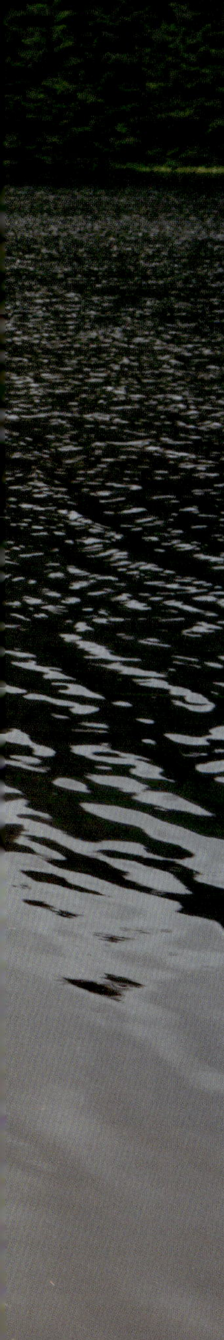

This picture was captured in
Scotland and has proved to
be Oliver's big sister Anna's
all-time favourite image. She
has it hanging in her home.
This is also one of those
images that has a picture of the
photographer actually capturing
it to accompany it!

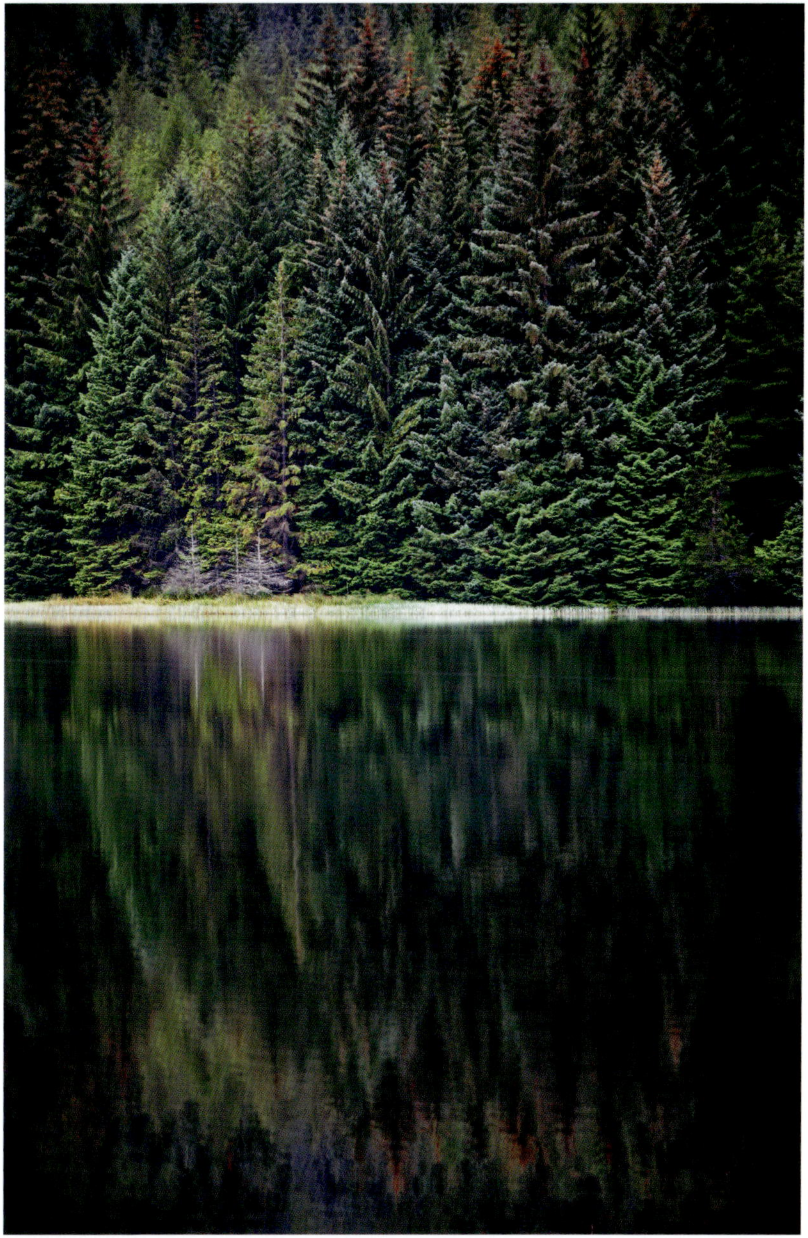

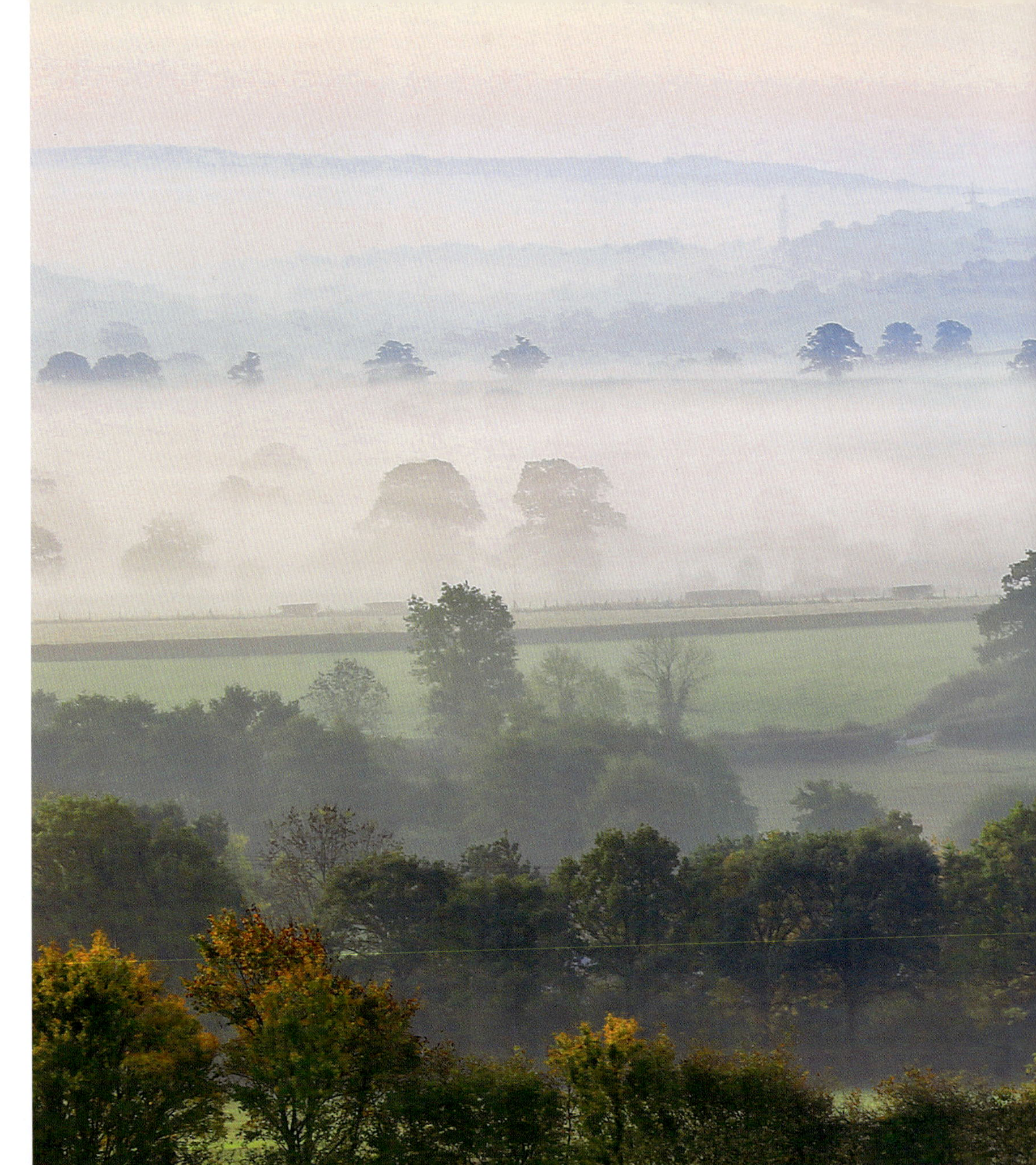

BLUE-GREEN MISTY FIELDS

This is such a gentle yet captivating image of the early morning mist floating on the fields. Oliver captured many photographs on this expedition, all of which he was very pleased with.

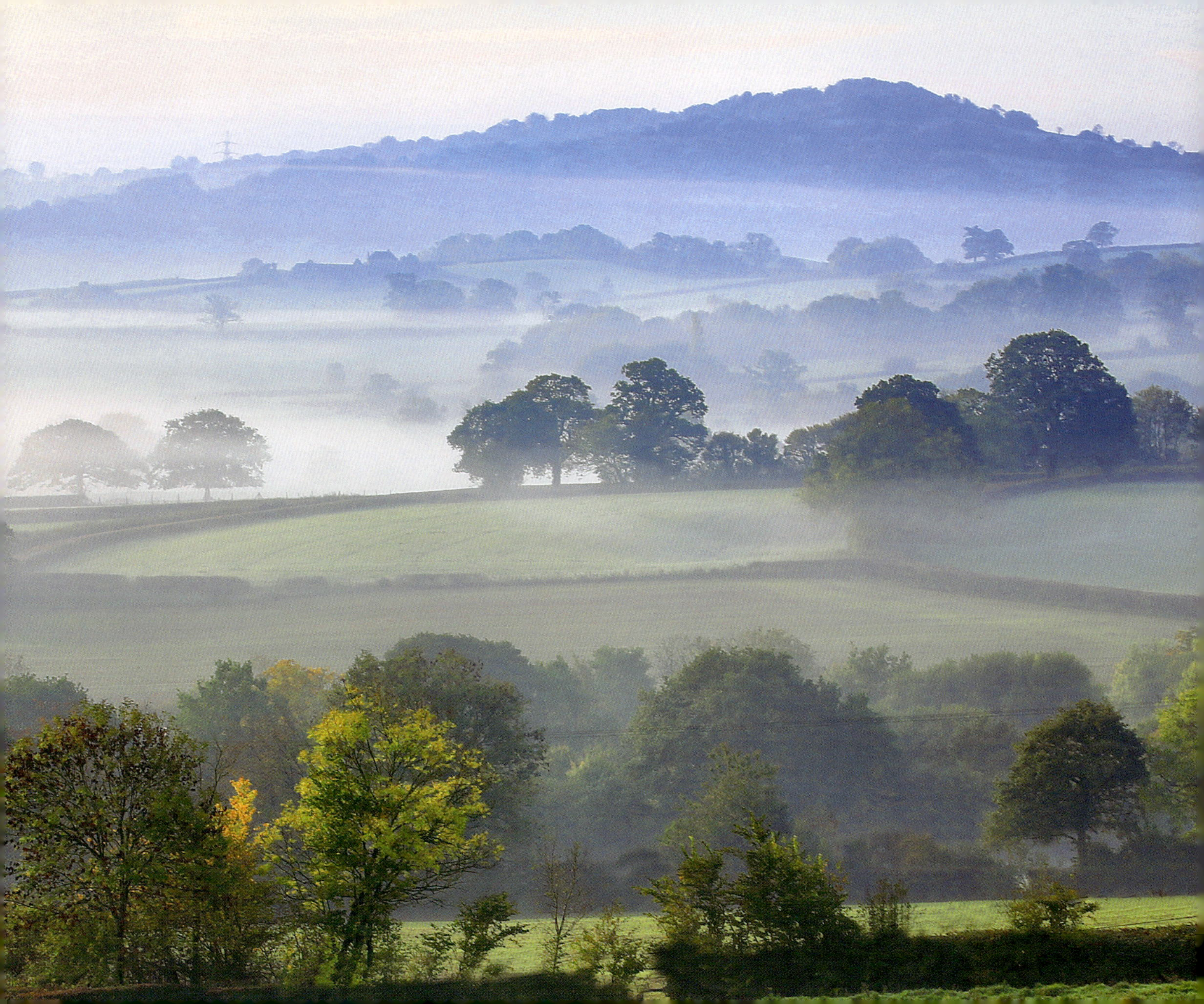

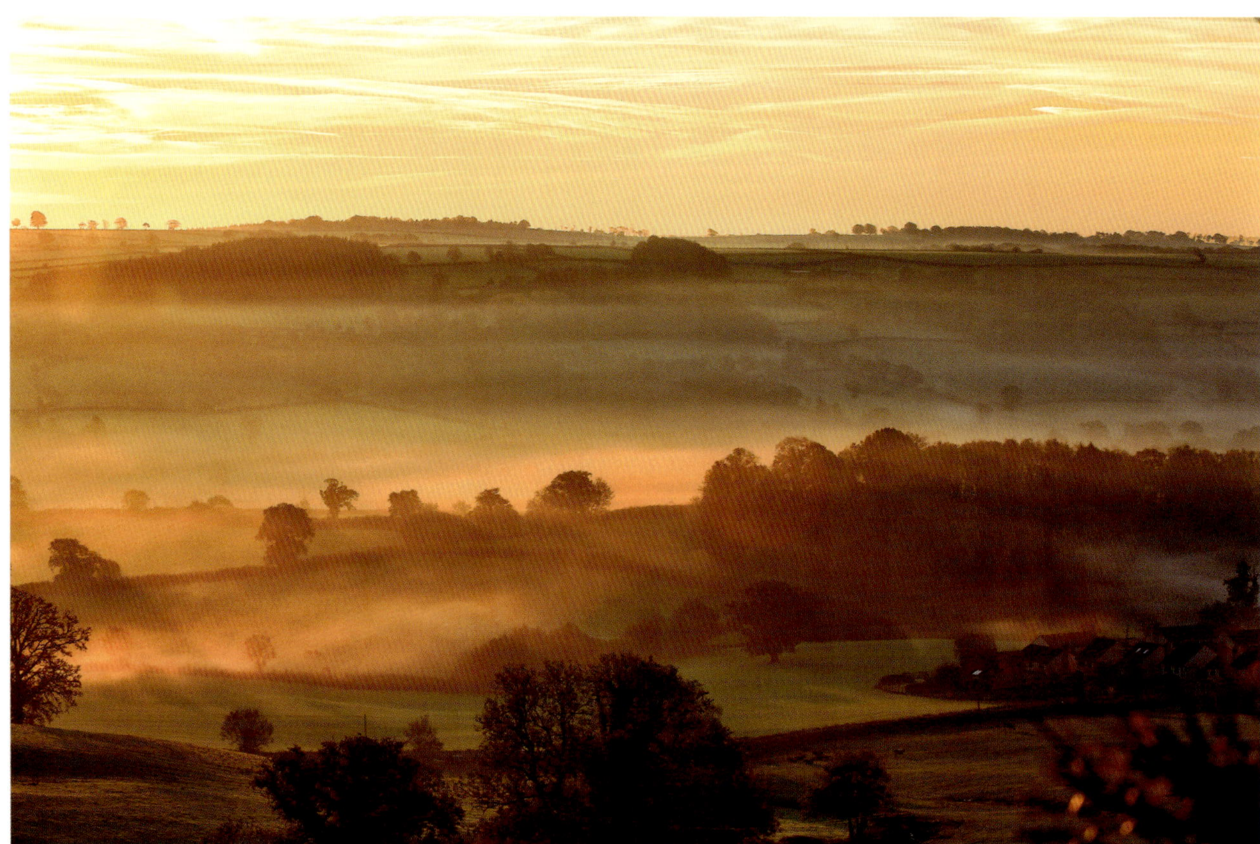

OUR GREEN AND
PLEASANT LAND
Oliver's favourite

"I really like this one. I got it on holiday in Wales. I love the trees and the fields, and everything is so green and the light is there, and you can see the white sheep like dots in all the fields."

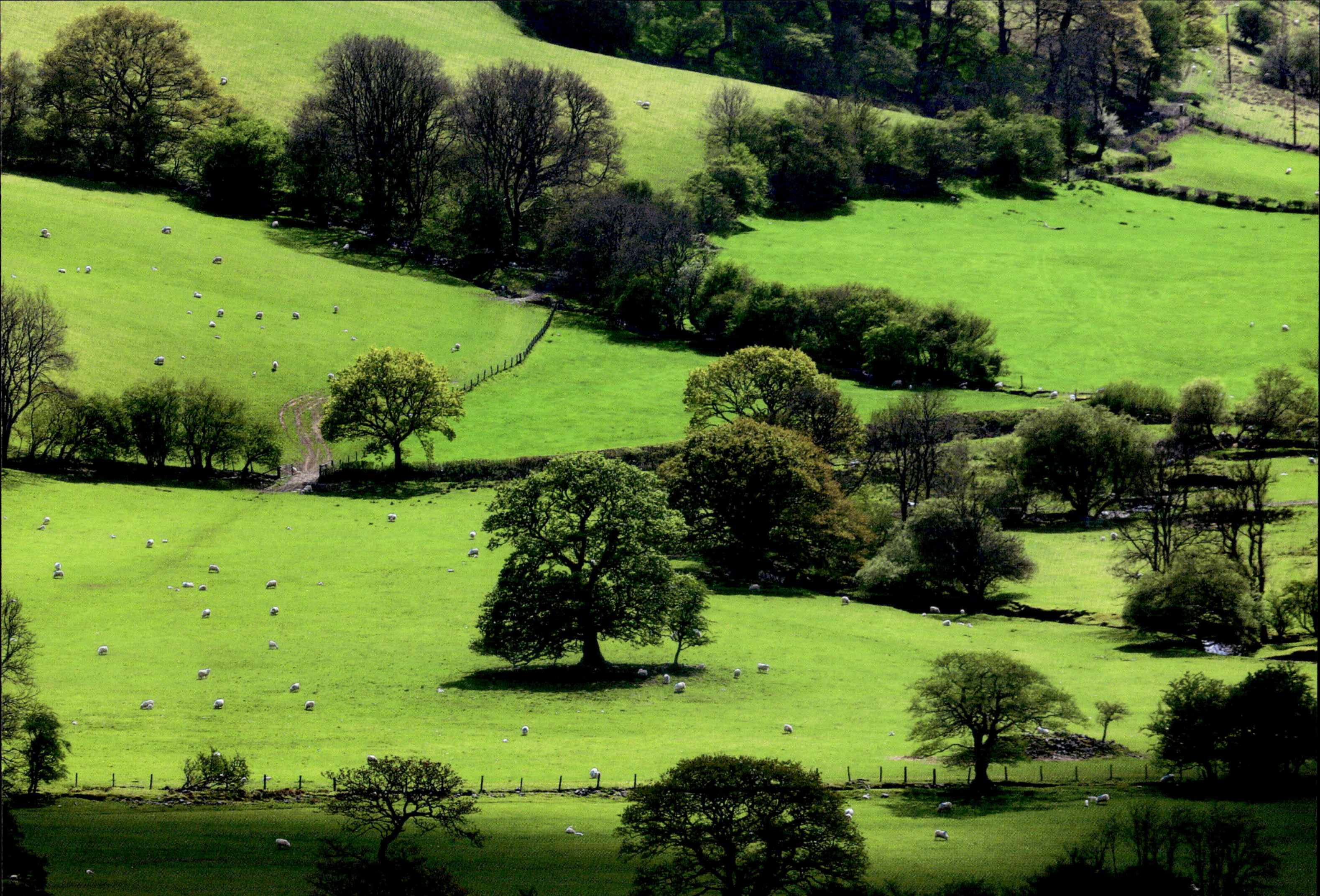

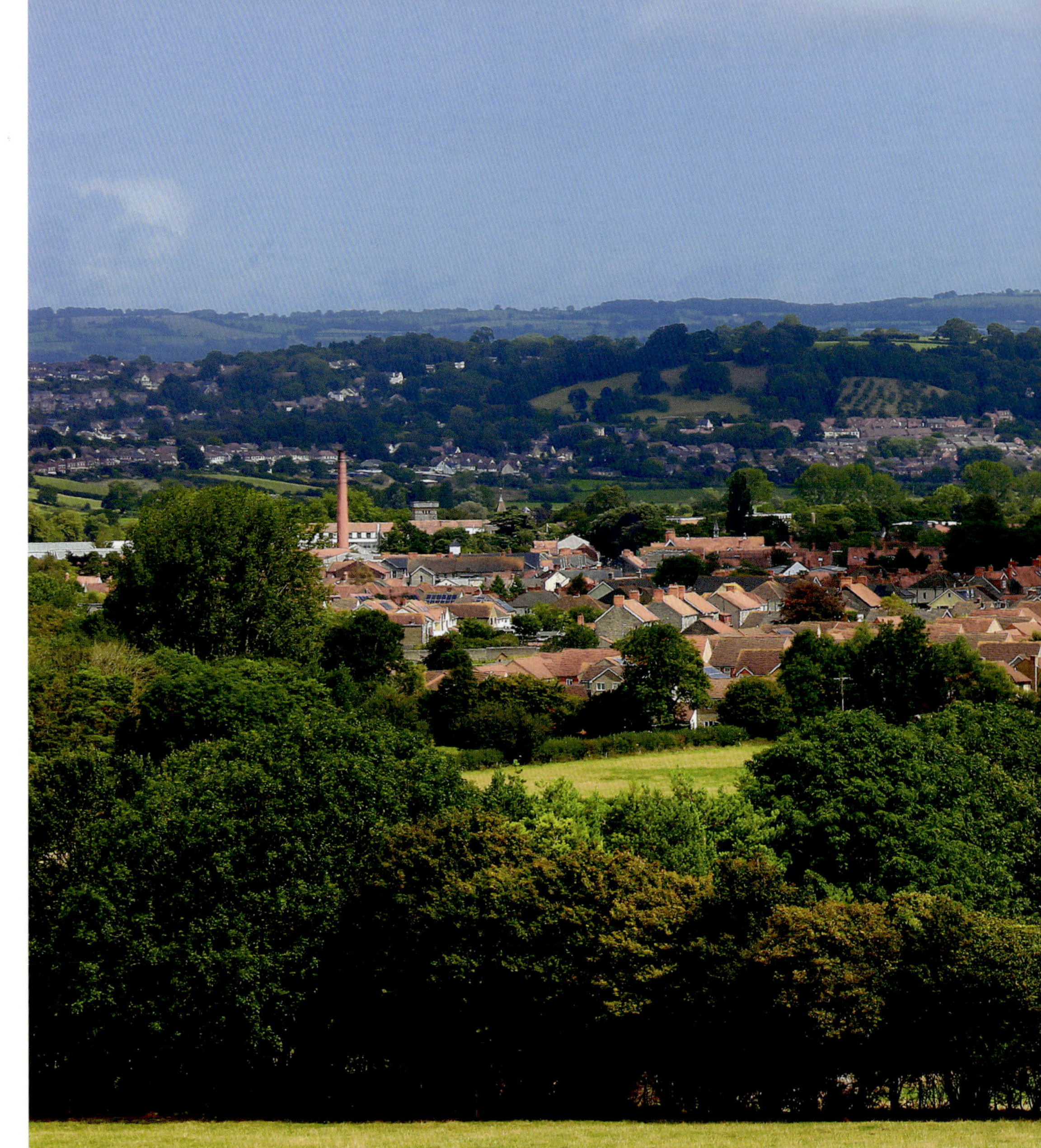

"We were driving to Glastonbury to get some pictures of Glastonbury Tor and on the way we stopped and I got out and looked over a gate to take this picture, because I could see it, rising up a long way away. You can see all the red houses and the green trees and the blue sky. It's a good picture."

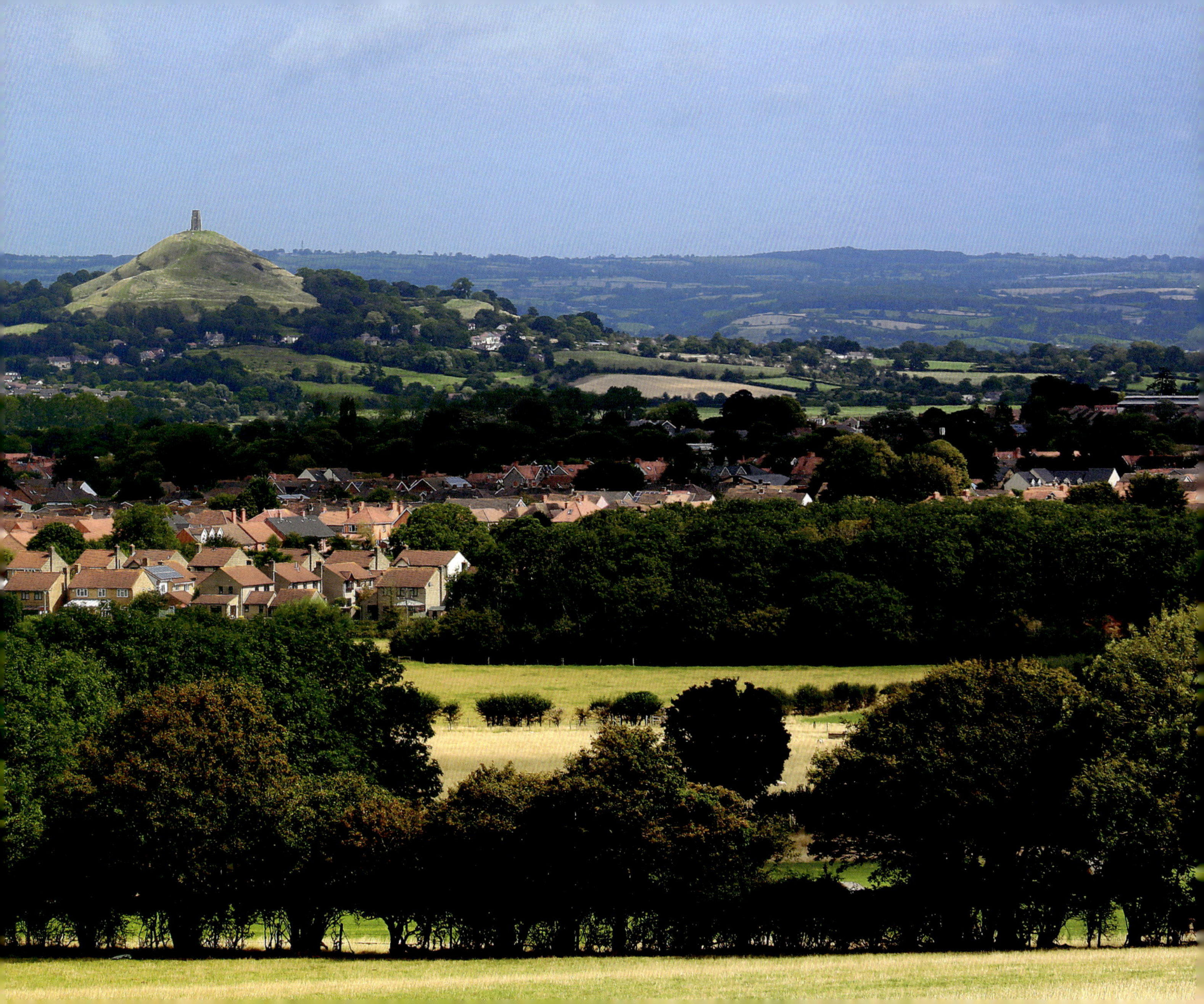

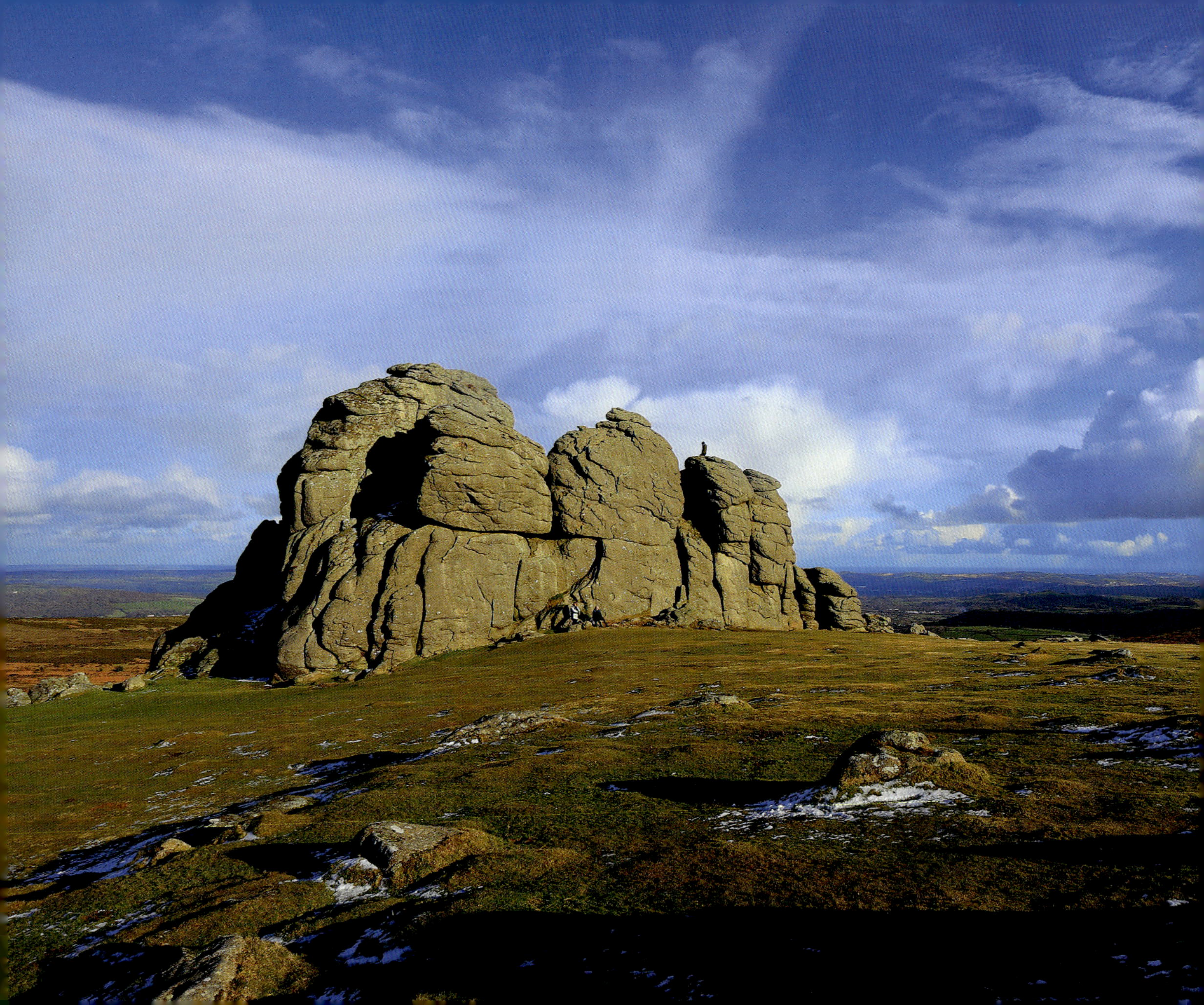

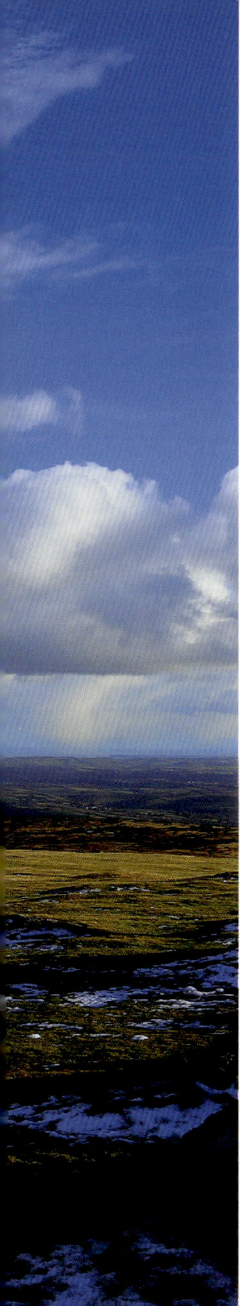

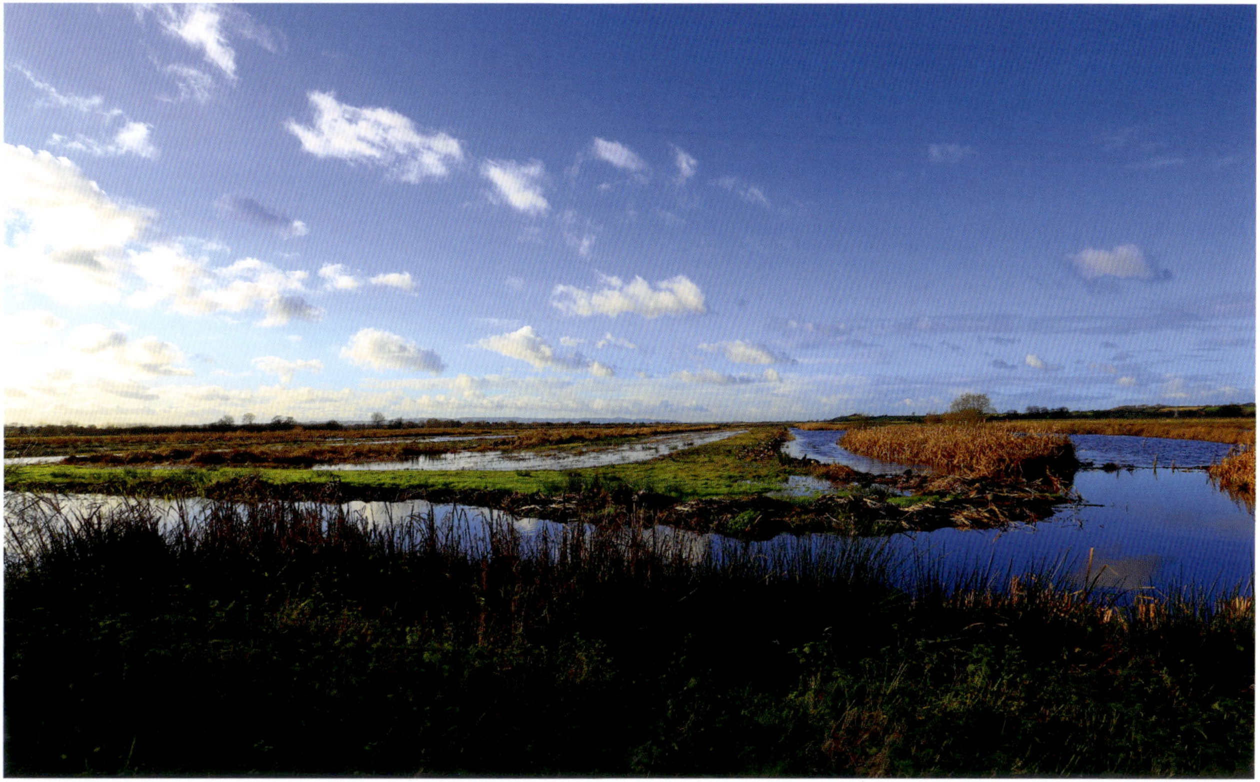

THE WETLANDS

We have many wetland areas
across our rather watery British
Isles, all teeming with wildlife if
you know where to look.

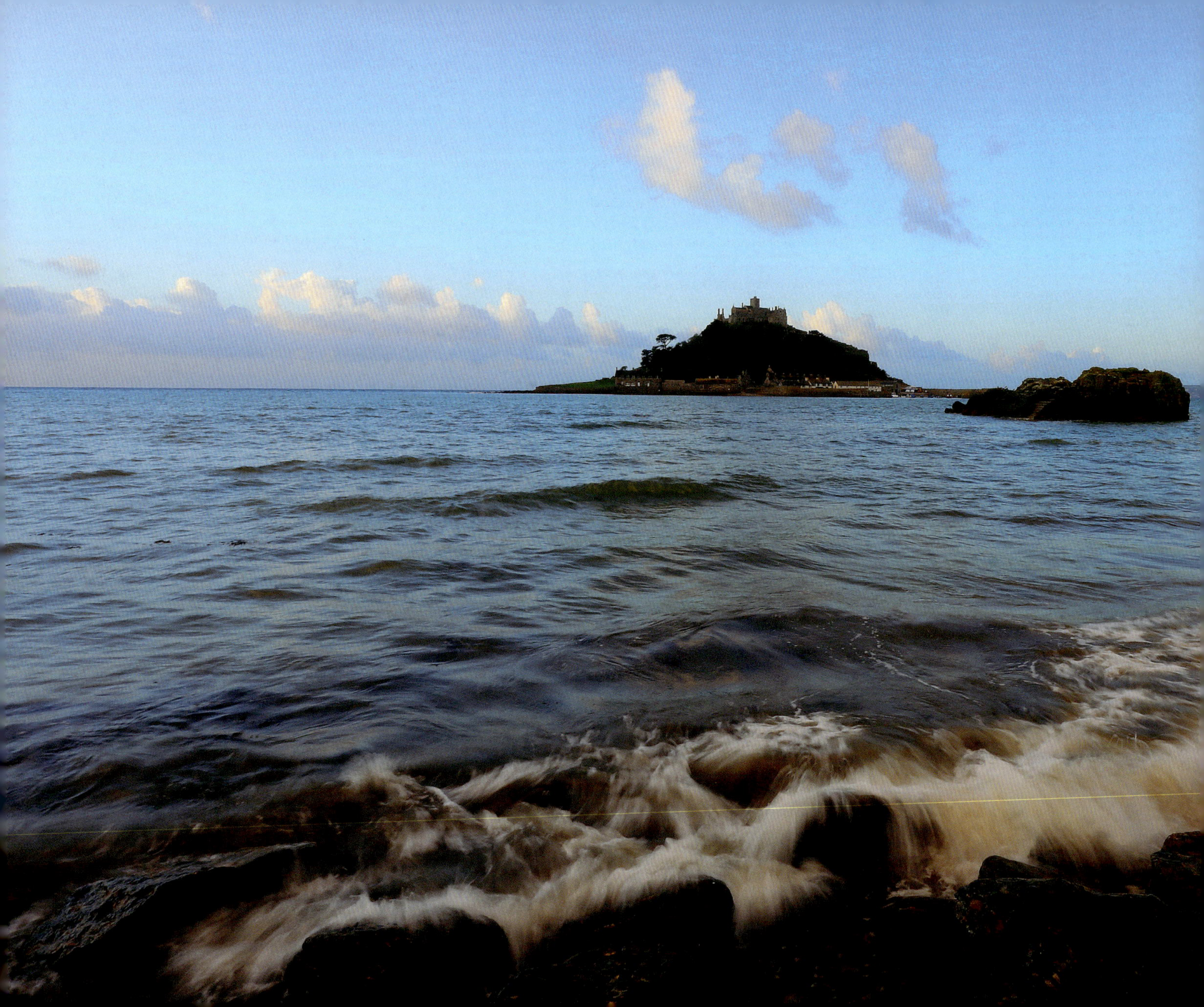

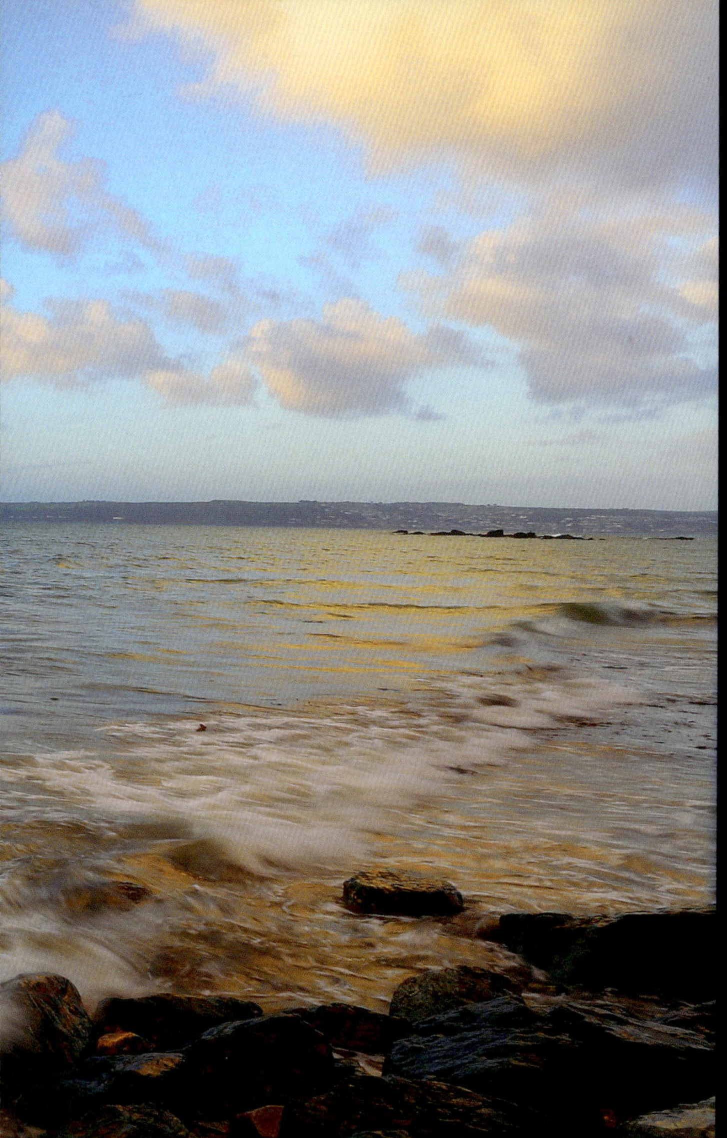

OH, I DO LOVE TO BE BESIDE THE SEASIDE

With so much shoreline all around us, we Brits do love the seaside. And for Oliver, the chance to combine his love of water with some chips or an ice cream is an opportunity not to be missed! What better joy can there be than to sit and watch the sea with a portion of freshly made piping hot chips in your hands?

Oliver will often sit for ages on a quayside to capture pictures of the boats, or sit on a beach or cliffs and take lots of images of crashing waves.

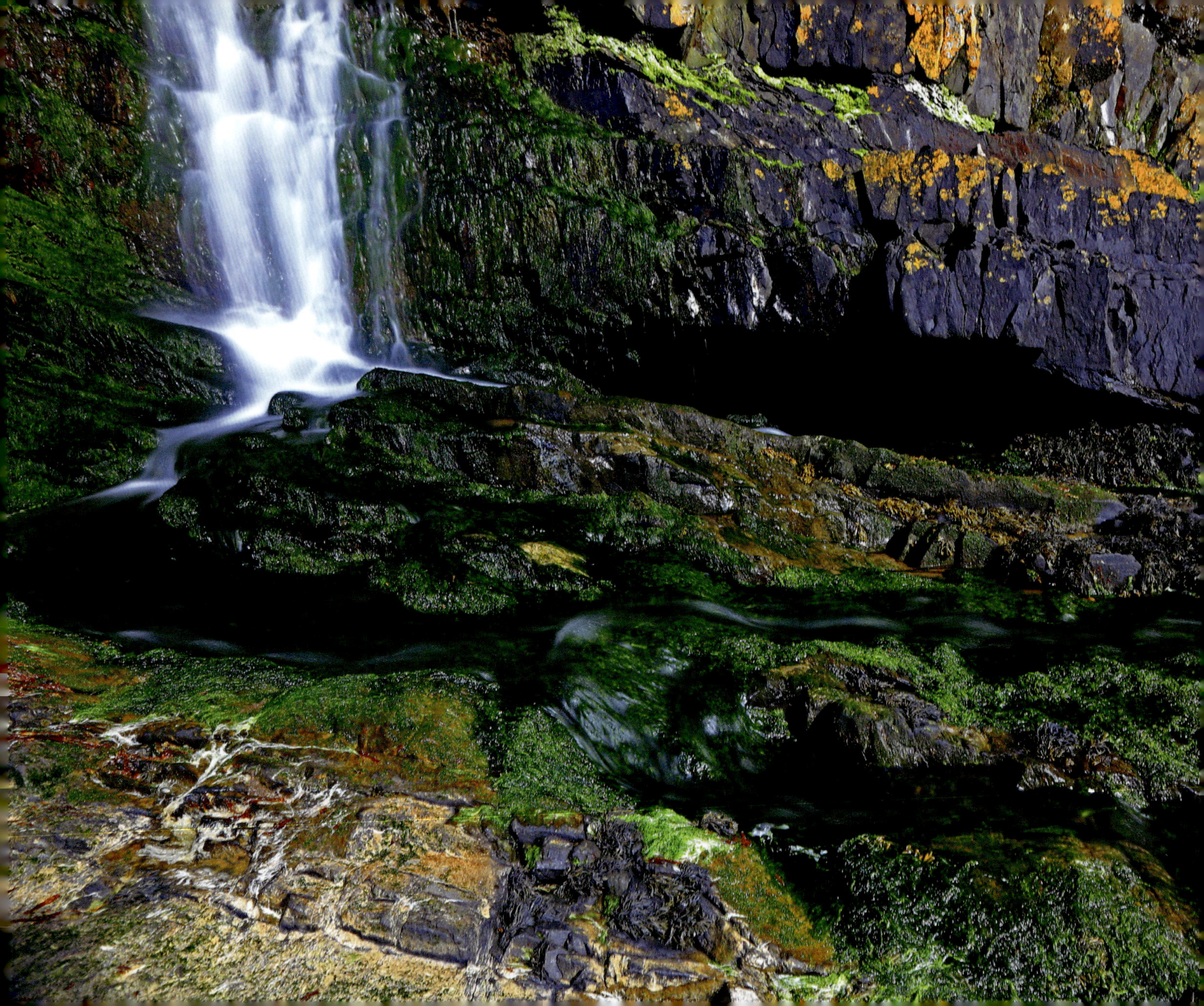

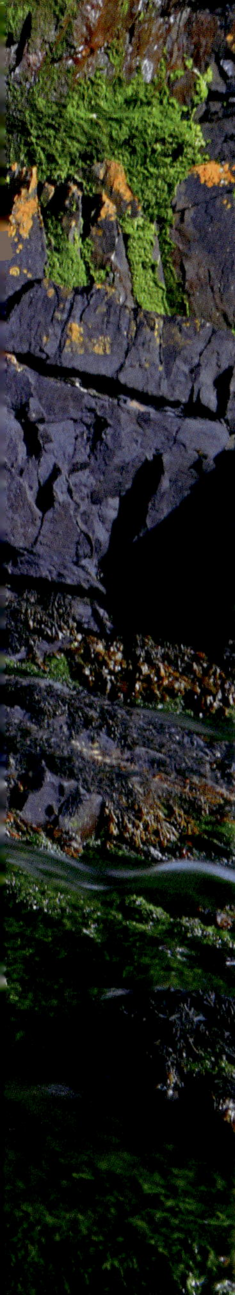

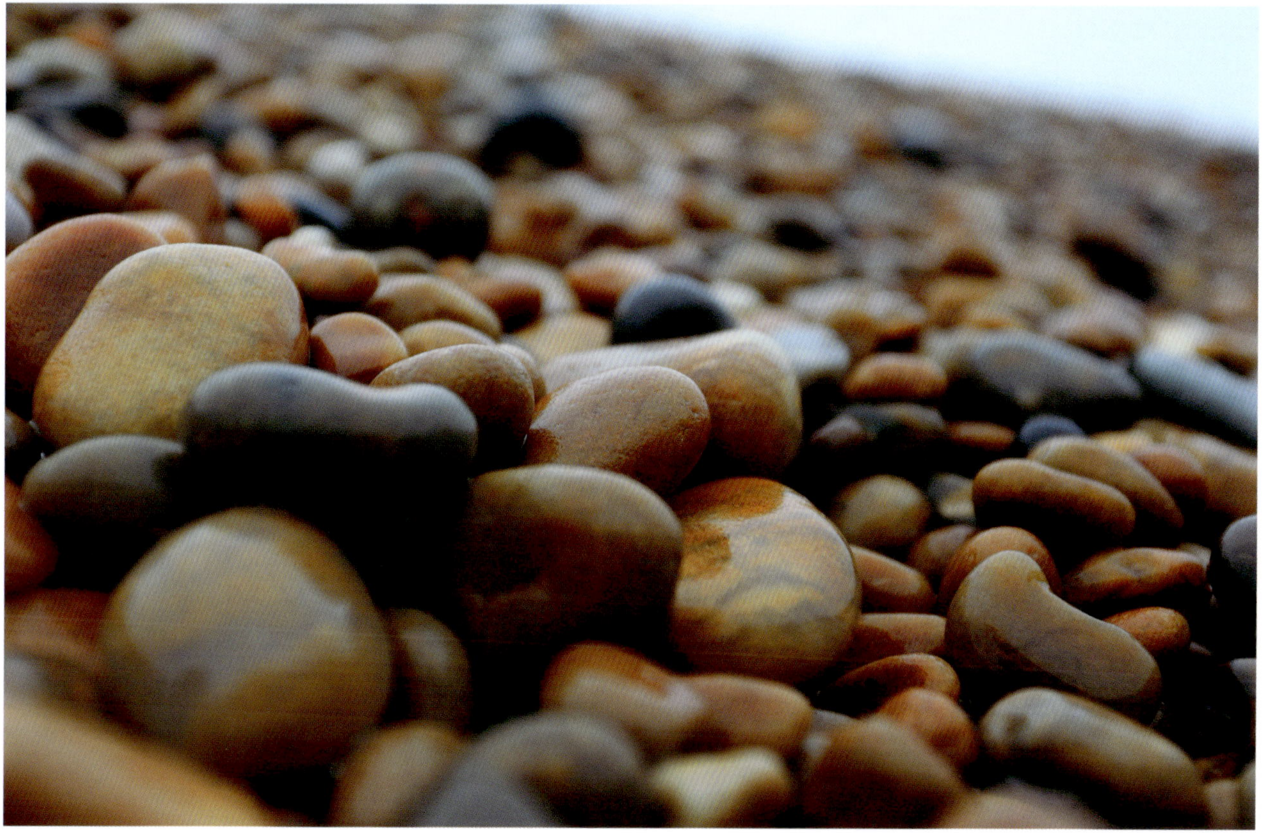

CEIBWR BAY, WALES – WATERFALL ON THE BEACH
Oliver's favourite

"I did a long exposure to get the flow of the water. I like the detail in the rocks, the waterfall, the dark green moss, the yellow lichen and purple rocks."

PEBBLES ON THE DORSET COAST

Oliver enjoyed the colours and variety of all the pebbles on this beach along the coast in Dorset.

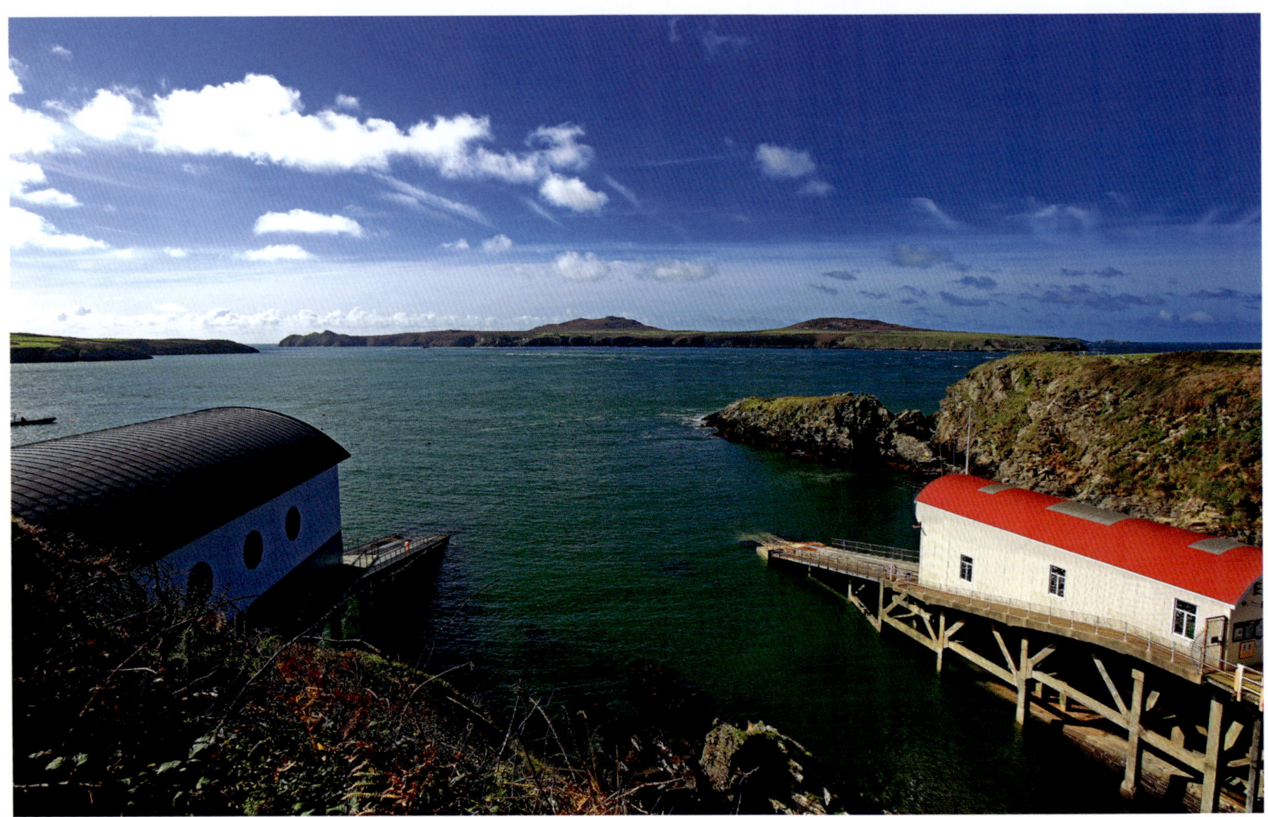

ST JUSTINIAN'S OLD AND NEW LIFEBOAT STATIONS, WALES

Oliver enjoyed walking a little way along the cliff path on the west coast of Wales and got this great shot looking down on the old (right) and new (left) lifeboat stations. He took a few different shots before he was happy that he'd got the angles he wanted.

HERRING GULL IN LOOE CORNWALL
Oliver's favourite

"This is a herring gull. They are very common in Britain on the coast. They steal people's chips! We were in Looe, Cornwall, with my sister Anna. I had my wide-angle lens on my camera to get the gull in focus in my foreground and the houses out of focus in the background."

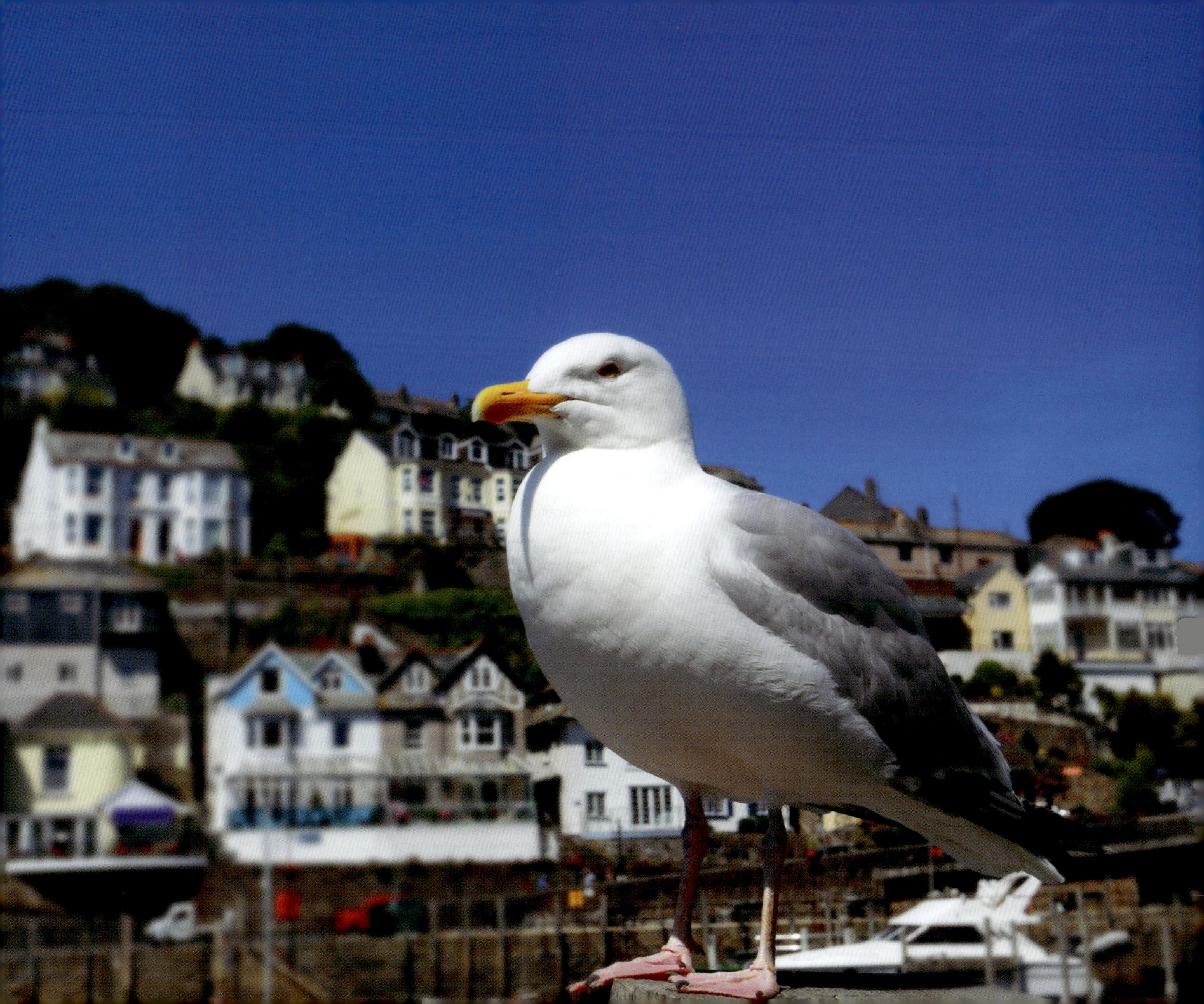

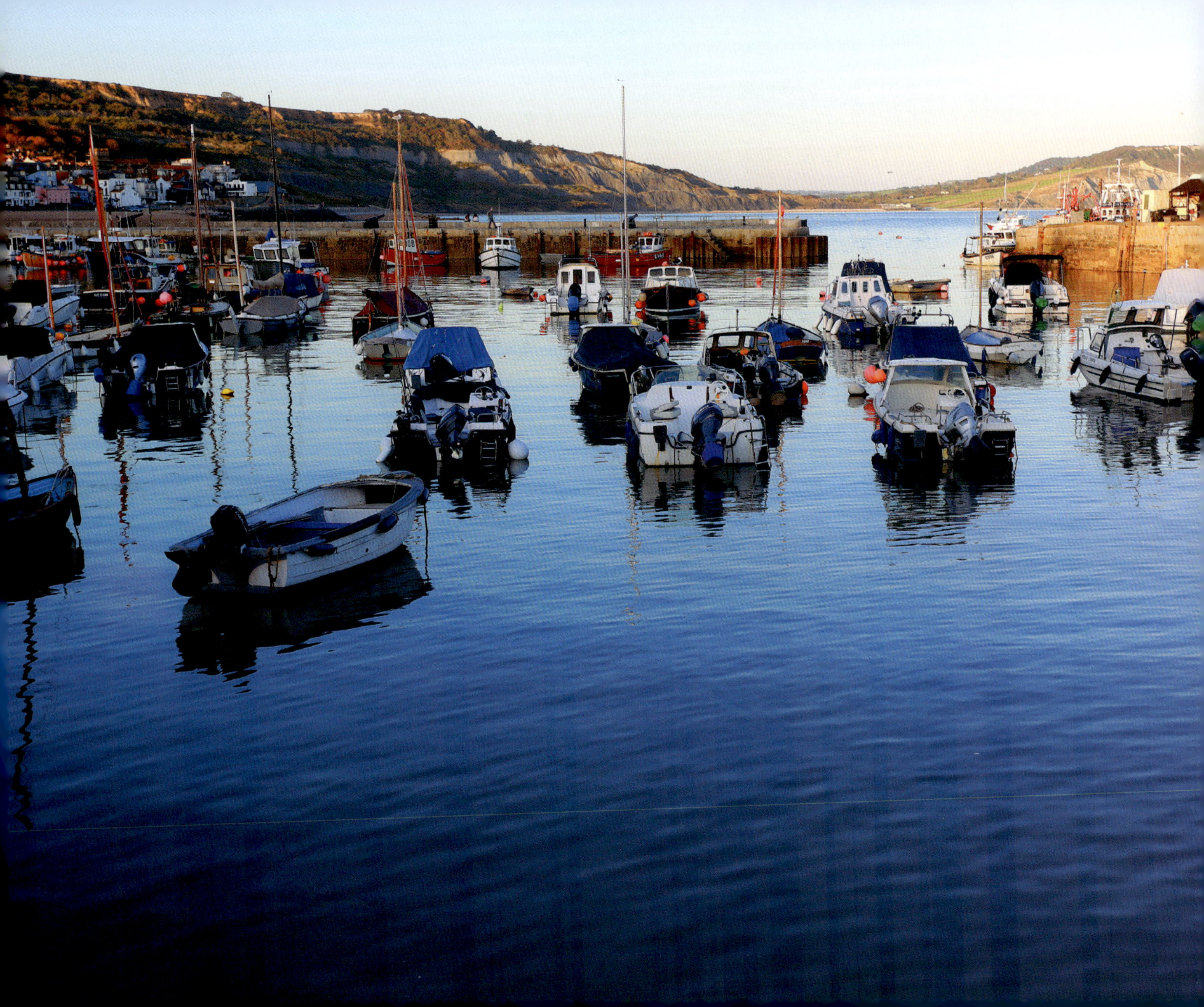

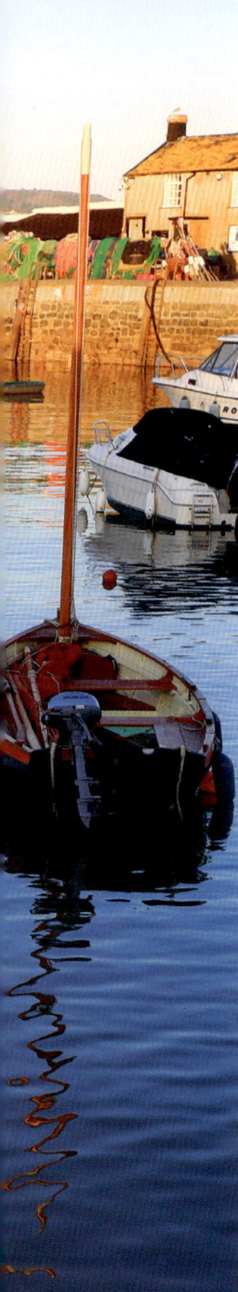

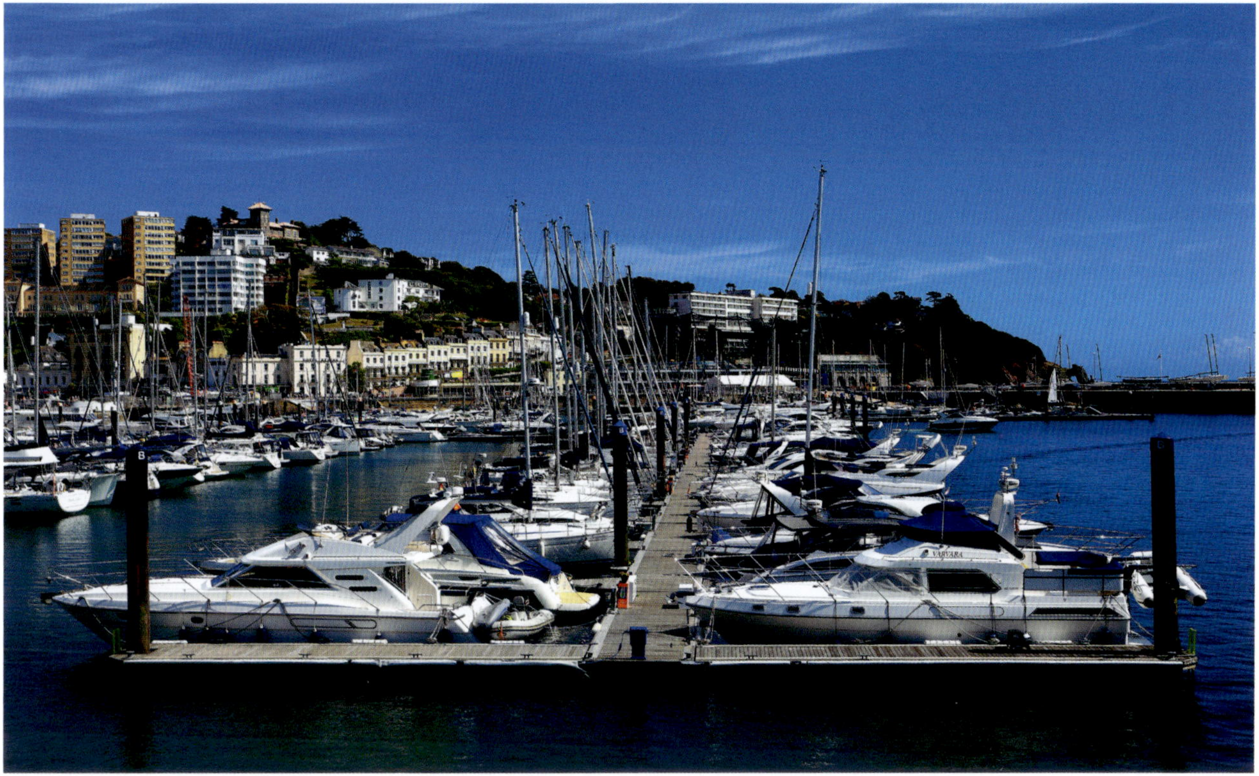

HARBOUR AT LYME REGIS

Oliver enjoyed a trip to this little harbour in the summer to take pictures, watch the sun go down and enjoy seaside chips and ice cream!

THE JET SETTERS OF TORQUAY

There are many very expensive boats and yachts moored in Torquay – Oliver thought they all looked pretty cool!

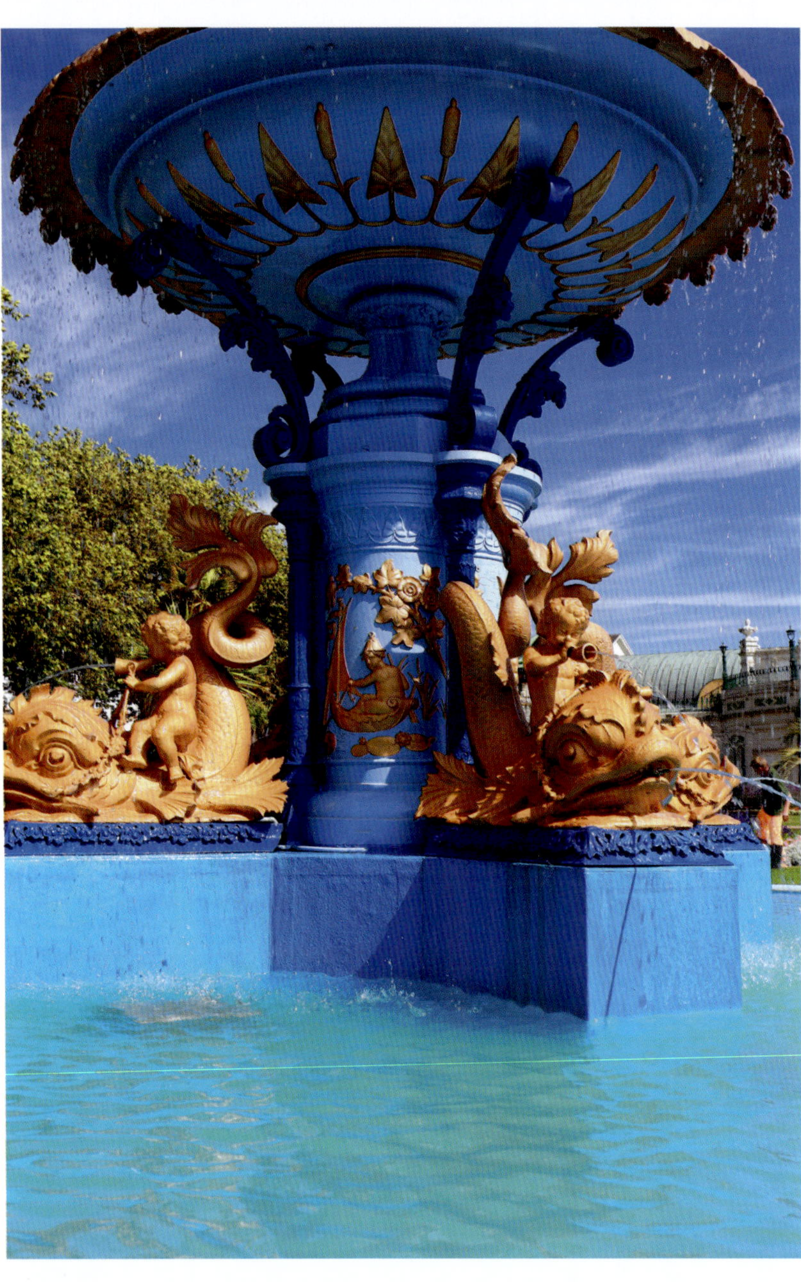

CAST-IRON FOUNTAIN IN PRINCESS GARDENS, TORQUAY, DEVON

Oliver's favourite

"I was out with my sister Anna in Torquay and I saw this ornamental fountain. I wanted to capture all the shapes and the patterns. There are bits curving over and I wanted to look up and get it all in the frame. You can see how I framed it up. I love all the blue, and I like the statues on both sides."

THE SMOOTH BLUE

Oliver used a tripod and long shutter speed to get this beautiful, relaxing image of the coast at Hope Cove in Devon.

CORNWALL – CLIFFS AND SEA

Oliver's favourite

"I like the turquoise and blue colours of the sea. I like the detail of the rocks and the water. I do like splashes!"

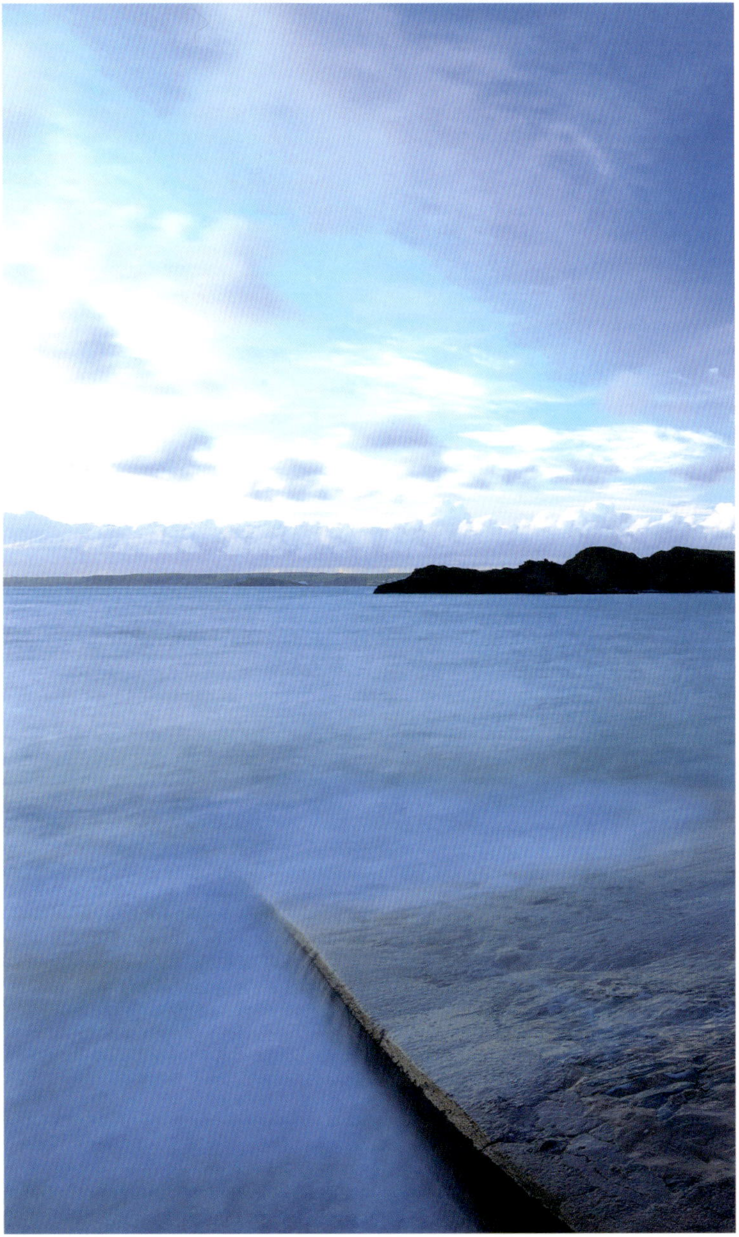

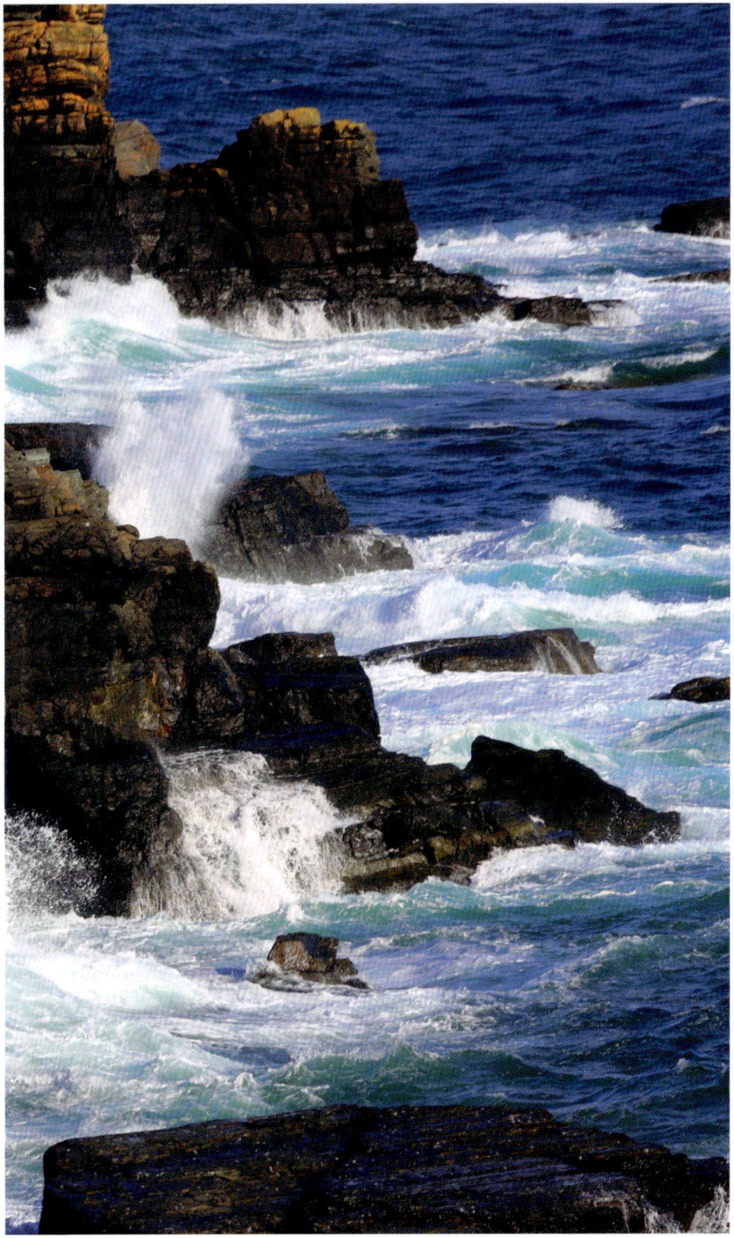

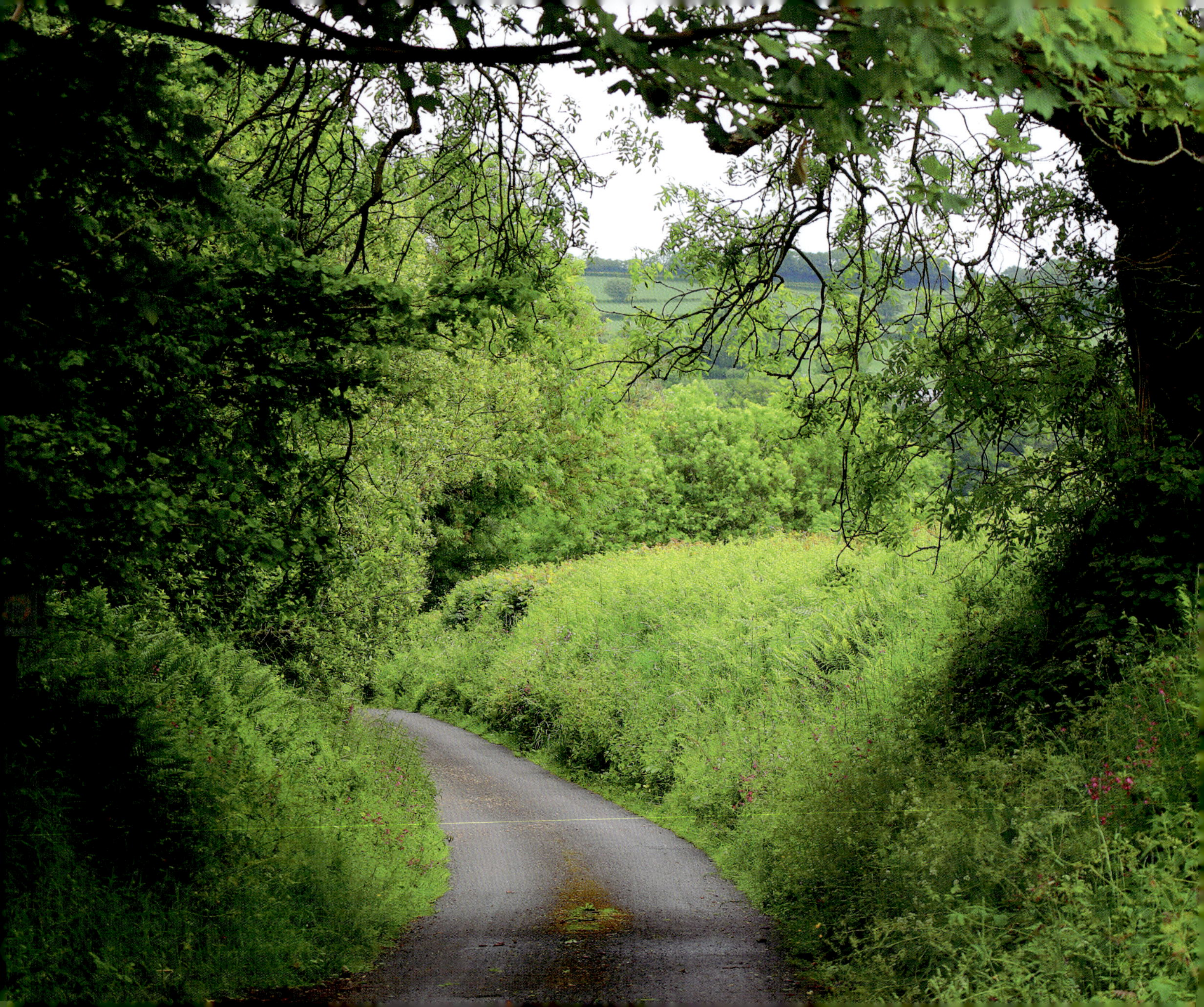

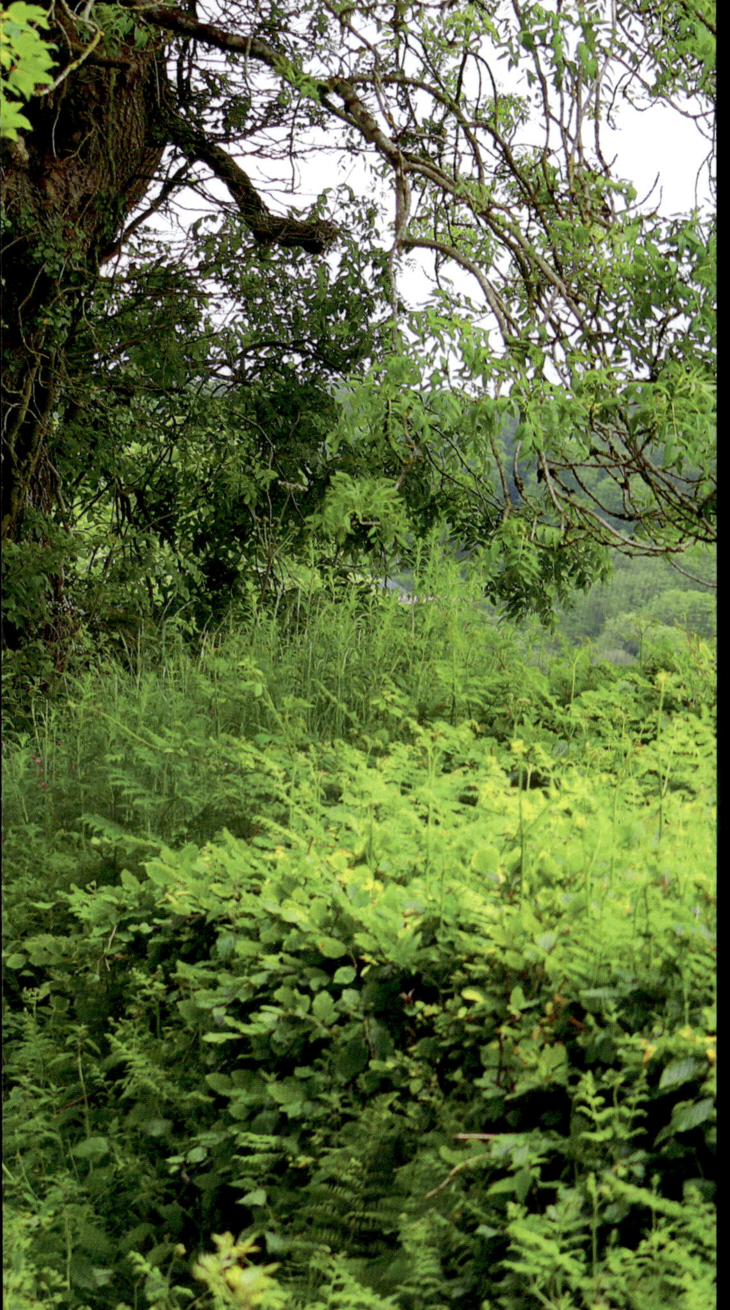

TAKE ME HOME, COUNTRY ROADS

Oliver does love a good path! He very frequently takes photographs of roads, lanes and paths and his followers seem to love them too! One's eye is often attracted to a road or path and we are frequently left wondering: Where might it take us? What might be around the next corner? Or over the hill? And we are drawn in…

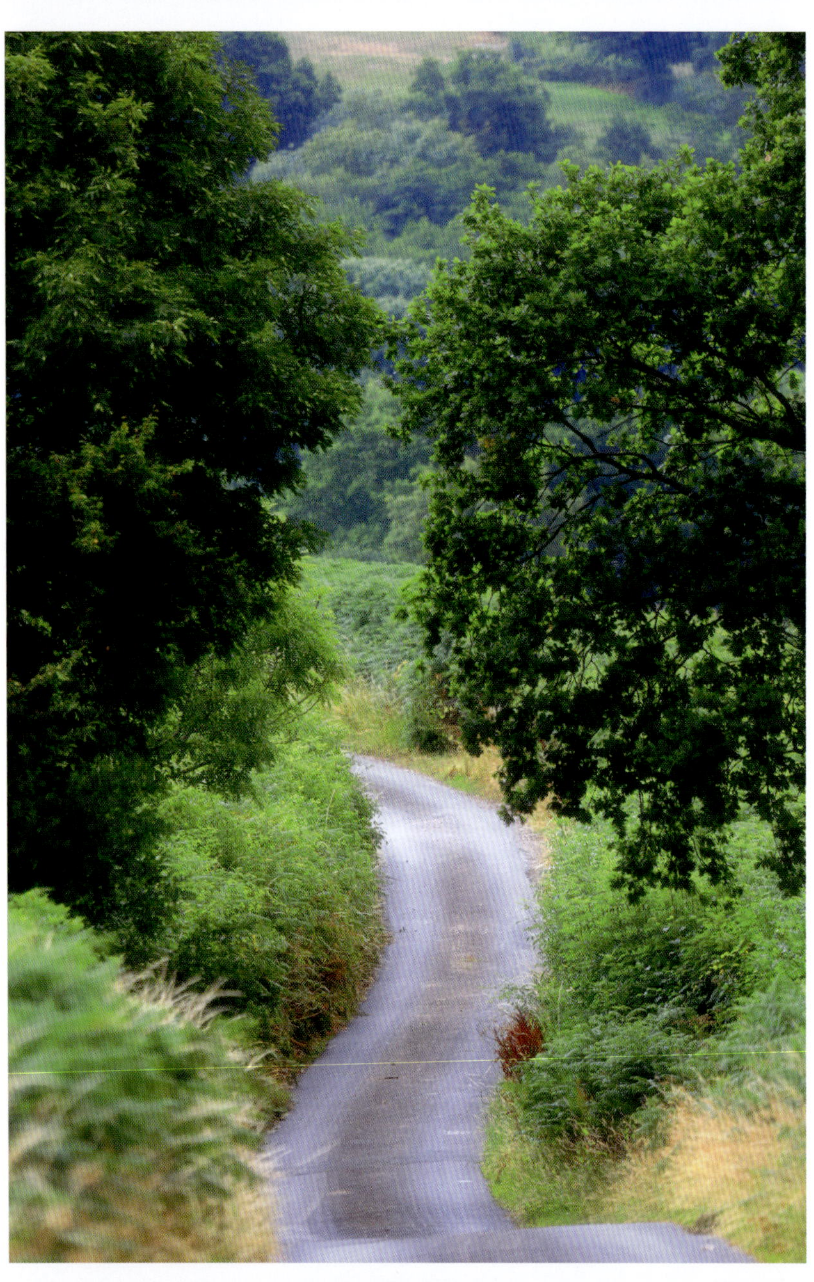

WINDING LANES

Britain is so very fortunate
to have so many thousands
of gentle, lush country lanes
to wander along whenever
you are so inclined – and for
Oliver to enjoy and photograph
throughout the year.

PATH THROUGH THE GREEN, QUANTOCK HILLS

THE ROAD TO OLIVER

This is the road that takes you
down the hill and into Oliver's
home village. He has captured
it many times and across all the
seasons, but this is one of his
favourites.

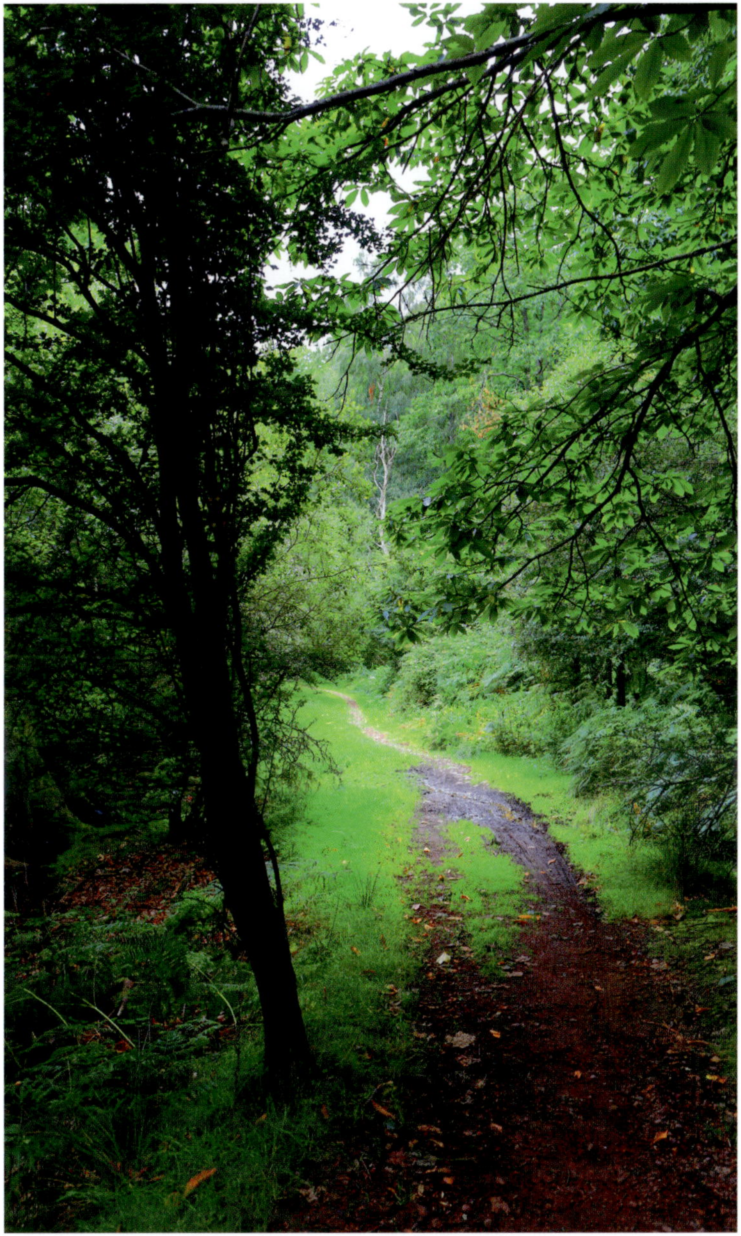

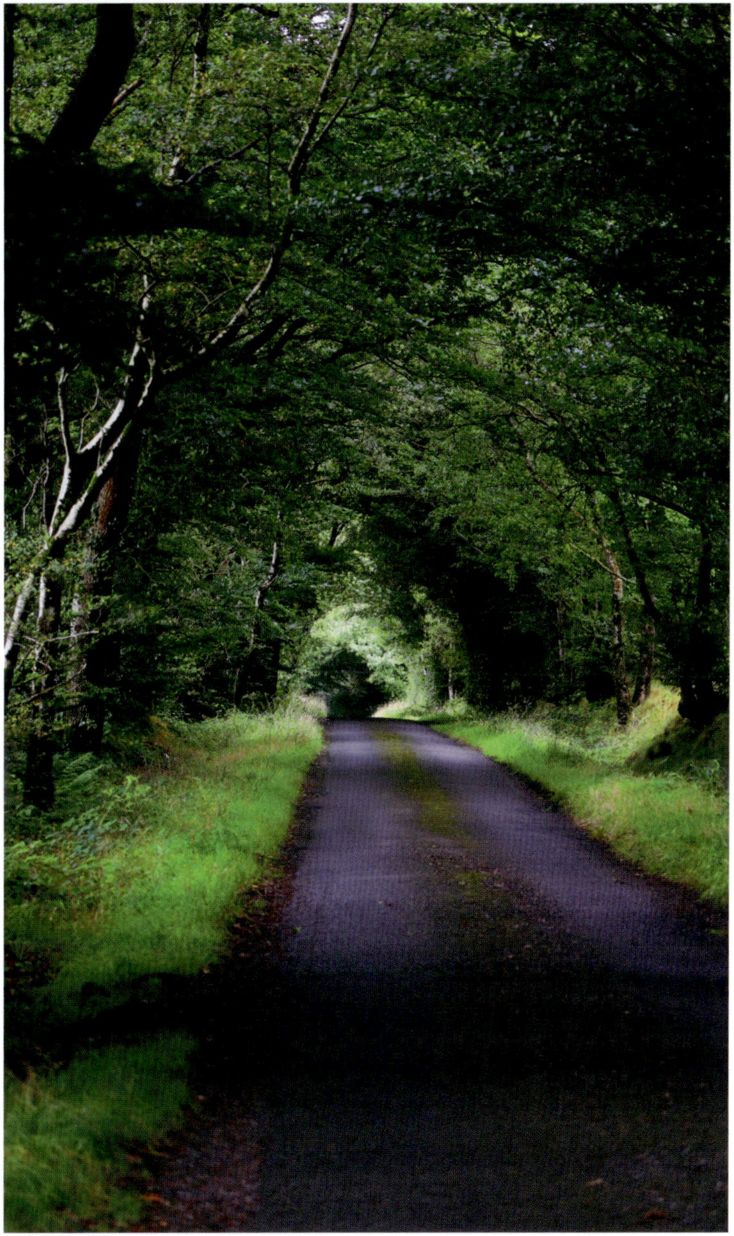

This image is one of those that could have been taken at a thousand different locations across Britain, featuring a typical British deciduous woodland. This is definitely Oliver's all-time bestselling image, both as a print and as a large canvas. It really is one of those pictures, especially when it is up on a wall in a large format, that makes you feel as if you could just walk right into it and along that path.

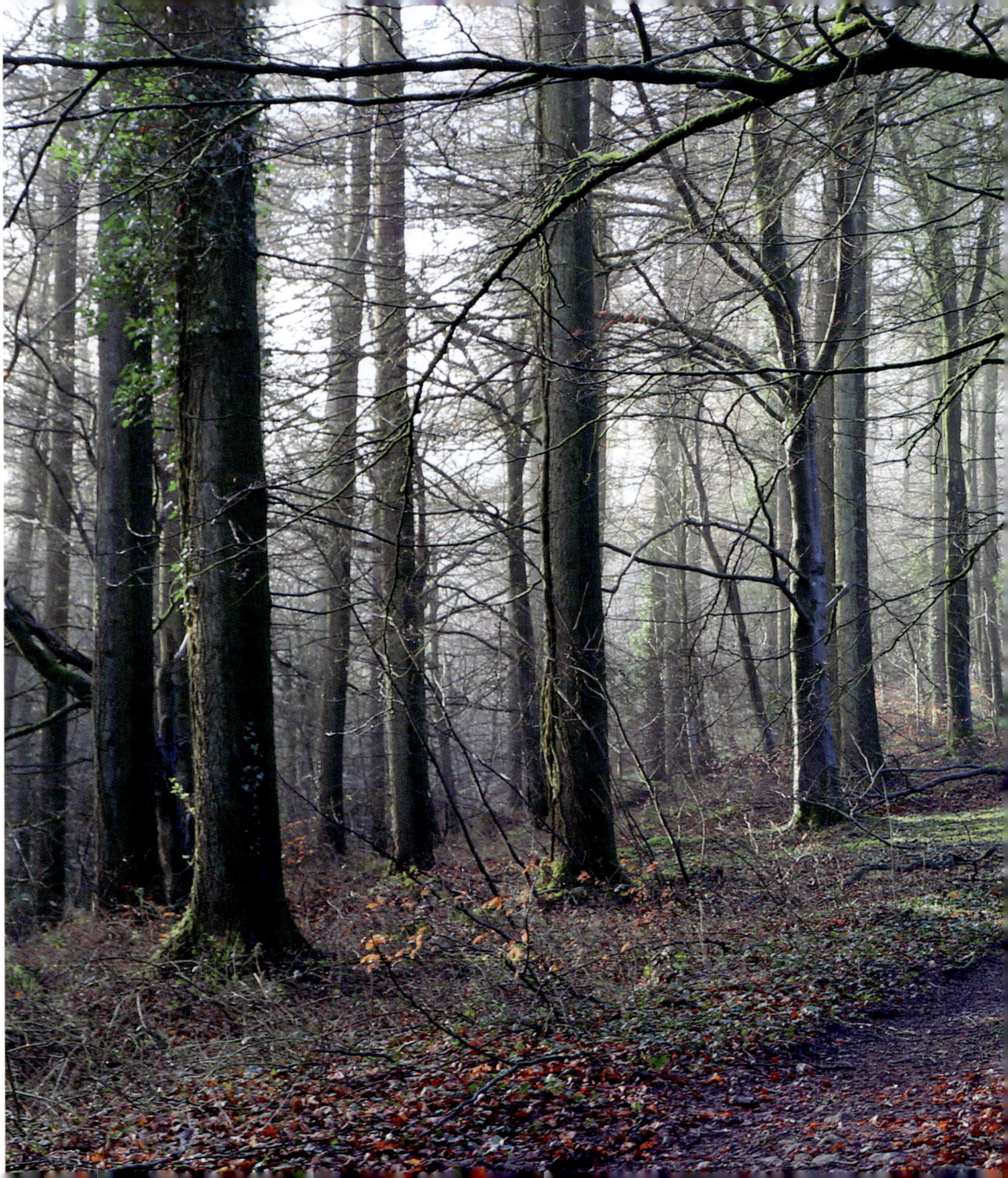

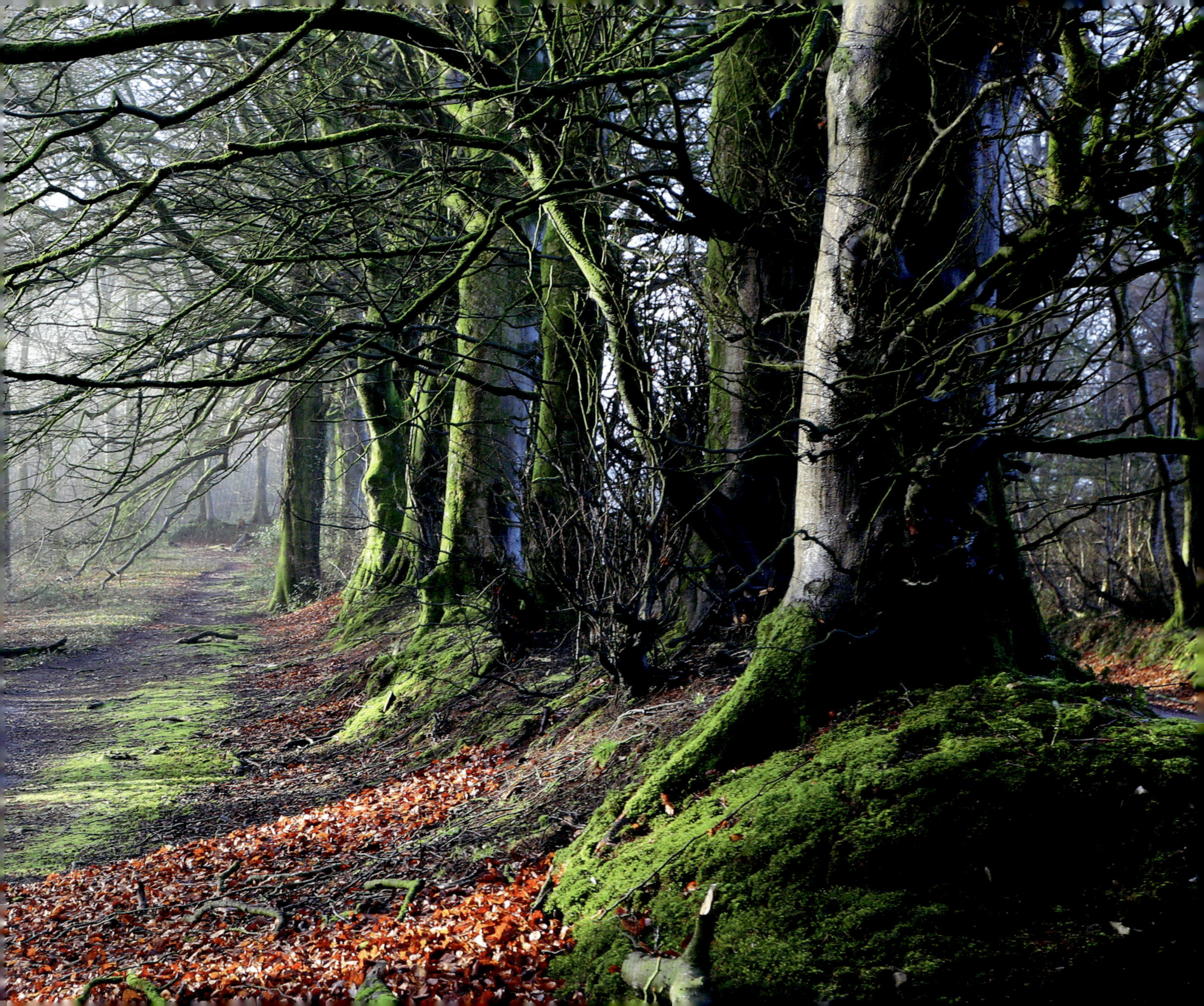

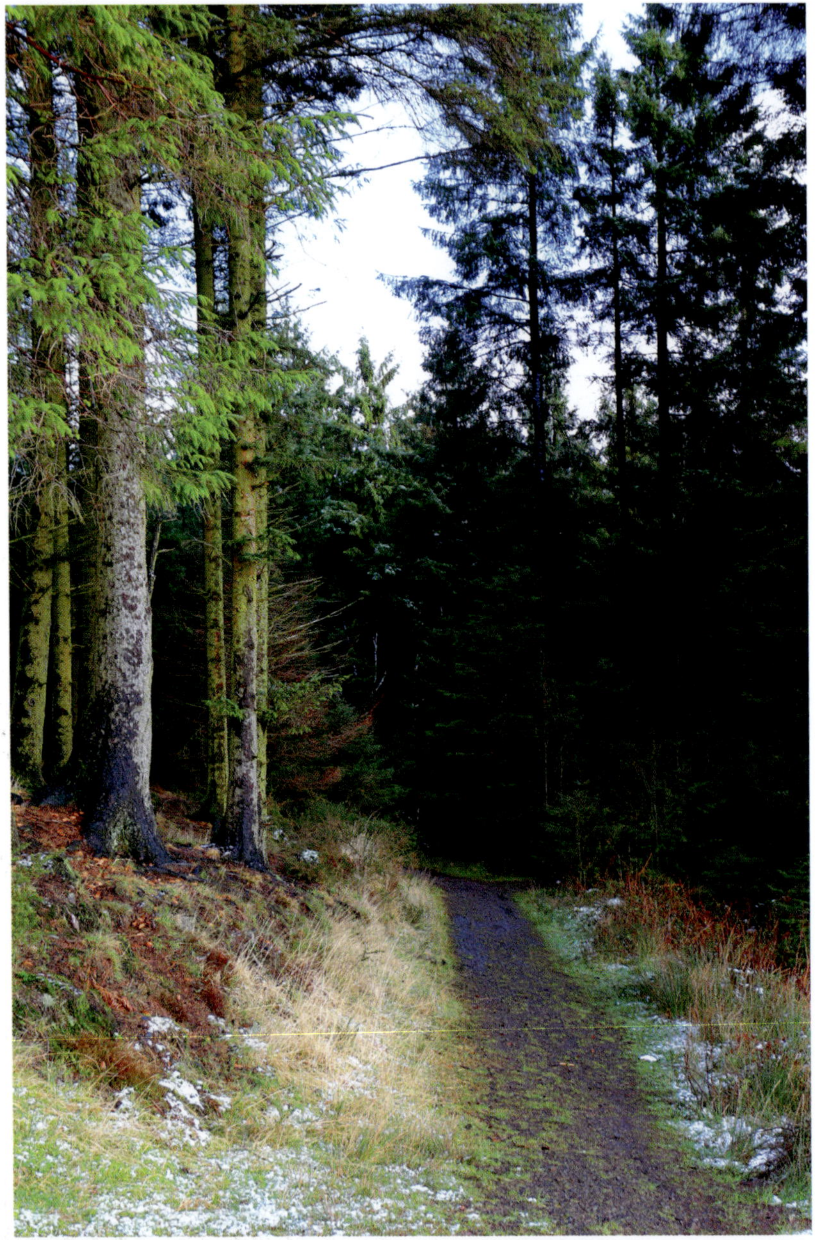

PATH THROUGH
THE PINES, BRECON
BEACONS, WALES

AUTUMN LANES
Oliver's favourite

"I think the road is cool; you can
'walk in' to this picture, and it's
very vibrant with the colours of
the leaves."

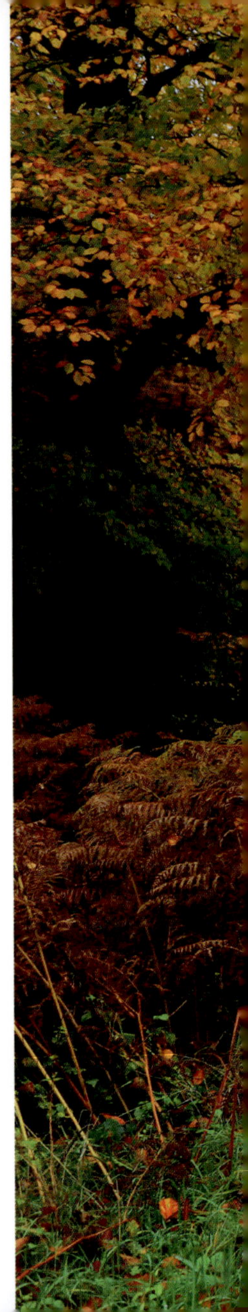

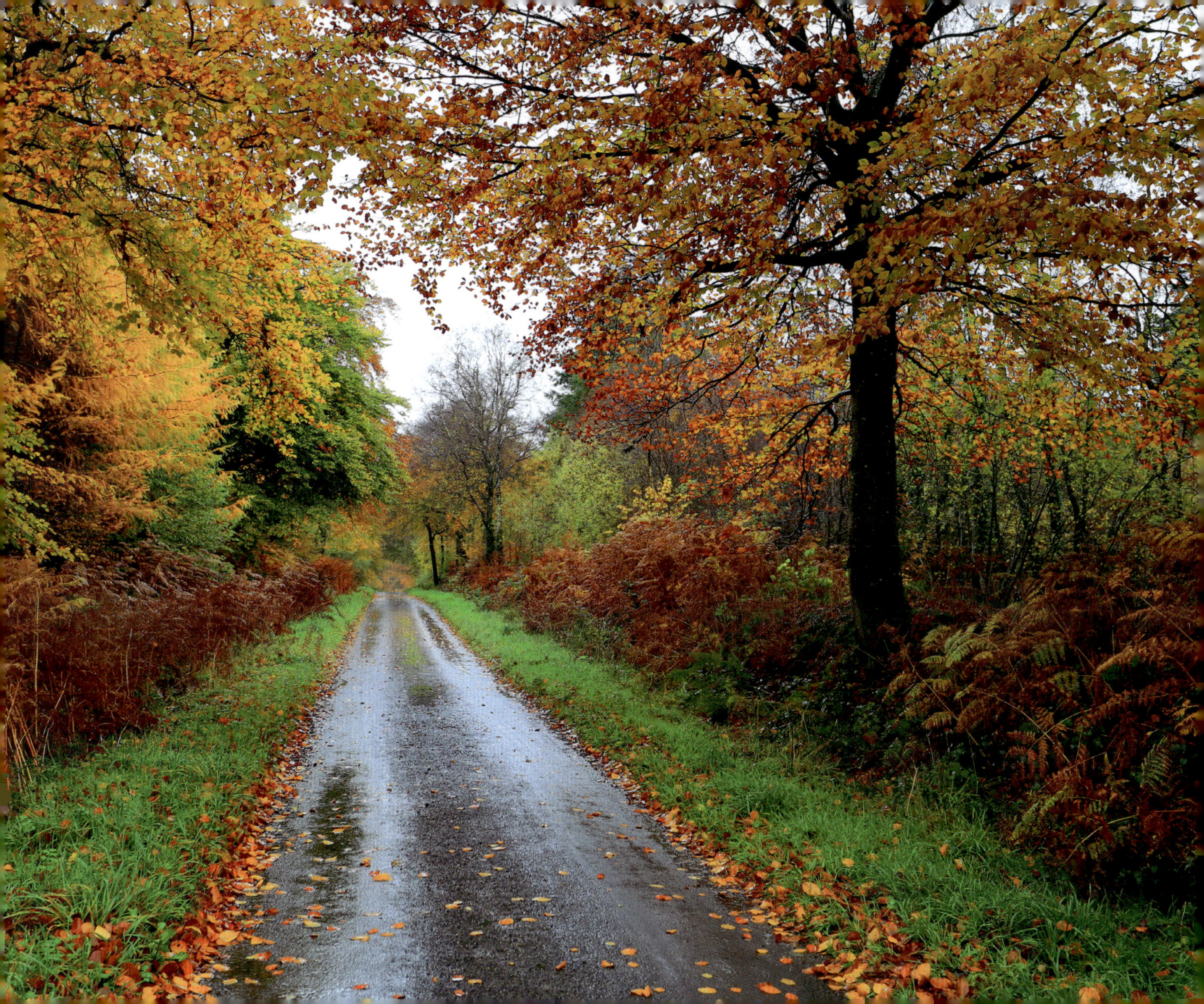

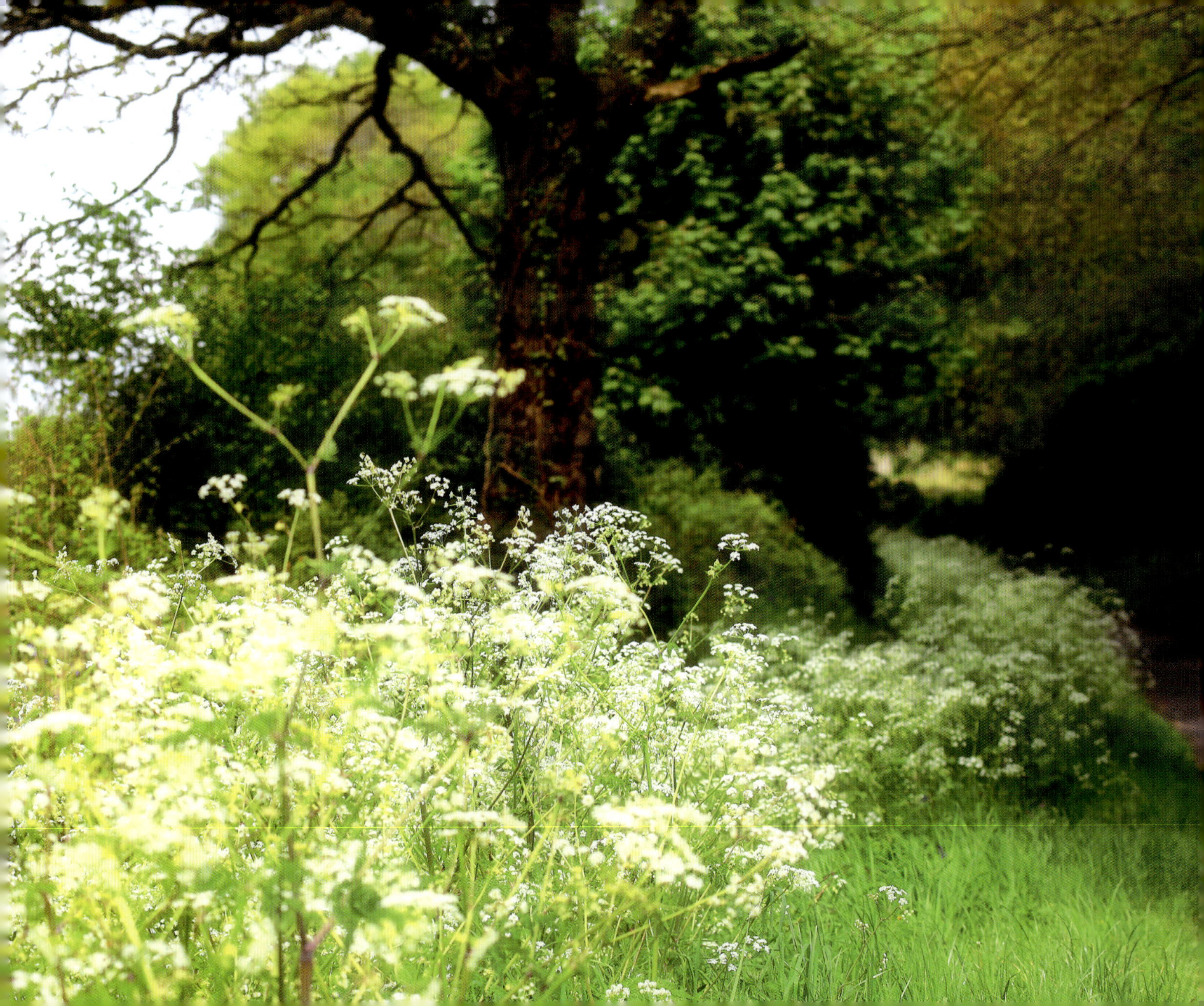

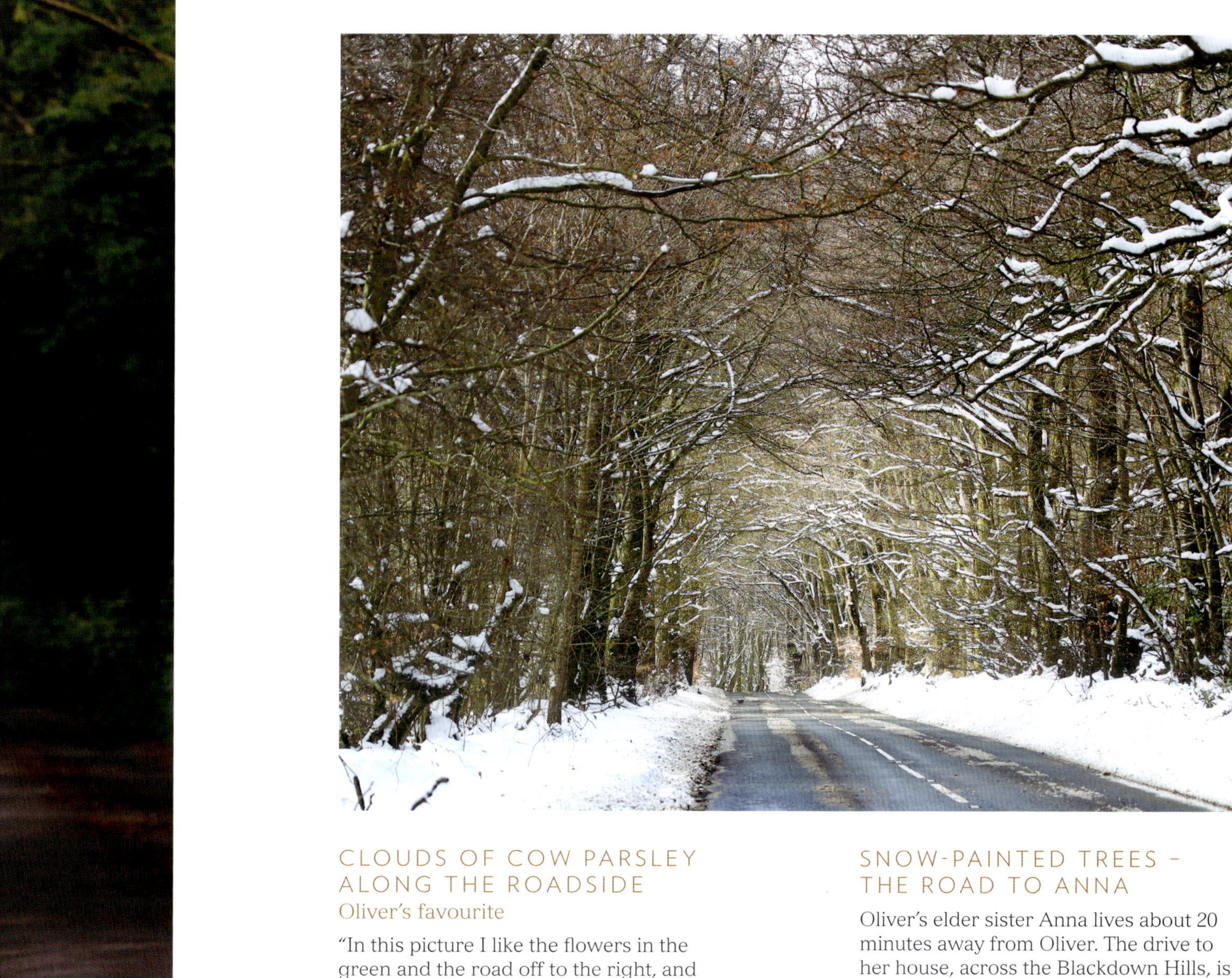

CLOUDS OF COW PARSLEY ALONG THE ROADSIDE
Oliver's favourite

"In this picture I like the flowers in the green and the road off to the right, and the curve of the road with the curve of the trees."

SNOW-PAINTED TREES – THE ROAD TO ANNA

Oliver's elder sister Anna lives about 20 minutes away from Oliver. The drive to her house, across the Blackdown Hills, is a beautiful tree-lined journey at any time of the year.

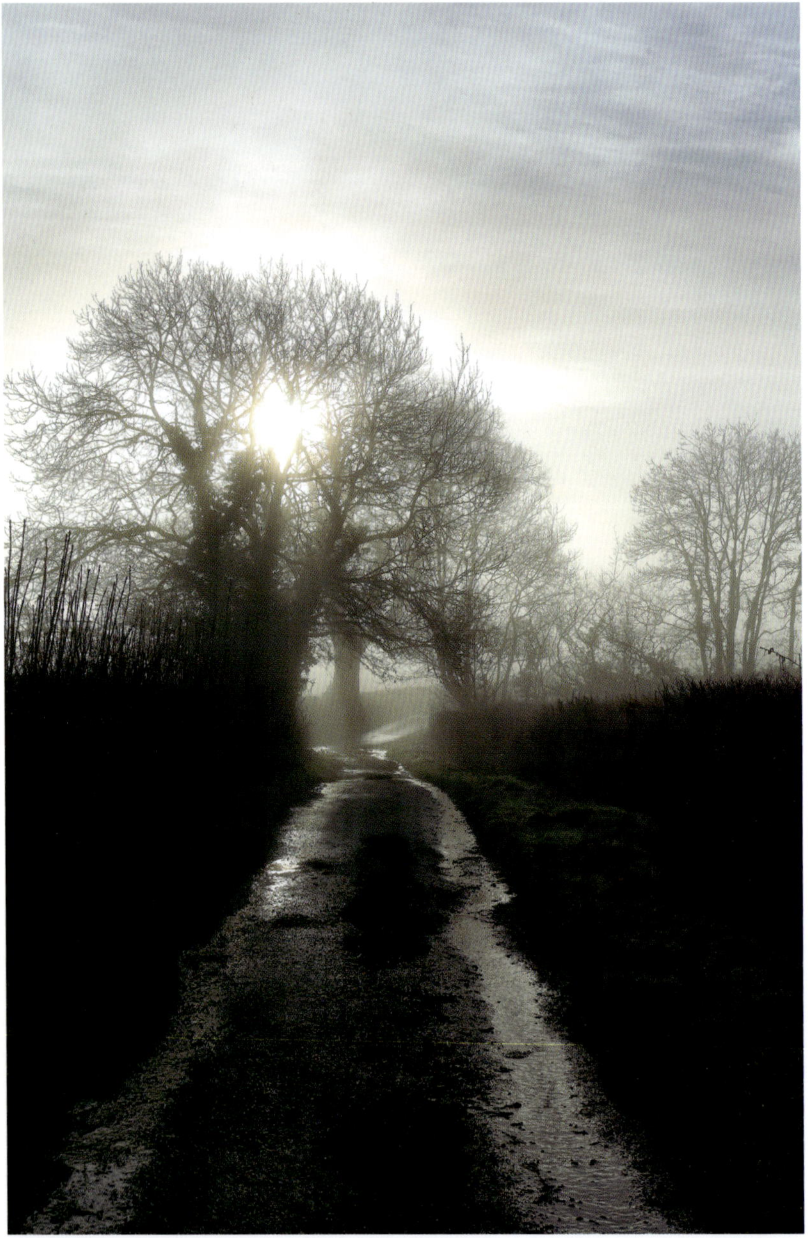

MISTY MORNING, BISHOPSWOOD

Oliver appeared downstairs at home one morning, coated and with camera bag on his back, saying, "I'm off out for a bit to get some pictures". His mother responded scathingly that it was a wet, cold, miserable, misty morning and that going out to take pictures was pointless. Oliver, undeterred, said he would be back within an hour – and returned as promised with this image amongst others, which ended up being one of his bestsellers! He also loved this comment from one of his Facebook followers when this image went up on his page: **Wynne Nicholls:** "You've taken me there Oliver… An early morning walk with the dogs, all wrapped up to keep warm and snug. Listening to the early morning stillness and occasional birdsong. Thinking of the warming hot chocolate awaiting me in front of the log fire as our walk ends and we return home. Bliss!"

SNOWY ROADS

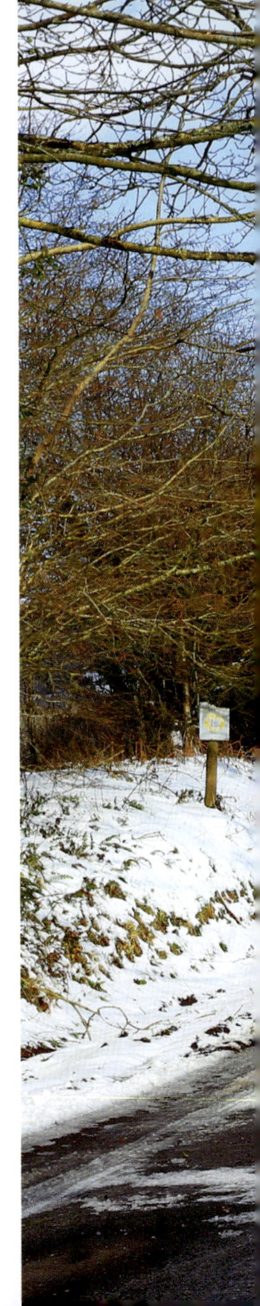

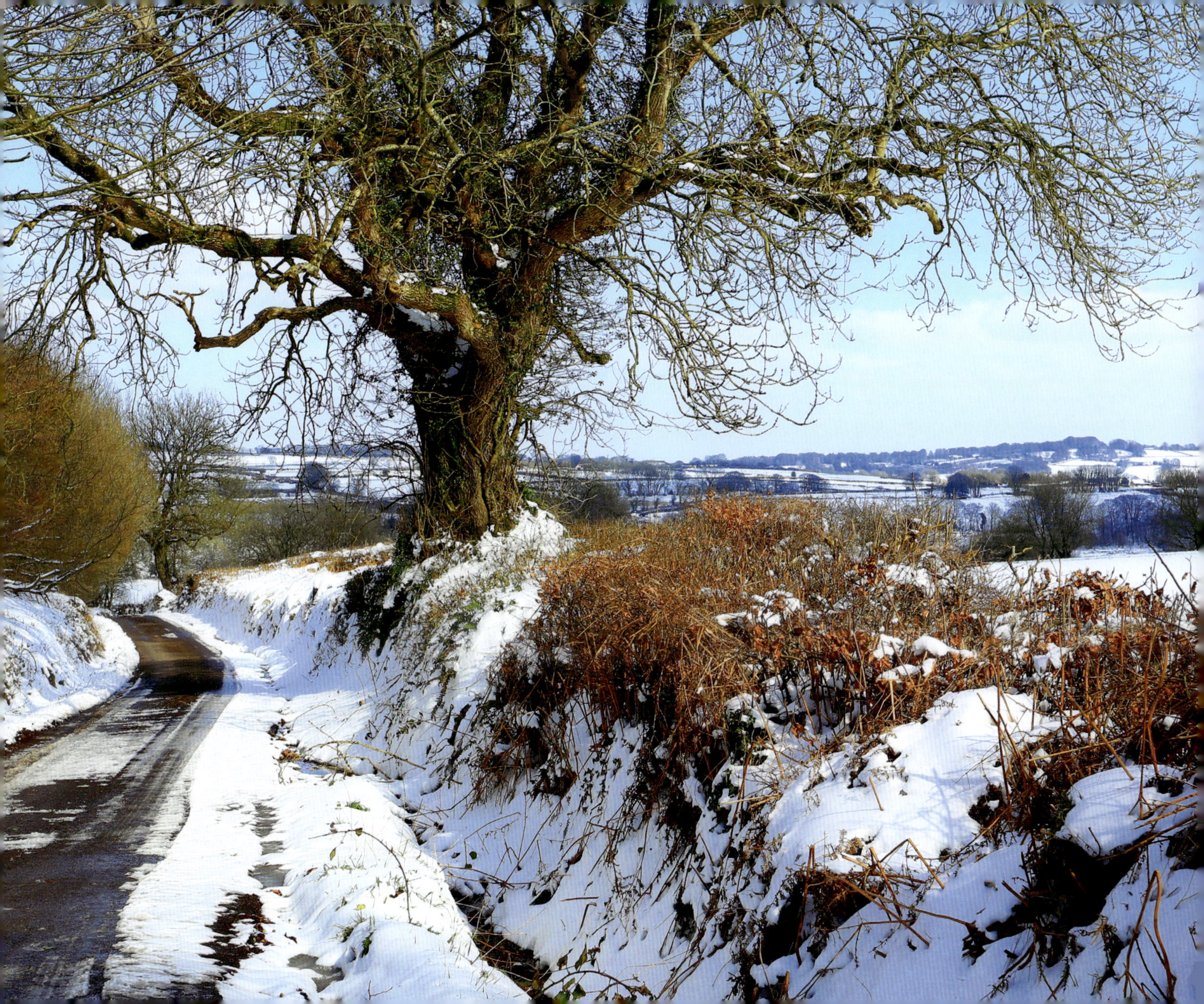

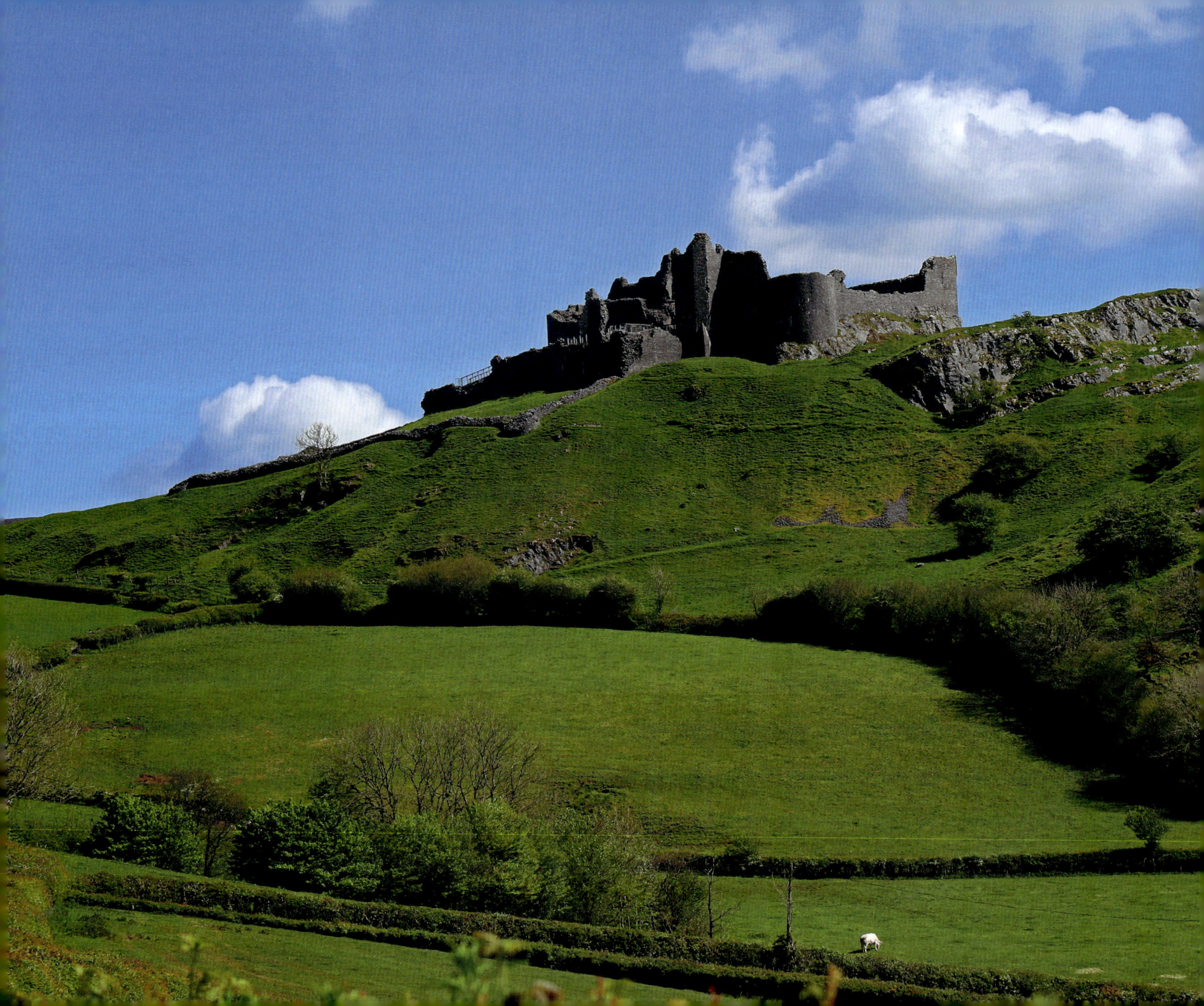

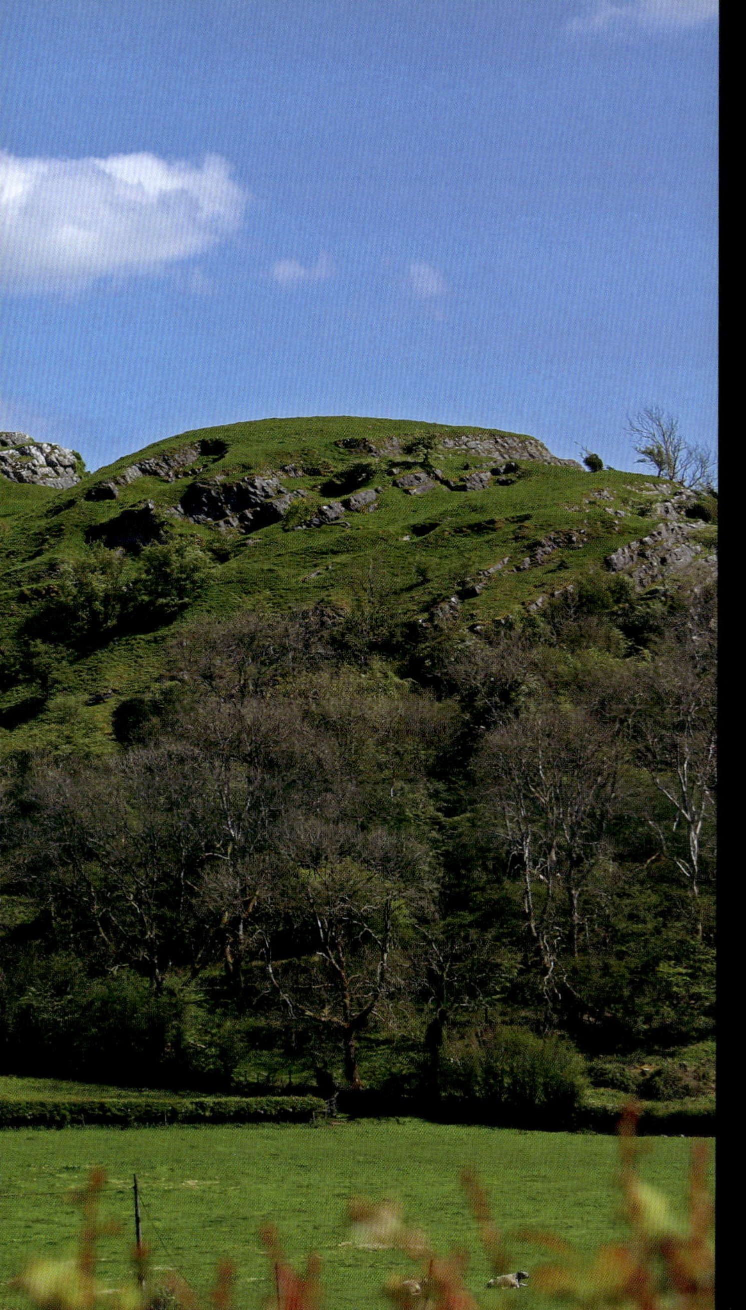

CASTLES, CHURCHES and CATHEDRALS

Oliver particularly loves visiting, walking around and photographing castles, churches and cathedrals. He loves the history and the look of these places and generally much prefers castle ruins to castles that still have people living in them! He likes to wander around the ruins at his own speed and usually captures lots of close-ups of the stonework, or the shapes of old doorways, archways and windows – hardly any pictures of the buildings as a whole. In churches and cathedrals, he spends a long time taking pictures from all sorts of angles, and again, his eye is usually drawn by light and shadow, shape and form. He also loves to walk around churchyards and read the gravestones to find out the names of the people who are buried there, when they died, and how old they were. He was fascinated on a visit to Wales a few years ago when in one tiny little churchyard he found many gravestones on which the Christian name and surname were the same – e.g. William Williams, Morgan Morgan, David David, Owen Owens and Humphrey Humphreys!

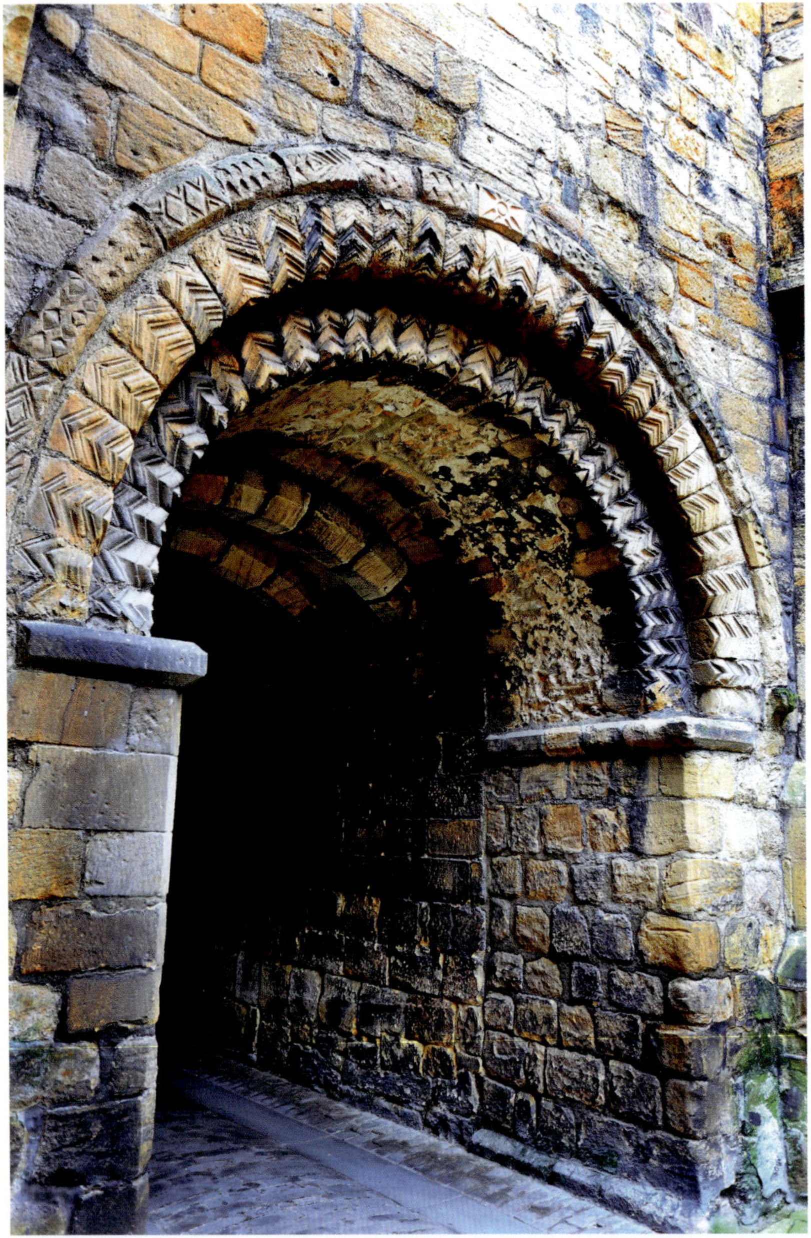

ALNWICK CASTLE ARCHWAY

Another shot from Alnwick Castle during Oliver's week in Northumberland. He took several pictures of this archway and was drawn in by all the shapes, patterns and colours in the stonework. Yves de Vescy, Baron of Alnwick, erected the first parts of this castle in 1096.

ALNWICK CASTLE, NORTHUMBERLAND
Oliver's favourite

"This is Alnwick Castle, where *Harry Potter* was filmed. I like this picture because I really like the walls; I think they stand out. I can see all the detail on the windows and the guttering and the brickwork. I like the arches and the shadows. It's a good shape."

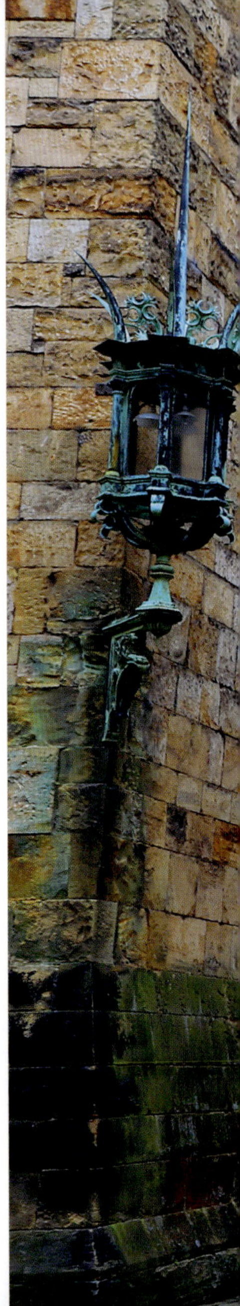

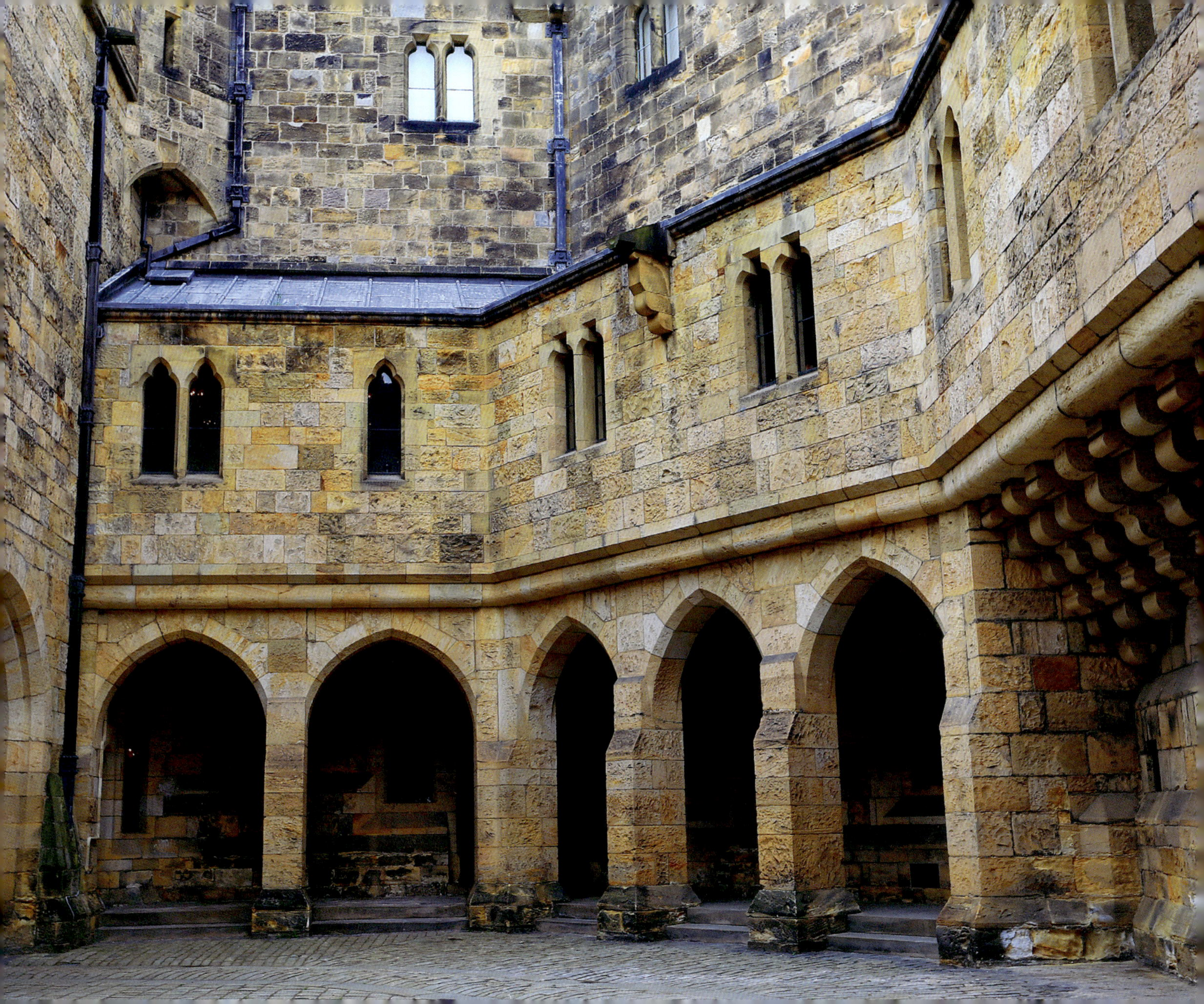

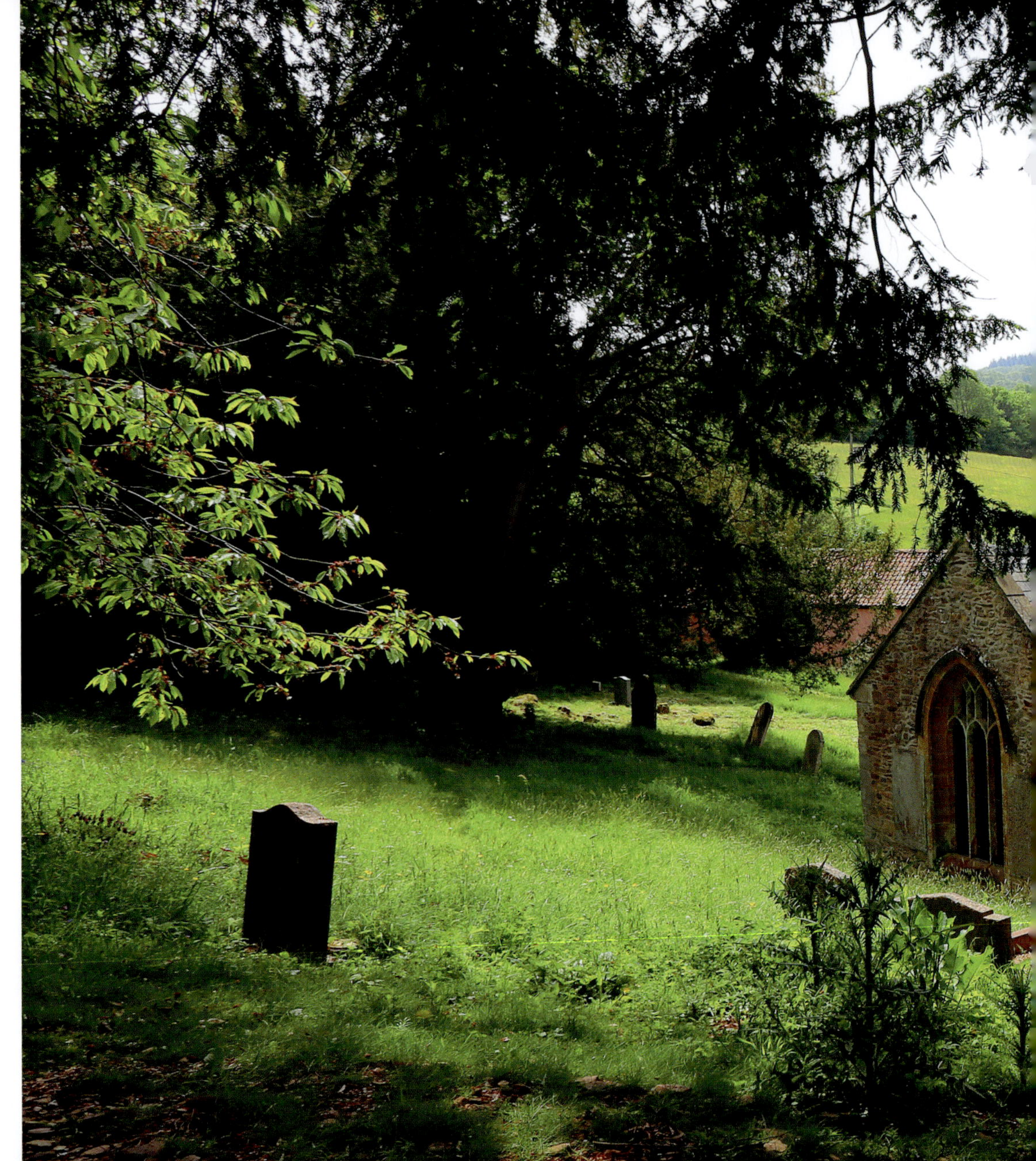

ALL SAINTS
CHURCH – AISHOLT,
QUANTOCK HILLS,
SOMERSET
Oliver's favourite

"This is a little church on the
Quantock Hills in Somerset.
I like churches. I stood under
a tree to get the right picture
that I wanted. The tree frames
around the church. That's what I
wanted – I like that."

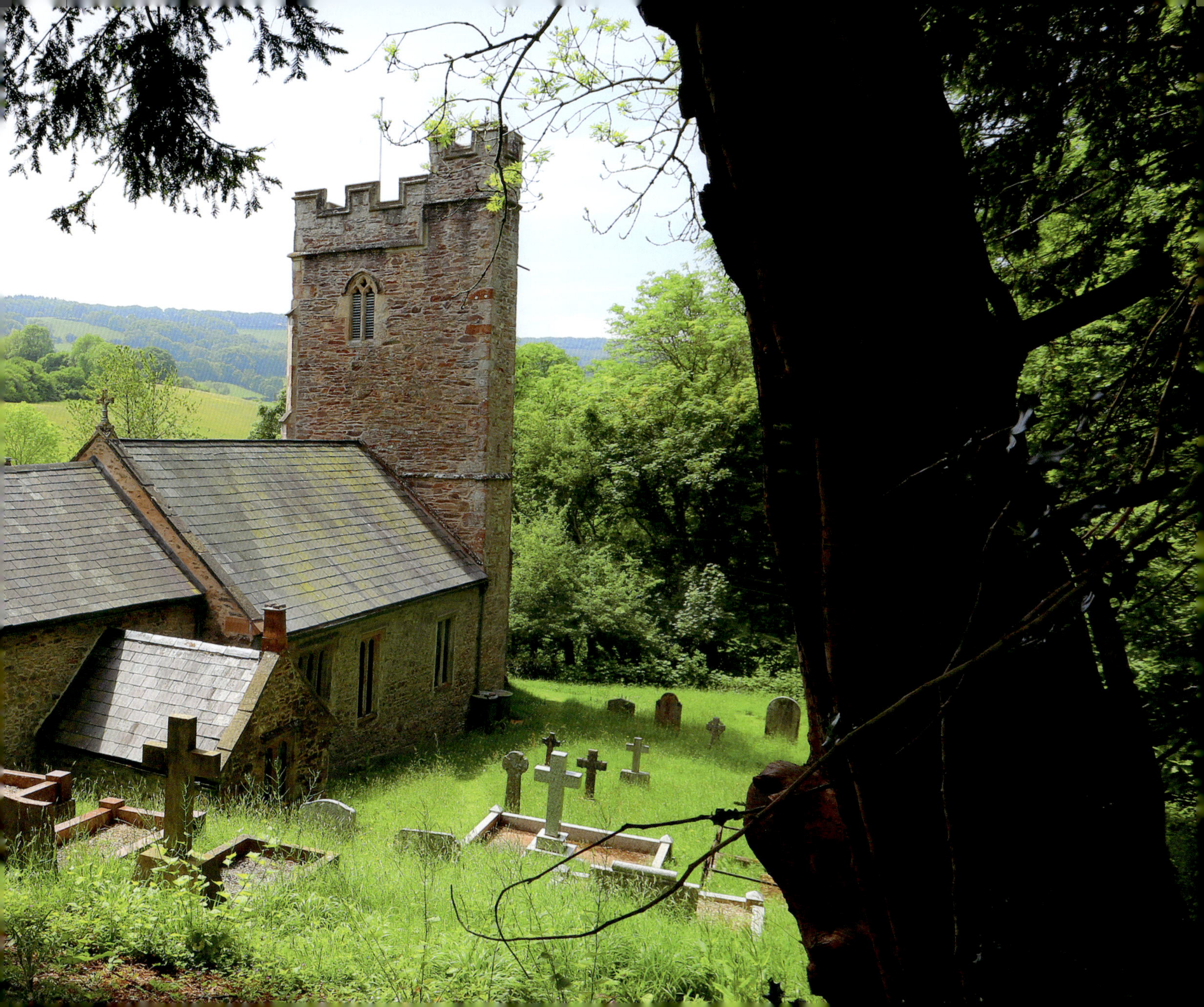

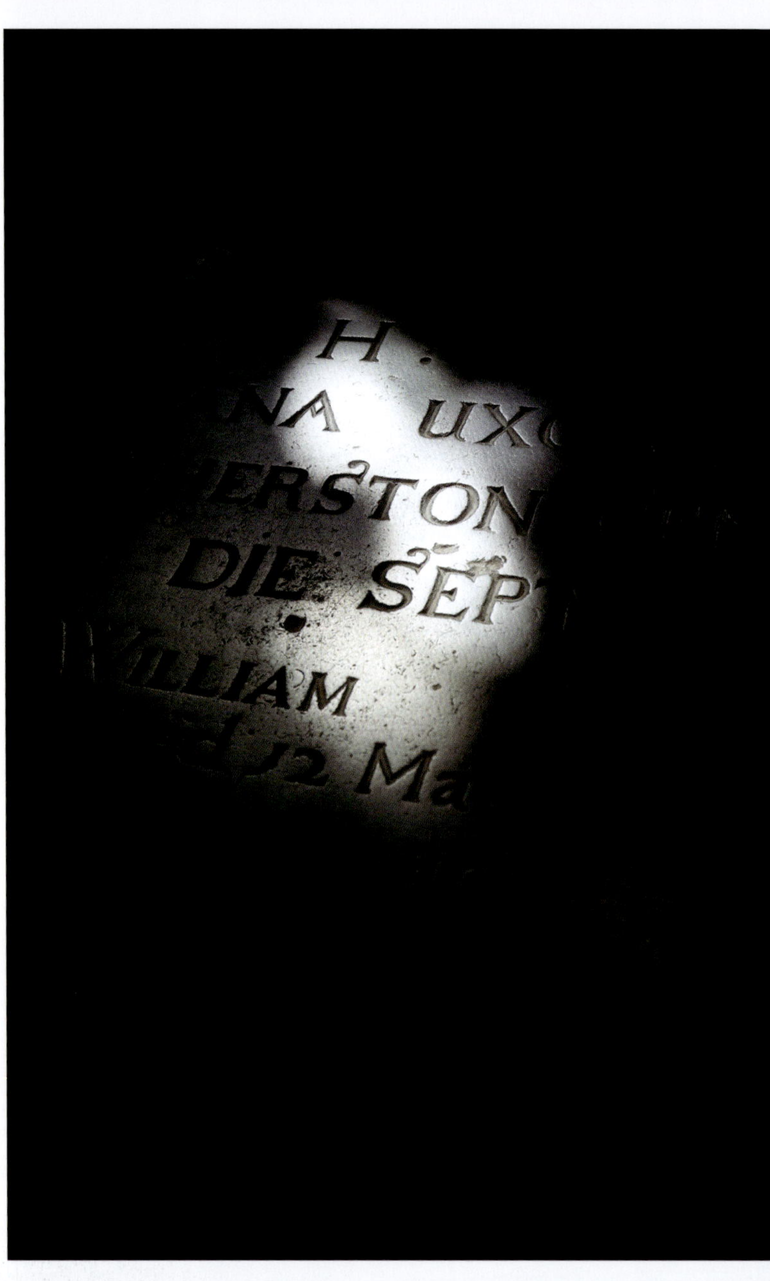

ENGRAVED FLOOR STONE OF WELLS CATHEDRAL
Oliver's favourite

"I saw the light on the stone on the floor and the writing. I love the light and the shadow on it. It's a cool picture."

CHURCH OF ST PETER AND ST PAUL AT ODCOMBE

Oliver has hundreds and hundreds of pictures from the inside of churches, often featuring their beautiful windows.

CHEDDON FITZPAINE PARISH CHURCH OF THE BLESSED VIRGIN MARY

As so often happens, Oliver's eye was drawn to the light from the window. He enjoys taking pictures of simple, plain glass church windows just as much as the big multi-coloured stained glass ones. The simple shapes and gentle light make this such a beautiful and peaceful image.

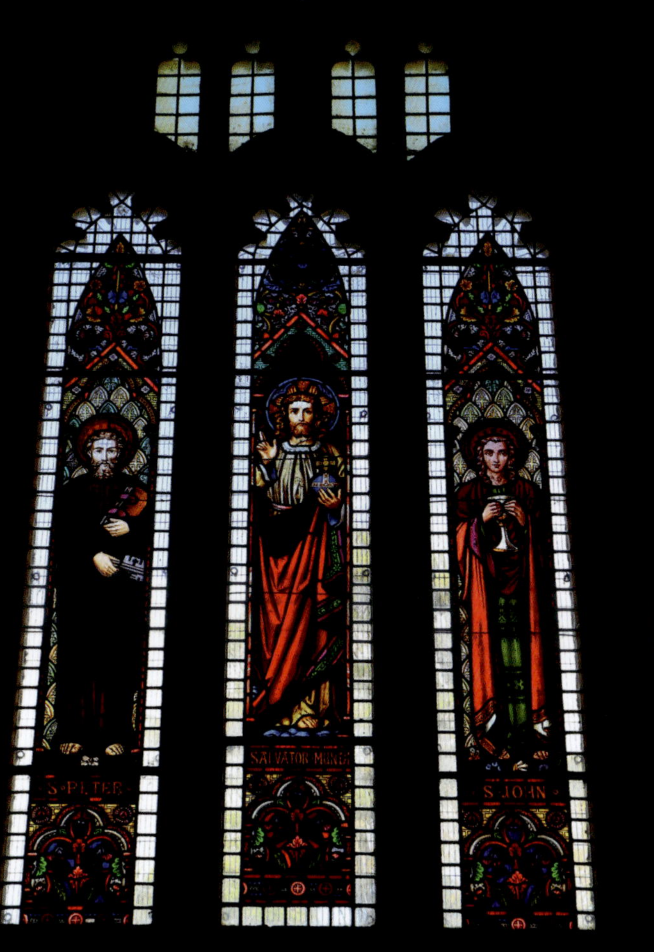

S. PETER
SALVATOR MUNDI
S. JOHN

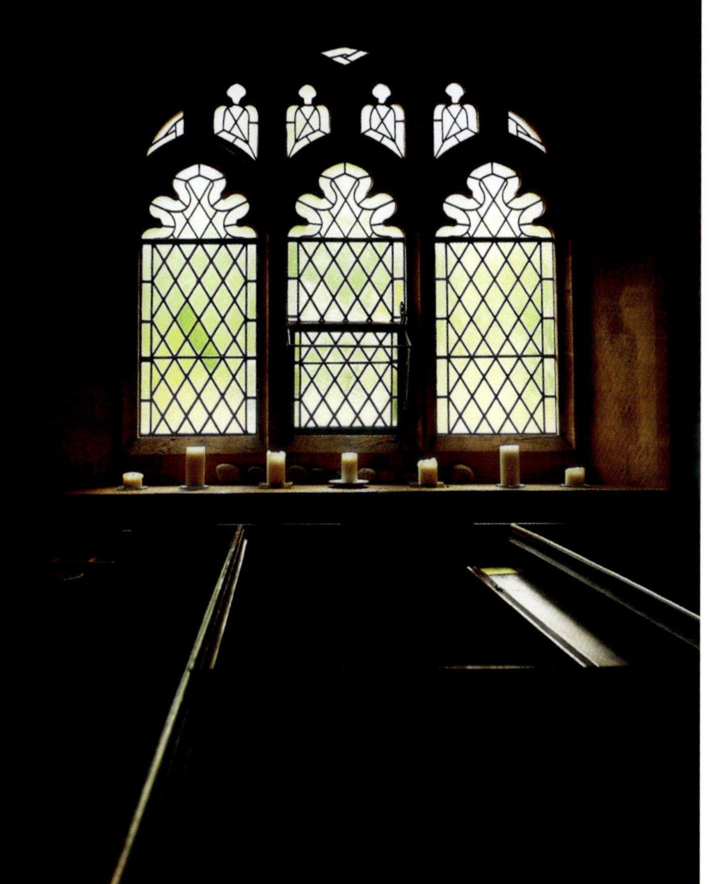

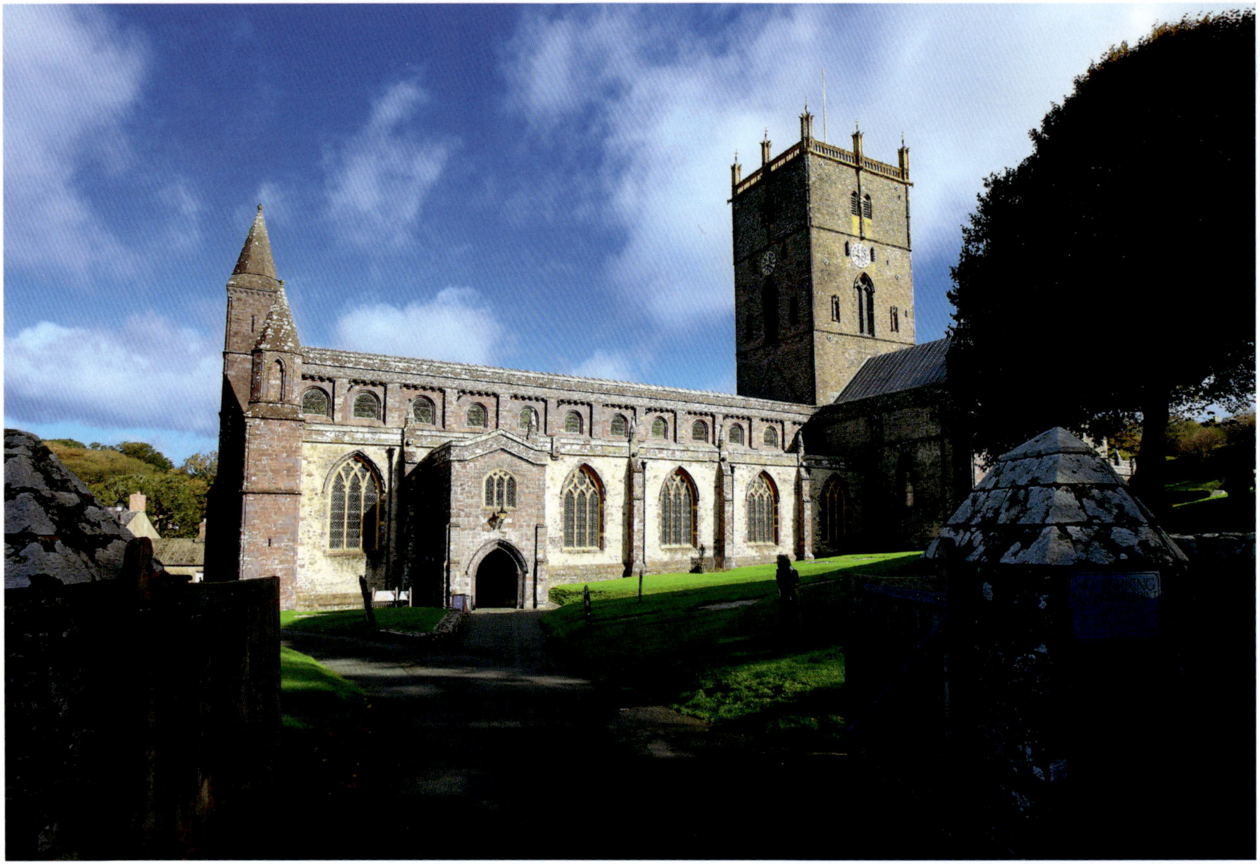

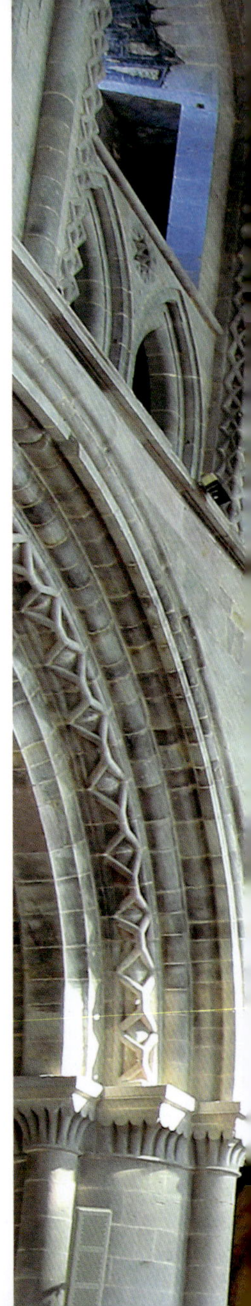

ST DAVID'S CATHEDRAL – THE AMAZING CEILING

In this picture, Oliver captured the feeling of vastness and glory, and the stunning and incredibly beautiful wooden ceiling. He spoke to a lovely gentleman guide who told him all about the ceiling and how it is still the original wooden ceiling with the original timbers from the 1500s, and has absolutely no nails or metal bolts in it at all! (Inadequate foundations and the effects of a 13th-century earthquake caused the walls at the west end of the nave to lean outwards, hence a wooden ceiling rather than a stone vault.)

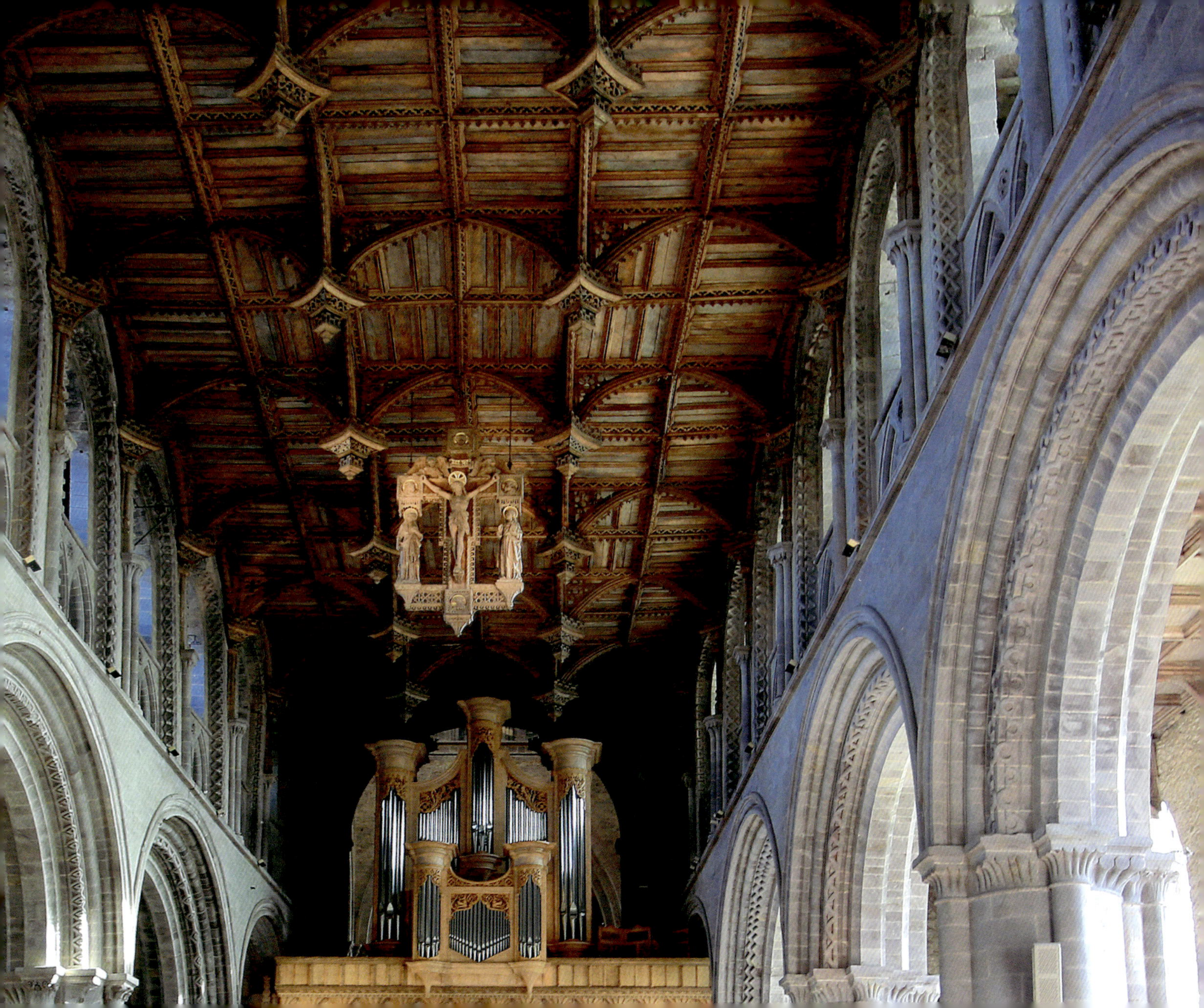

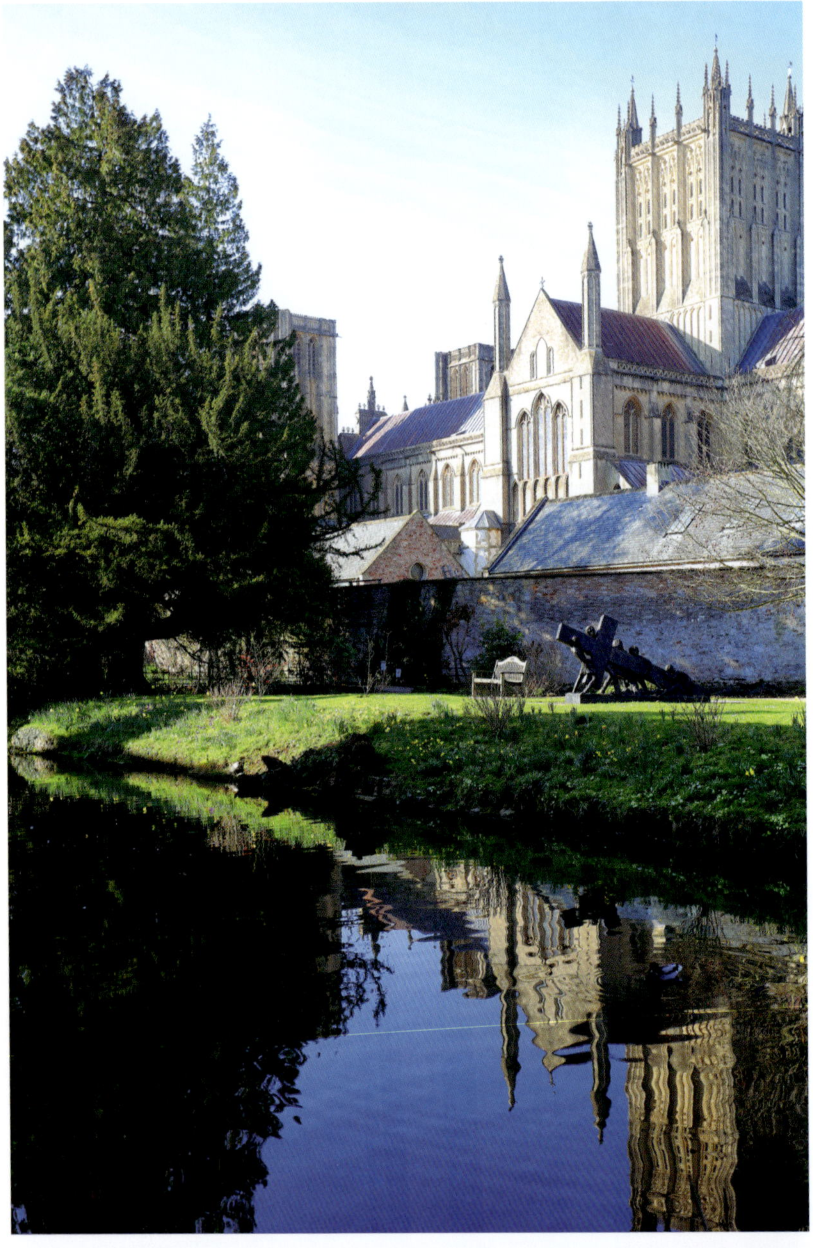

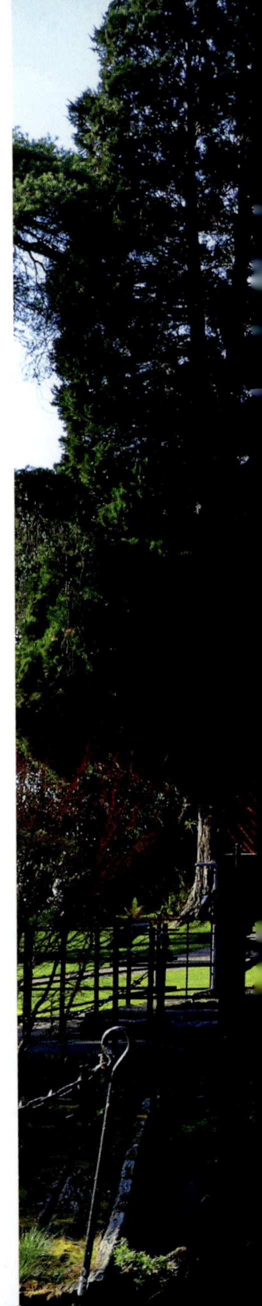

WELLS CATHEDRAL, SOMERSET

We have included several pictures of Wells Cathedral, partly because it is impossible to narrow down so many fabulous images to only one or two and partly because it is Oliver's favourite church/cathedral. Built between 1176–1450 to replace an earlier church that had been on the site since 705, Oliver has never taken a picture of the front – the best known view of the building. He much prefers interior images and these other views from behind and across the water.

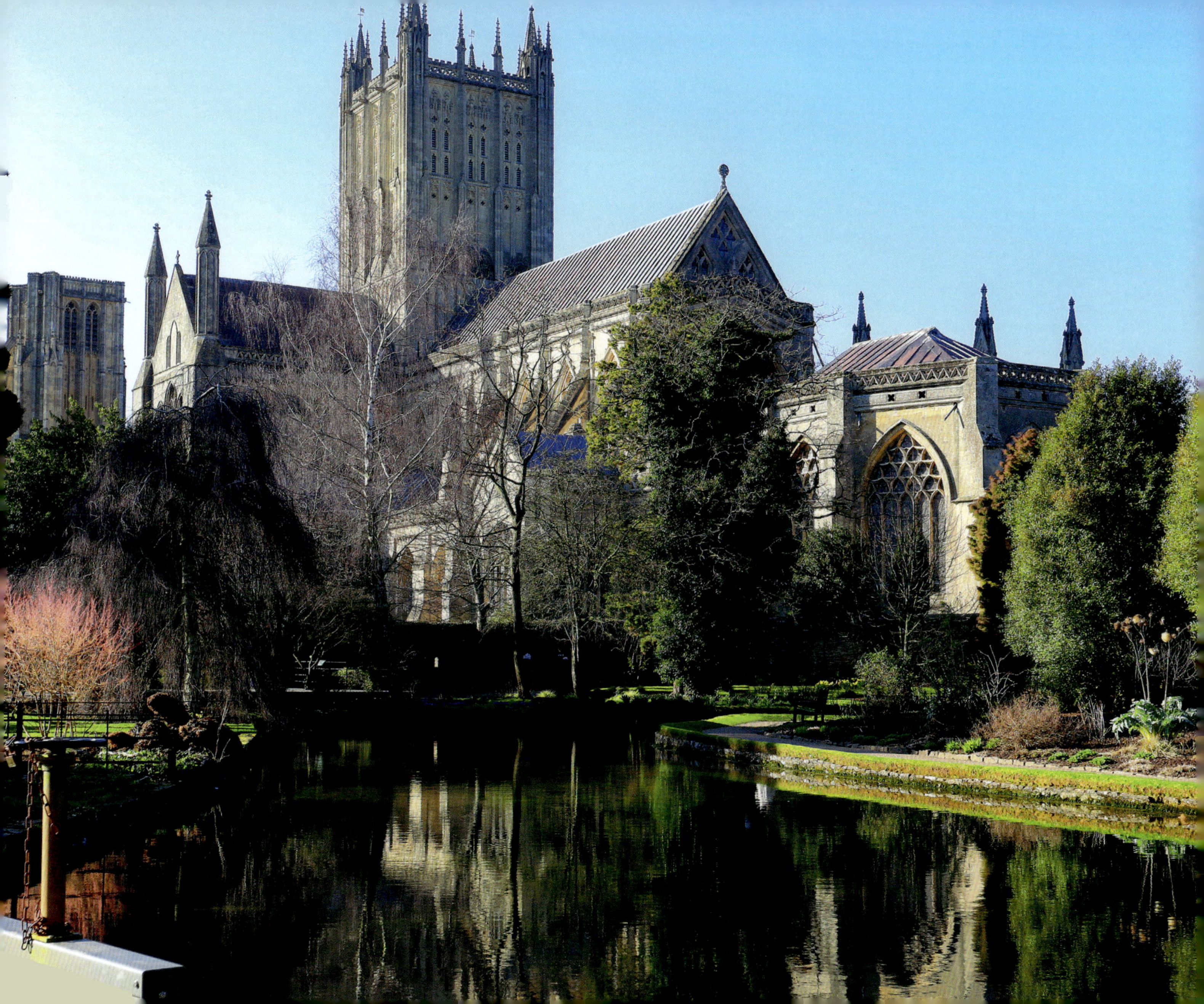

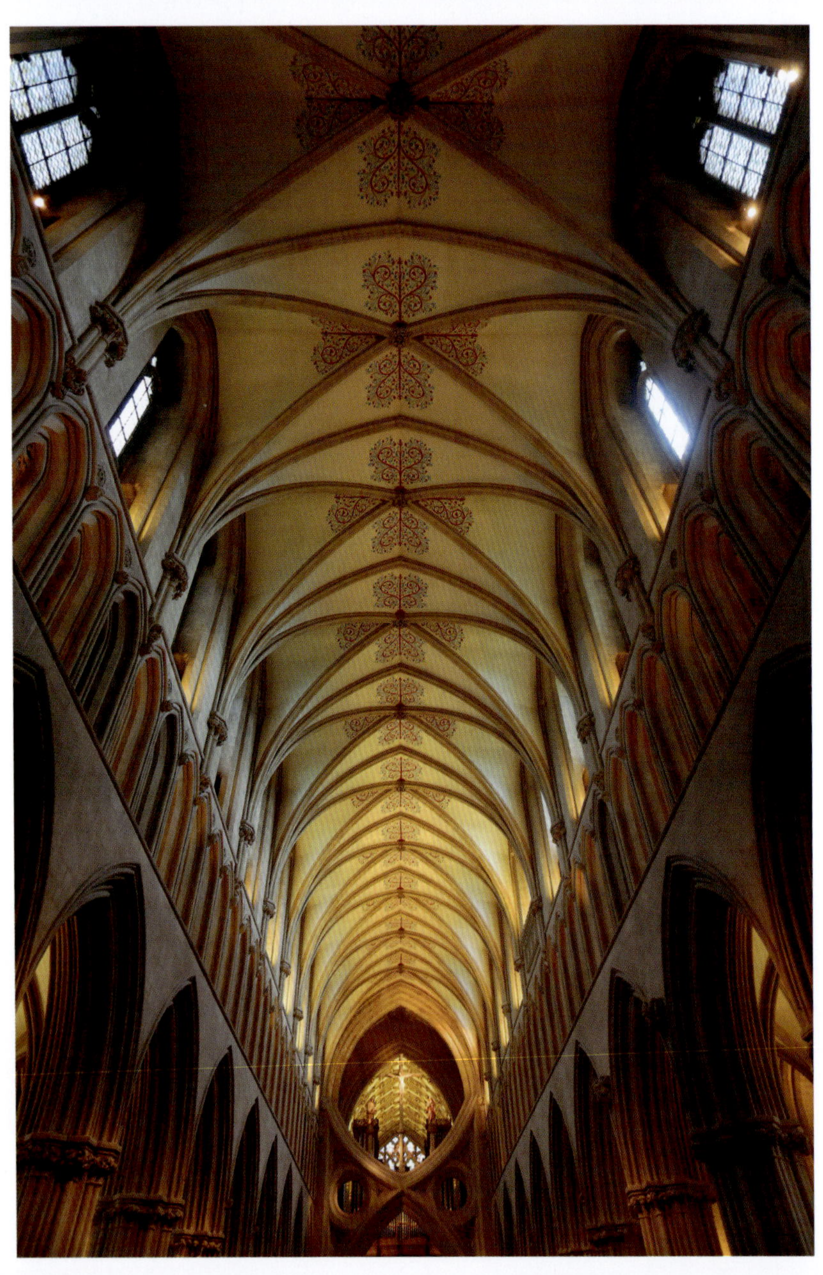

WELLS CATHEDRAL – THE VAULTED CEILING
Oliver's favourite

"I really like going to Wells Cathedral; I get different pictures every time. The ceiling is huge and I like the colours of this one – actually I like this picture best because I love all the windows, and all the arches, and I love the light."

WELLS CATHEDRAL – THE VIEW FROM THE GROUND
Oliver's favourite

"I put my camera down on the floor to look at it from that angle, because I like the floor slabs and looking up at the arches. I really like churches. This is a great picture."

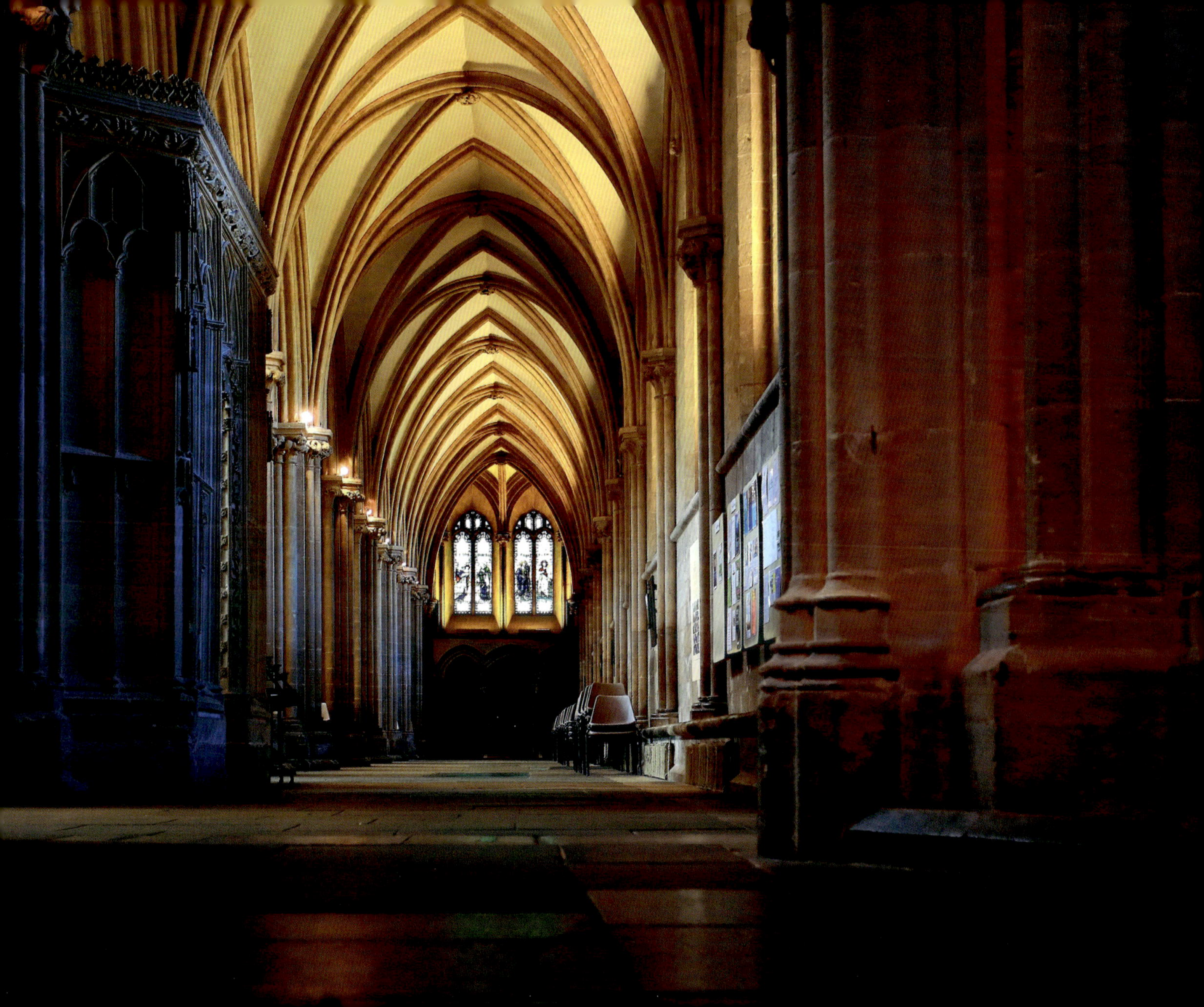

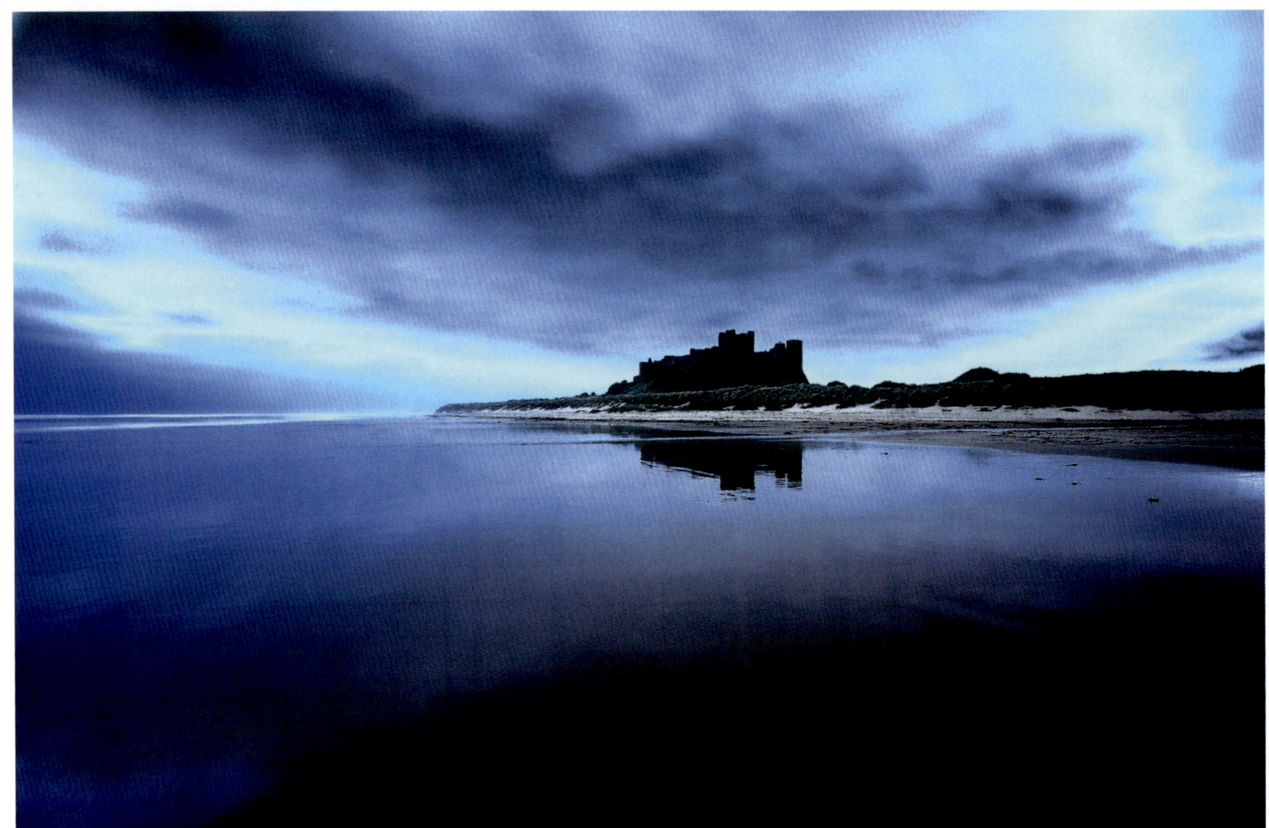

BAMBURGH CASTLE, NORTHUMBERLAND

Oliver took lots of pictures of this castle from different angles on different days and at different times of day, but this was his favourite of the set. It has also proved to be an extremely popular image with his followers. It was taken from the beach side of the castle across the wet sand, with a stormy-looking evening sky, and shows a great reflection.

CASTLE STALKER, LOCH LINNHE, APPIN
Oliver's favourite

"I like this castle in the mist, and it's natural looking. I like the green in the foreground and the misty day. We couldn't go in the castle but it still looked good for my picture."

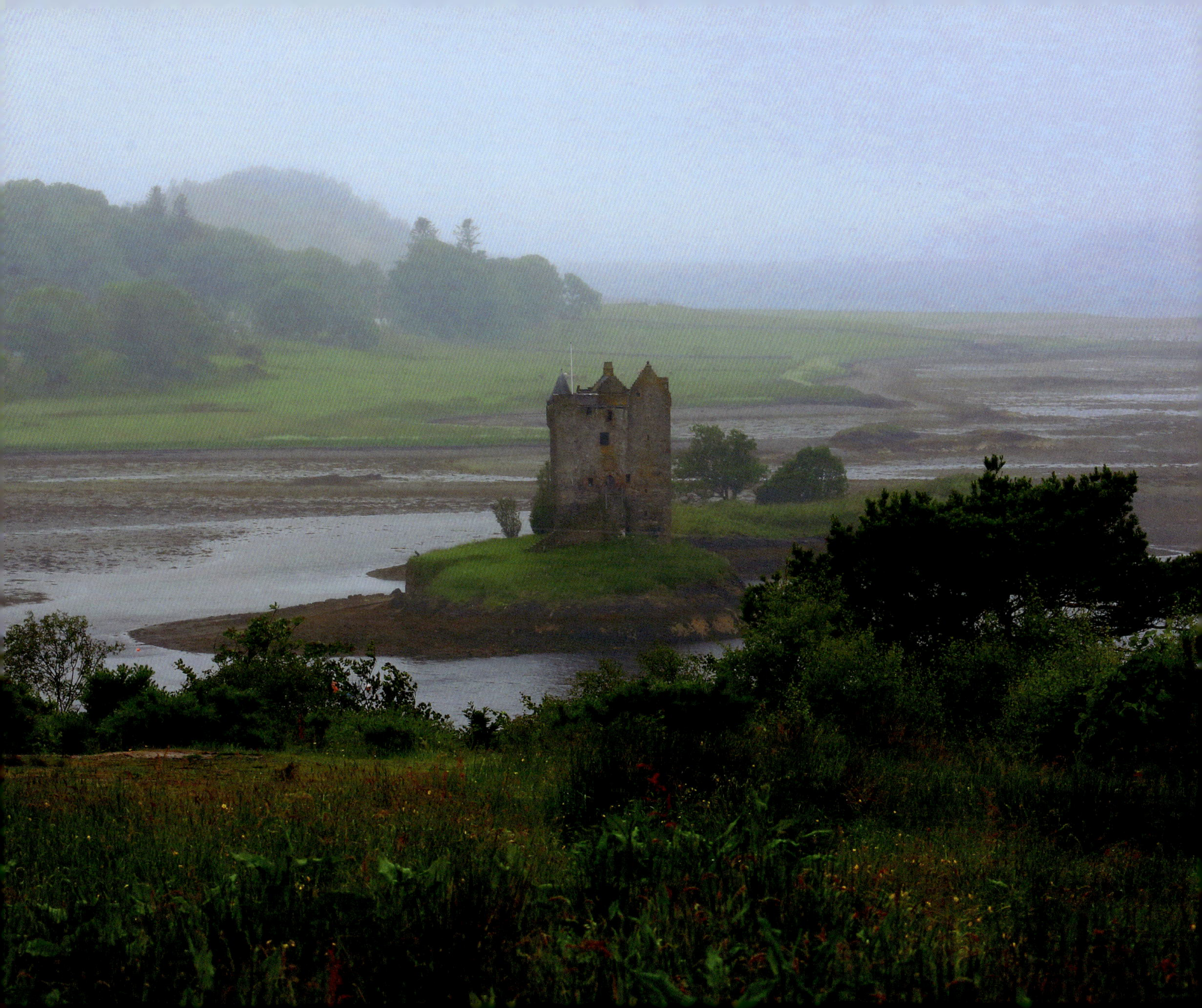

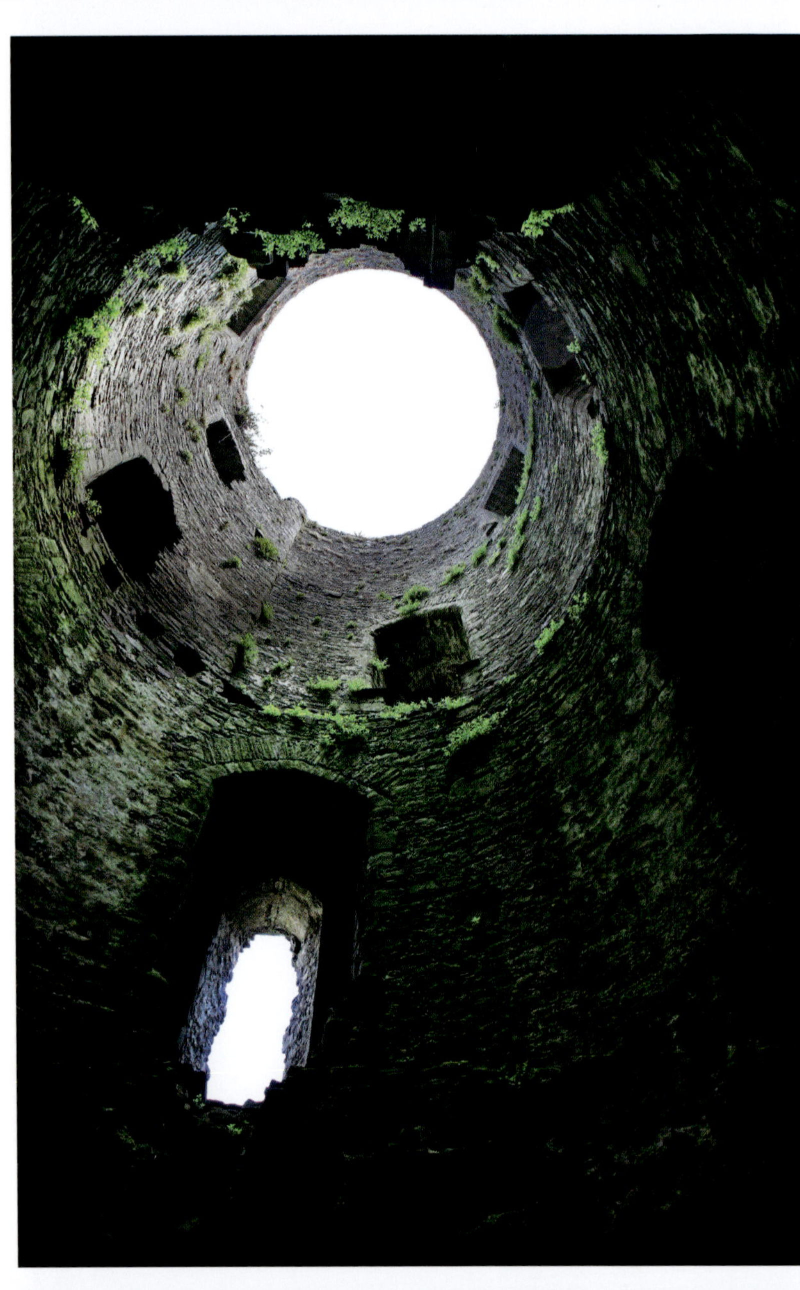

TRETOWER CASTLE – INSIDE THE TOWER

A great 'Oliver shot' from inside the tower looking up.

TRETOWER CASTLE, POWYS

Another of Oliver's favourite castles. Originally built at the beginning of the 12th century, it can be found near Crickhowell in Wales. It is actually 'Tretower Castle and Court', with a wonderful large and beautifully preserved medieval house on the same plot, which Oliver also loves to explore.

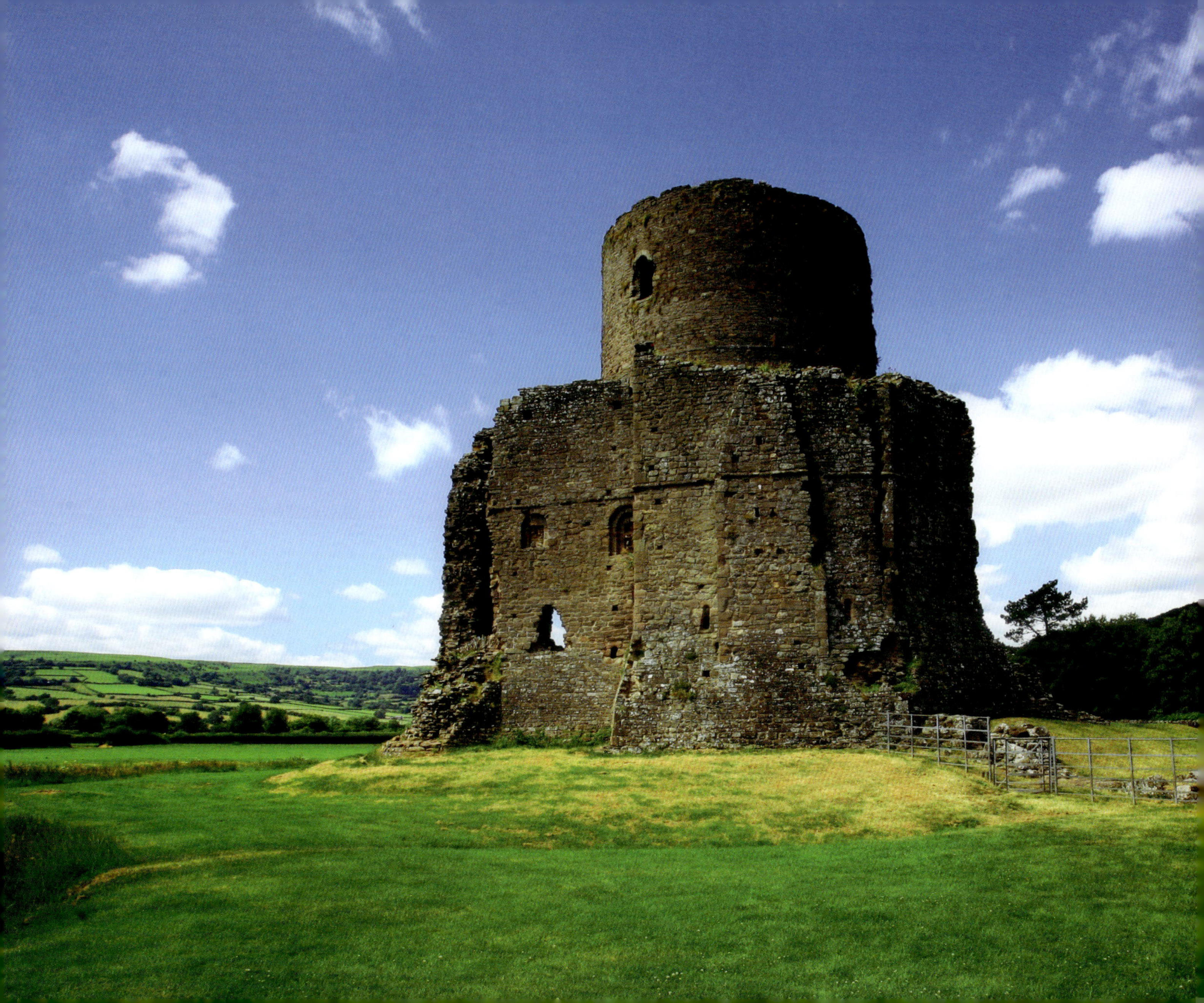

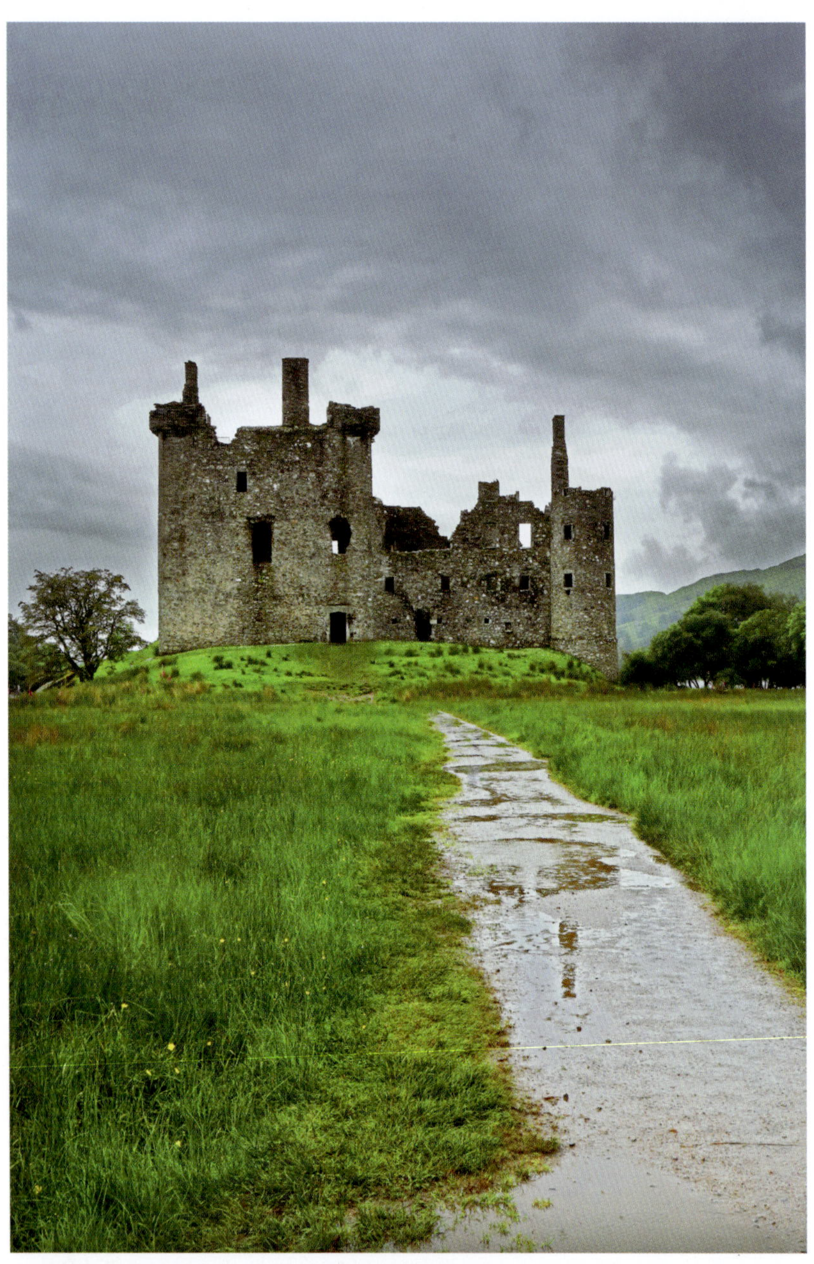

KILCHURN CASTLE, LOCH AWE, ARGYLL AND BUTE

It was a very wet miserable day when Oliver visited Kilchurn Castle on Loch Awe. But he said the stormy sky just made it look better and all "moody".

OLD GRAVESTONE UNDER A TREE IN A CHURCHYARD
Oliver's favourite

"I have got lots and lots of pictures of old gravestones. This is one of my favourites. I like the dark green leaves and the ivy around it and the white stone. I like the gravestone in the middle of it all – it's different. I like walking around the churchyards and looking at the graves – it's really interesting!"

RAGLAN CASTLE, WALES
Oliver's favourite

"I have been to Raglan lots of times – it's a great castle. This is where some of the TV series *Merlin* was filmed. In this picture I really like the arches, looking through to the next one and the next. I like the detail on the wall and the different colours of the bricks and the stone. It's a good picture." [Oliver loves the TV series *Merlin* and has every single episode of every season on DVD!]

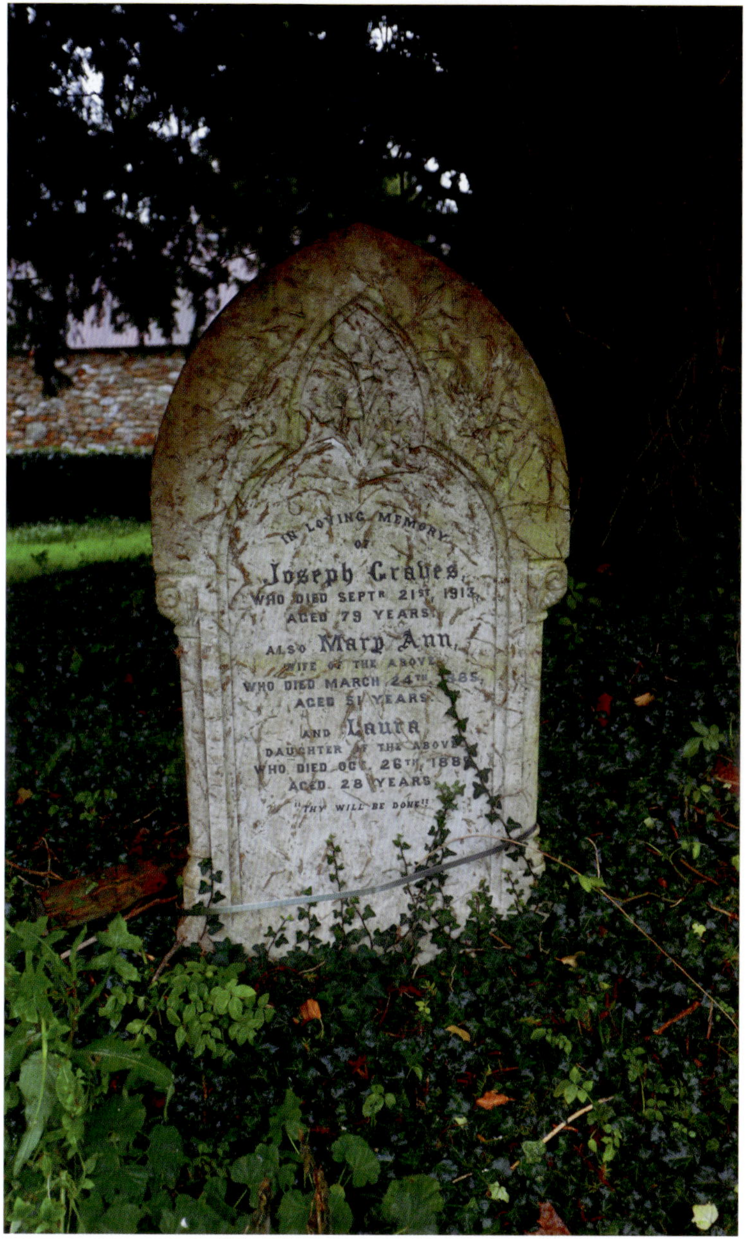

IN LOVING MEMORY
OF
Joseph Graves,
WHO DIED SEPTR 21ST, 1913,
AGED 79 YEARS.
ALSO Mary Ann,
WIFE OF THE ABOVE,
WHO DIED MARCH 24TH, 1885,
AGED 51 YEARS.
AND Laura
DAUGHTER OF THE ABOVE,
WHO DIED OCT 26TH, 1889,
AGED 28 YEARS
"THY WILL BE DONE!!"

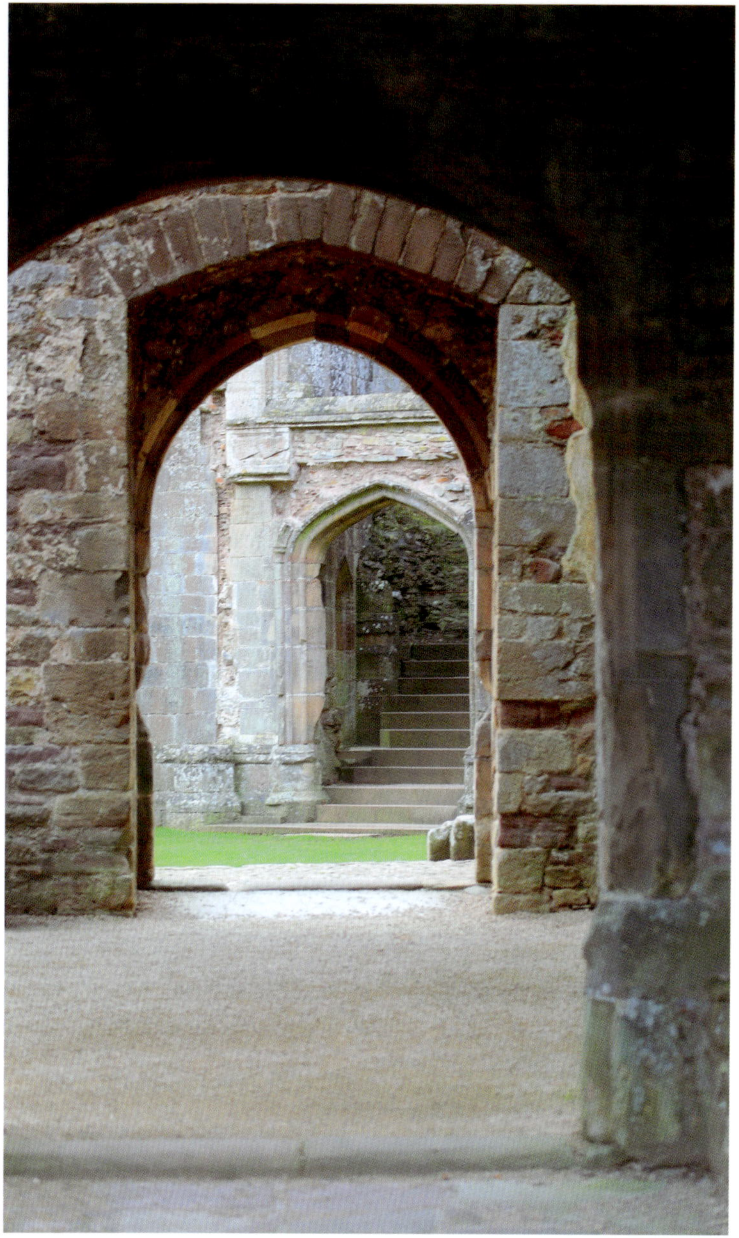

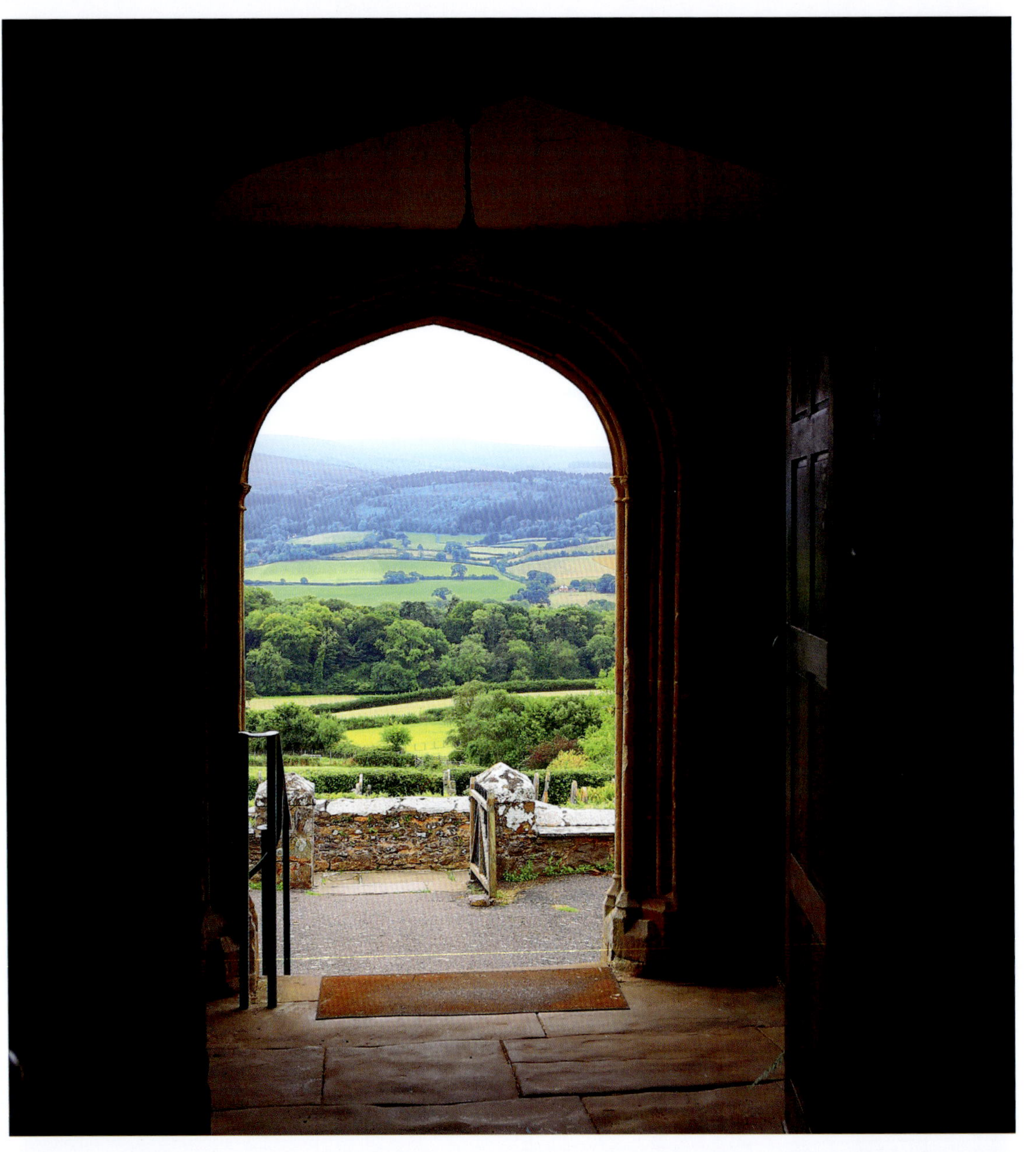

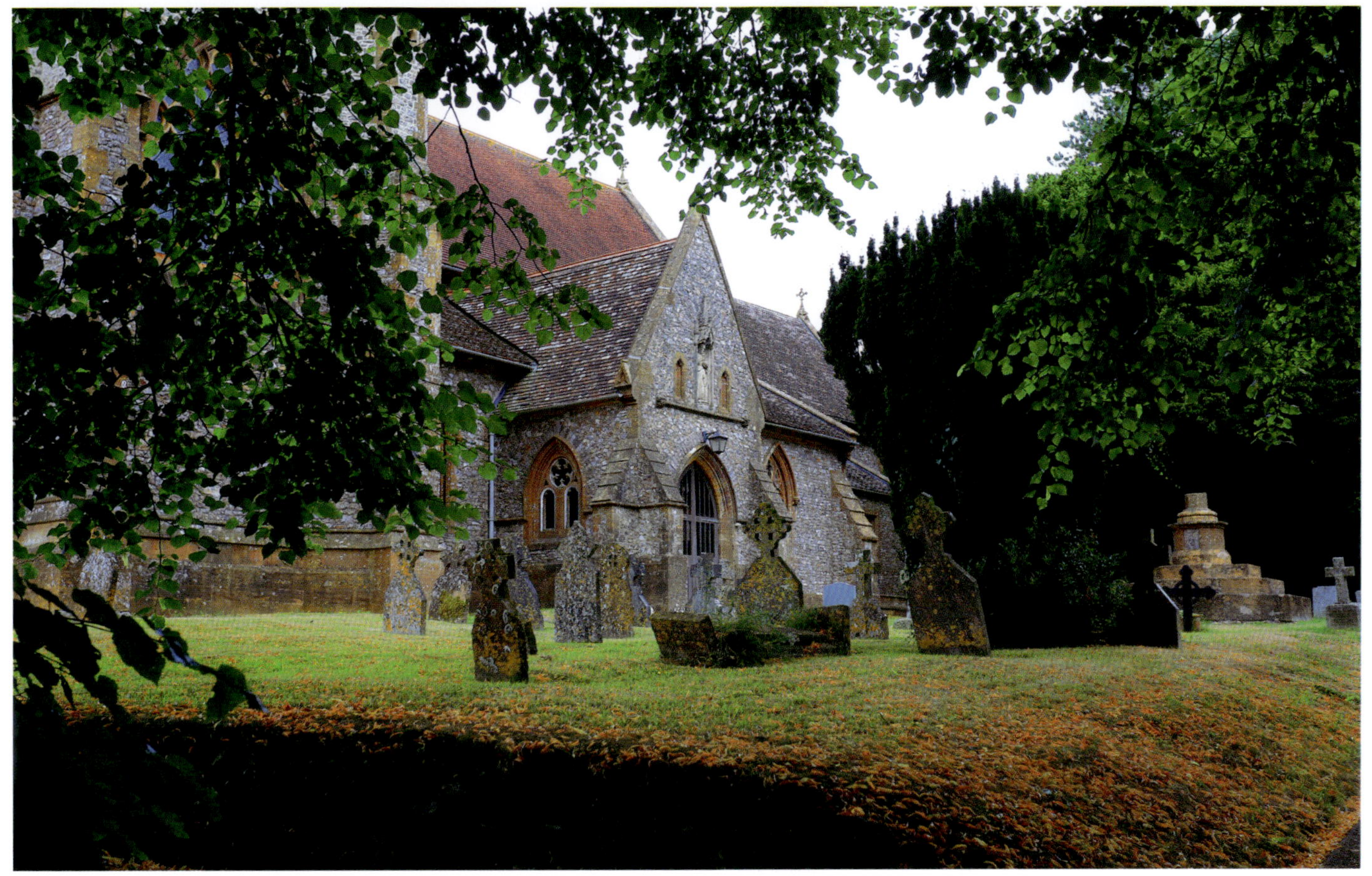

CHURCH OF ALL SAINTS, SELWORTHY, LOOKING OUT ACROSS EXMOOR

Oliver's favourite

"I really like this picture because I like that it's looking through the big old doorway and out to all the scenery in the distance. It's beautiful."

CHURCH OF ST MARY, BUCKLAND ST MARY

This is such a typical country church and churchyard, surrounded by greenery and trees. You cannot think of the British countryside without imagining a country churchyard popping up here and there.

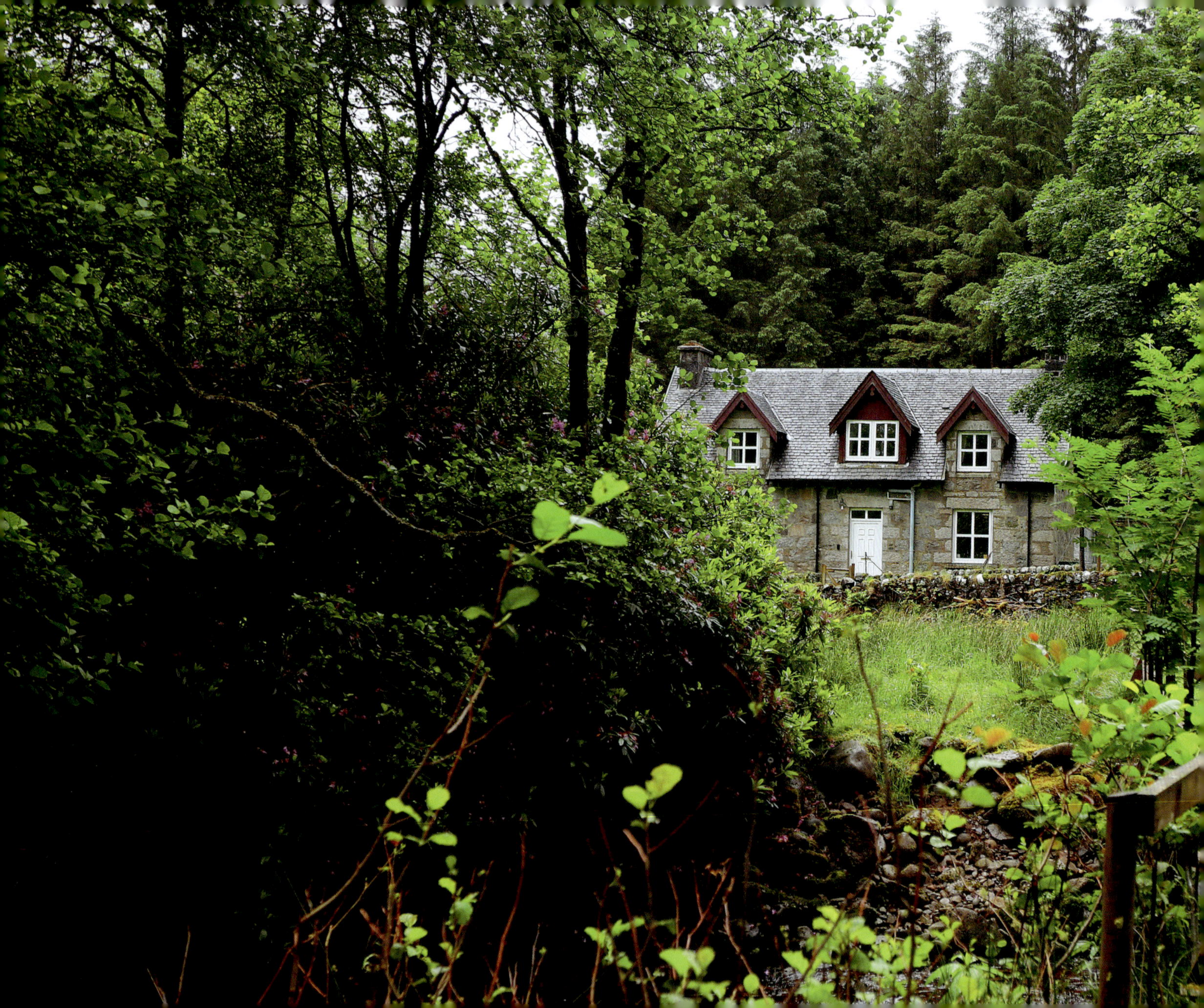

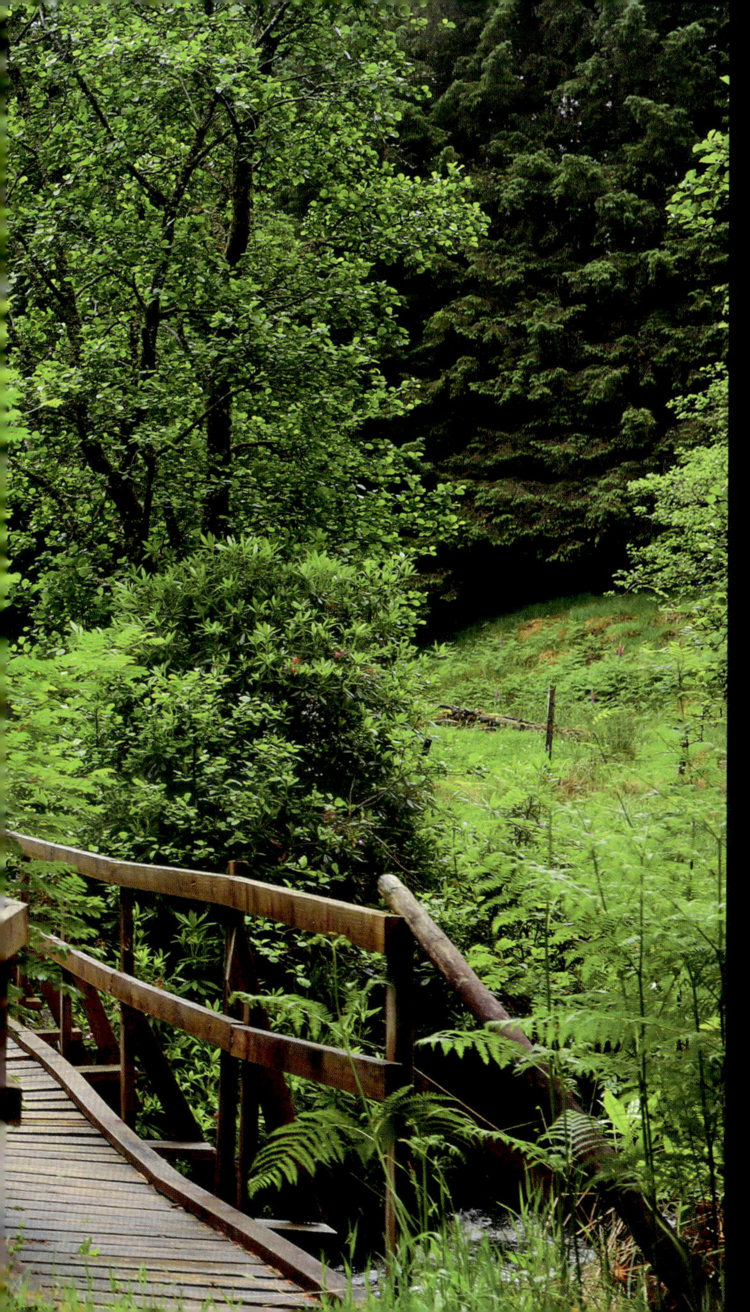

COUNTRY RESIDENCES

Oliver was born and raised in and around the countryside and it is here that he feels most at home. He envies those who live in large country residences with lots of land and huge gardens, and combined with his love of history he loves to visit and take pictures of stately homes and old picturesque thatched cottages, many of which are hundreds of years old. He also loves houses and homes that are exquisitely nestled into nature and often after complimenting himself on the quality of an image he has just captured, one can hear him say "That would be a nice place to live, wouldn't it?" As always, his eye is drawn by light, shape, and form. He captures many images of old stone steps and long walls in the gardens of grand homes open to the public, and is unable to resist the light and reflections he notices in the lakes, garden pools and water so often found there.

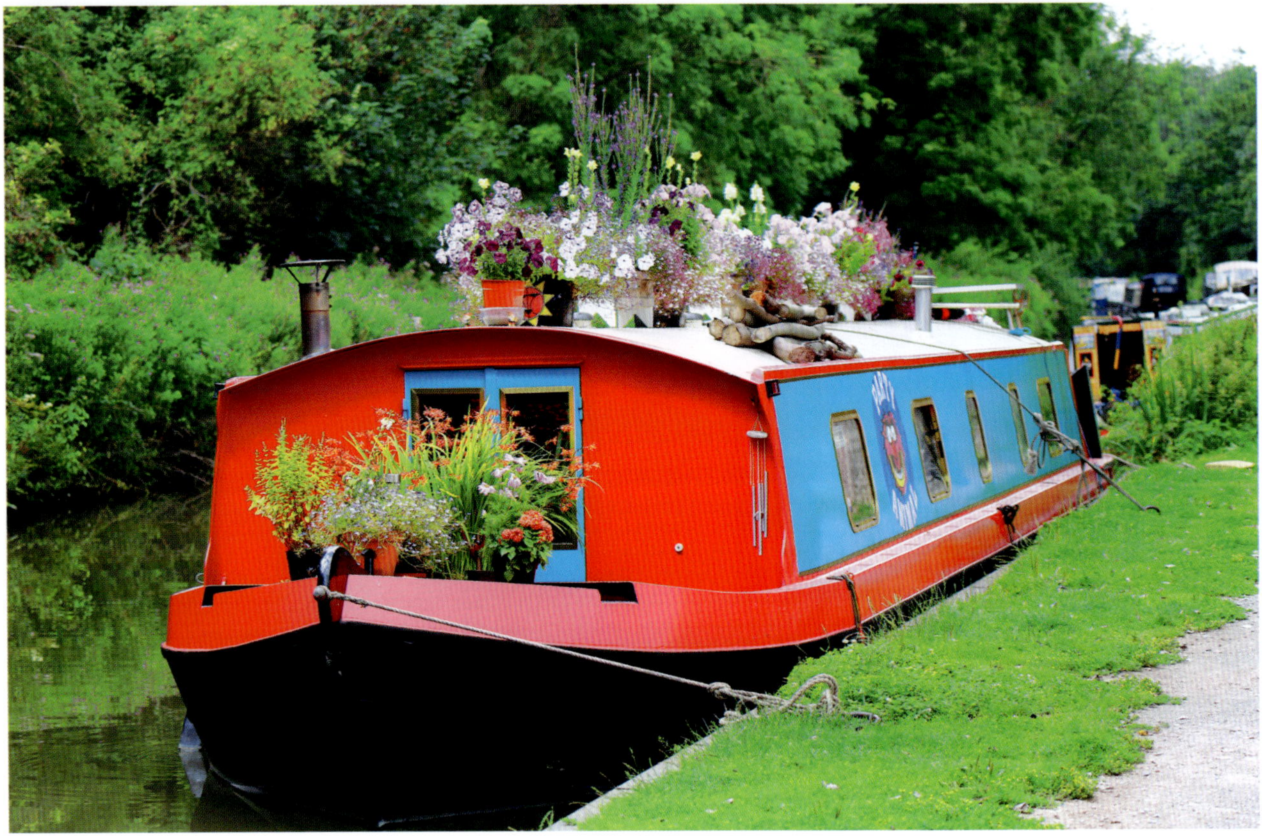

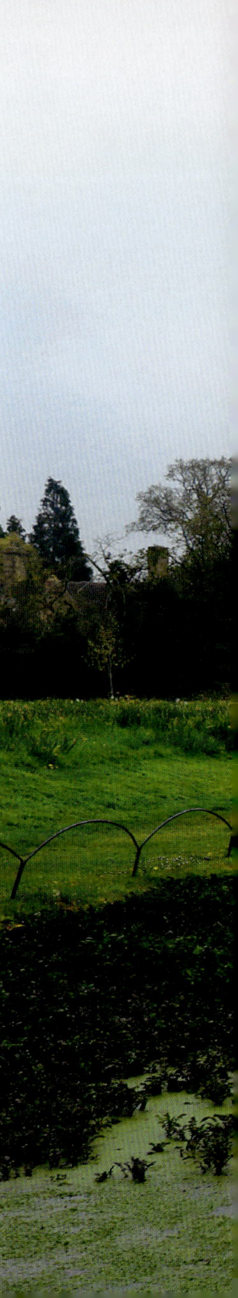

BARGE ON THE KENNET AND AVON CANAL, WILTSHIRE

A beautiful houseboat, complete with its own floating garden!

BARRINGTON COURT GARDENS
Oliver's favourite

"The reason I like this picture is I like the different colours and the contrast. I like the trees and the lines and the wall in front. Look at the colours on the wall and the green in the water."

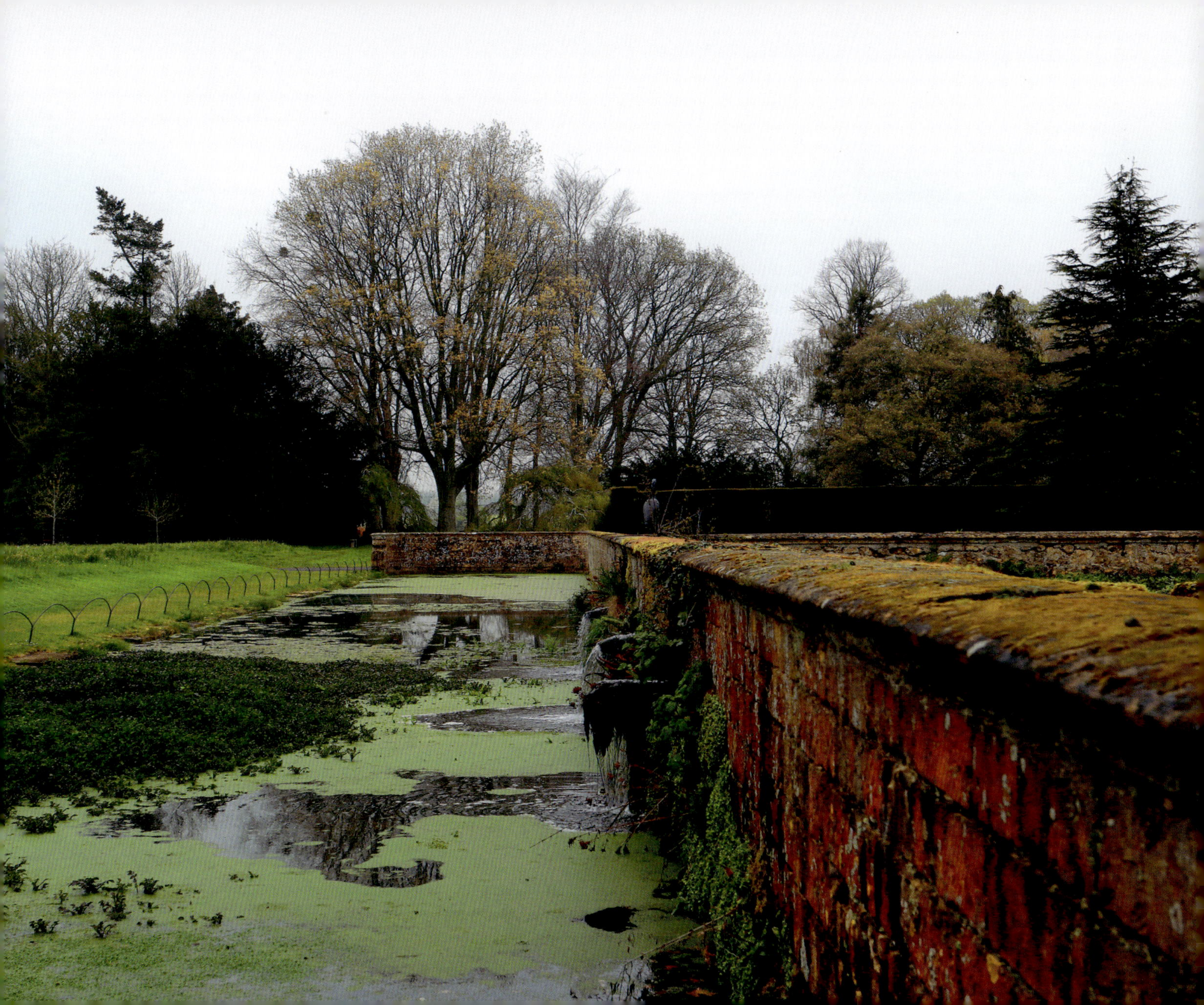

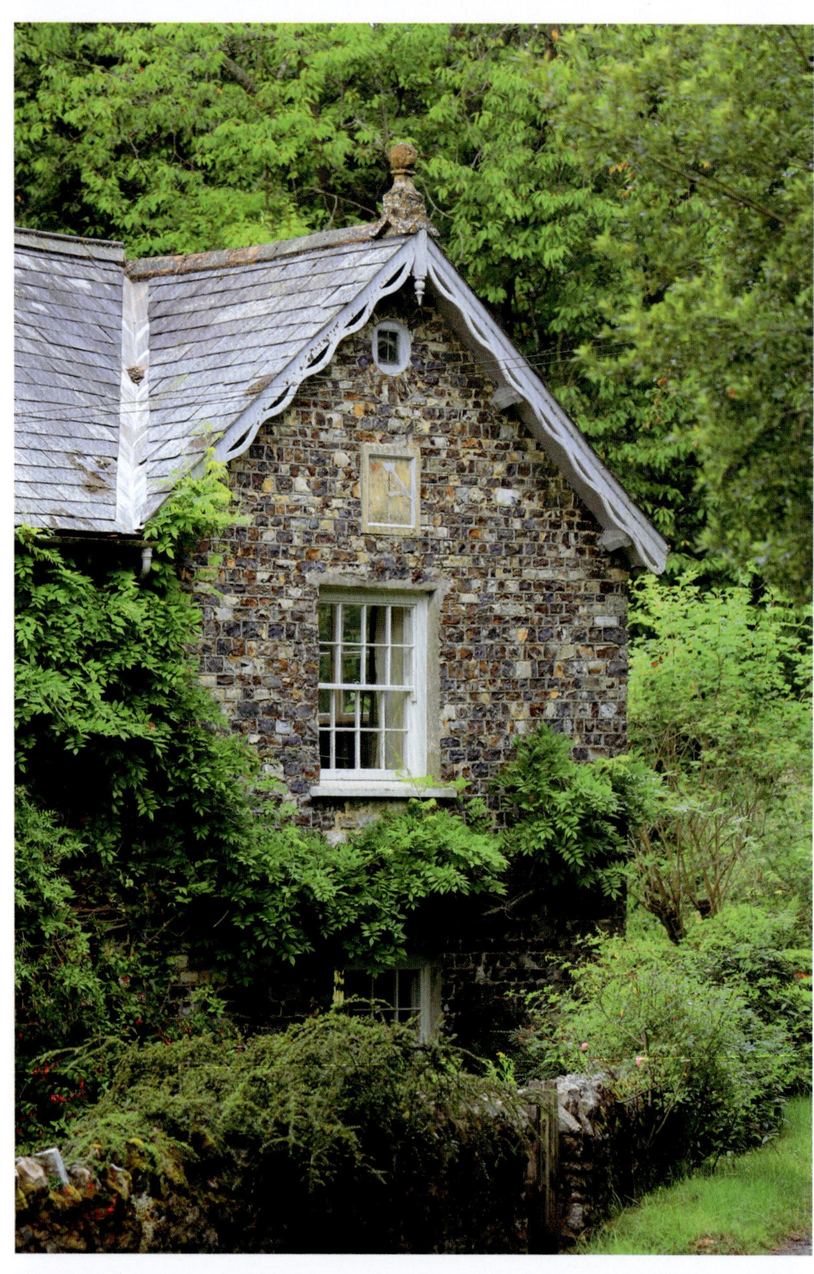

HOUSE IN THE COUNTRYSIDE WITH SUNDIAL

Oliver liked this house, tucked into the greenery. He didn't notice until examining the picture afterwards that it had a sundial on the wall above the window with 'Tempus Fugit' engraved at the top.

HESTERCOMBE HOUSE AND GARDENS
Oliver's favourite

"I like the shapes and the curves and the plants in this one. I like the different colours. It's actually quite vibrant."

TYPICAL COTTAGE GARDEN ENTRANCE

Oliver didn't even get out of the car to get this picture! He just wound down the window, took it and said, "Okay, I'm done." It's now one of his most popular greetings cards.

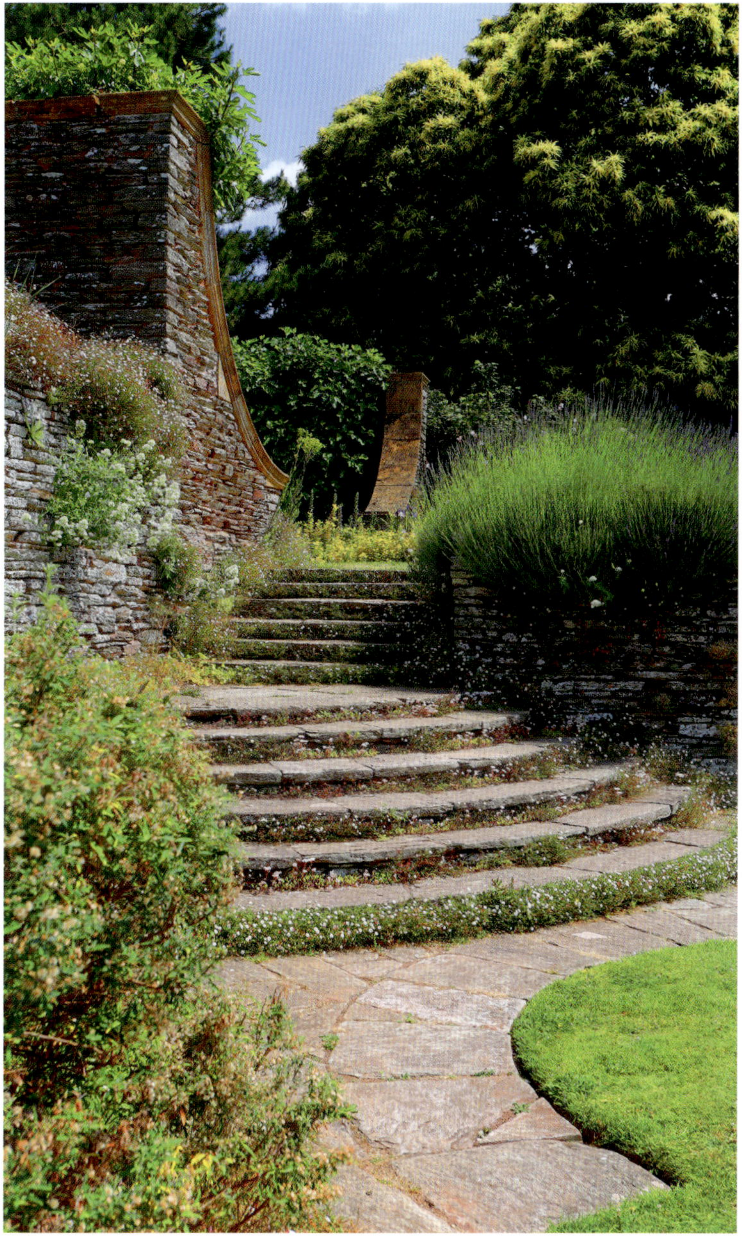

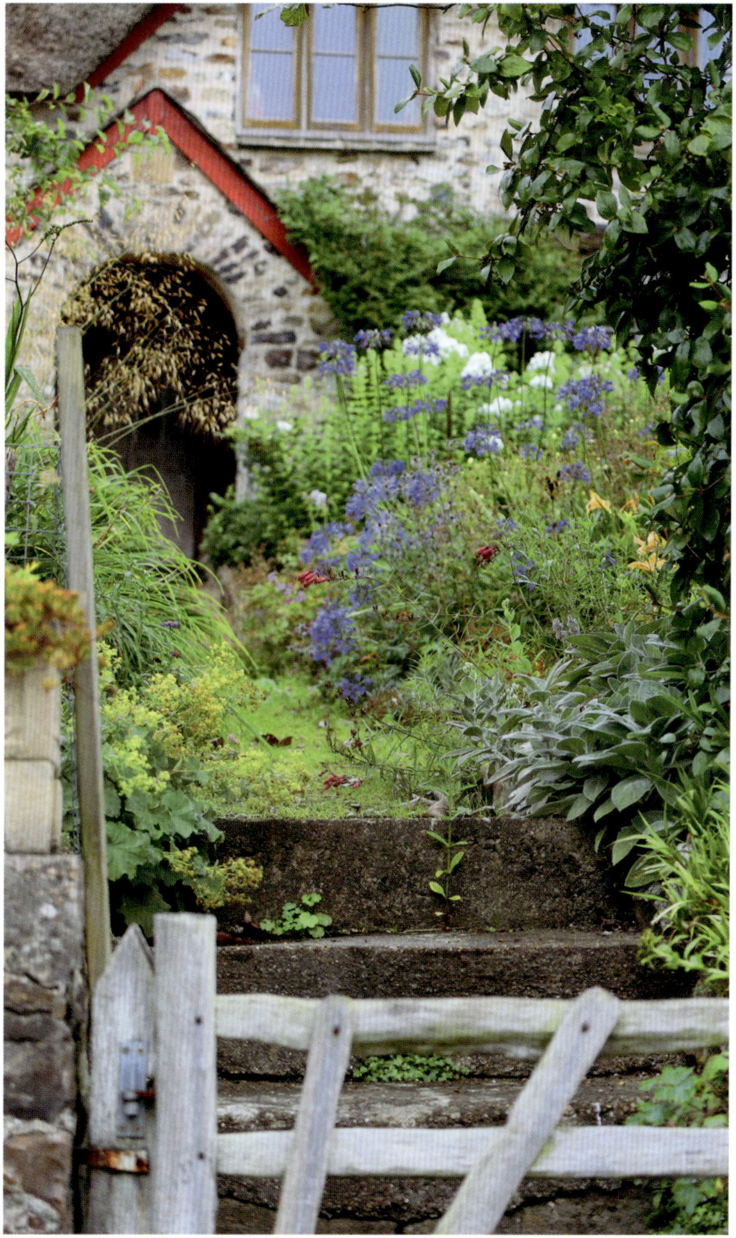

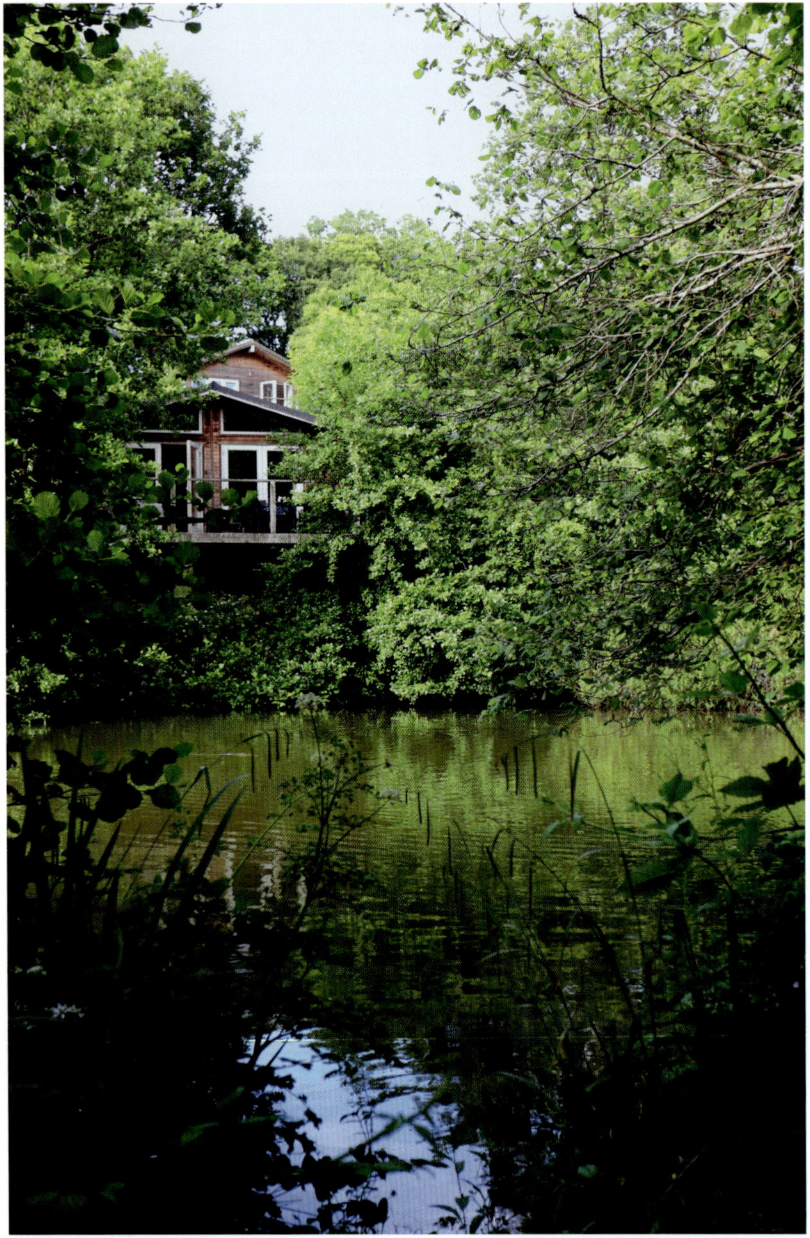

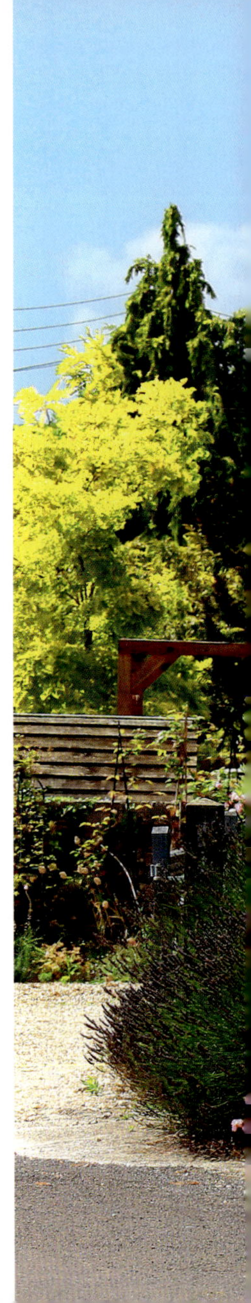

The West Country is just one
of the areas of Britain full of
delightful thatched cottages
like this.

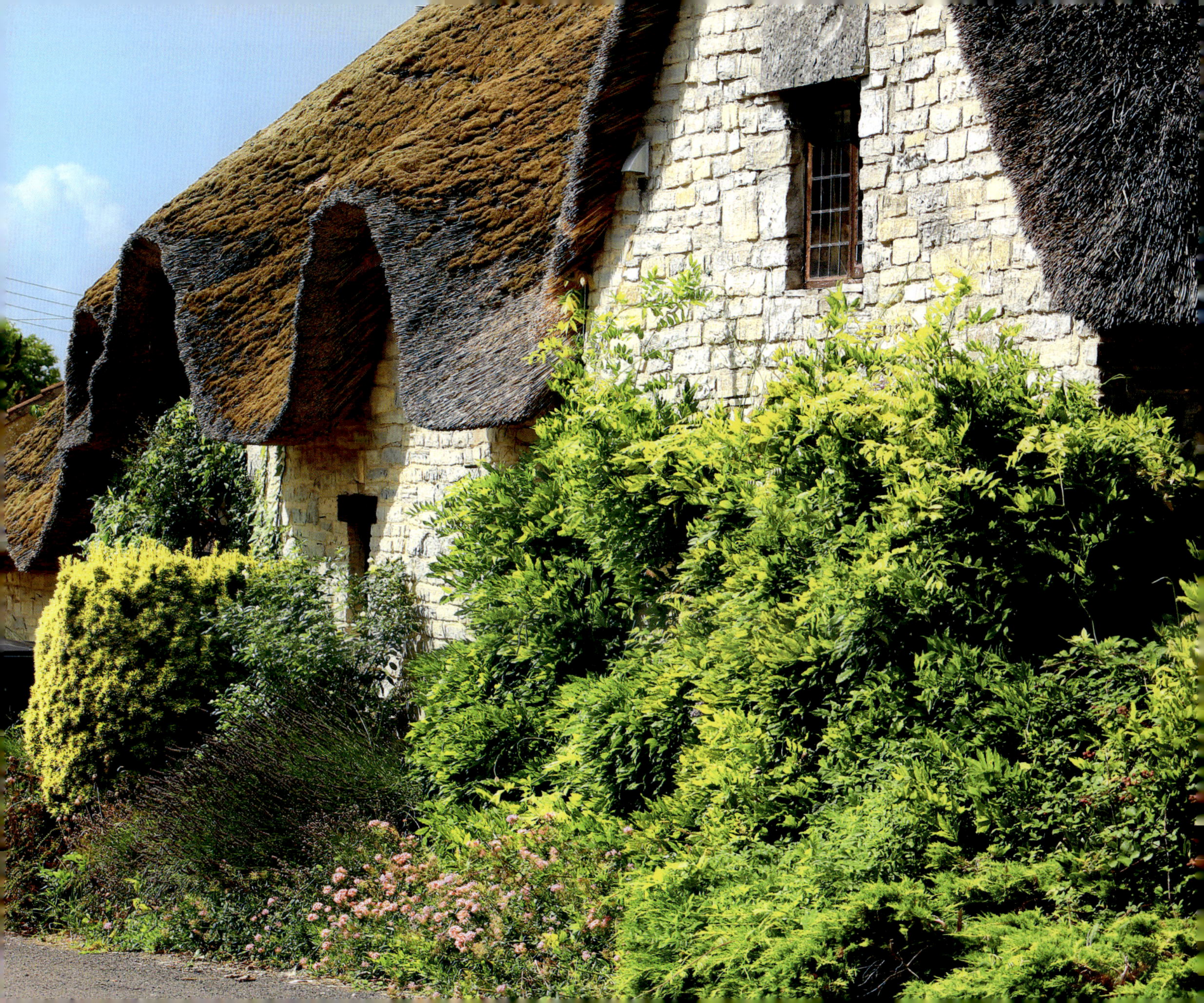

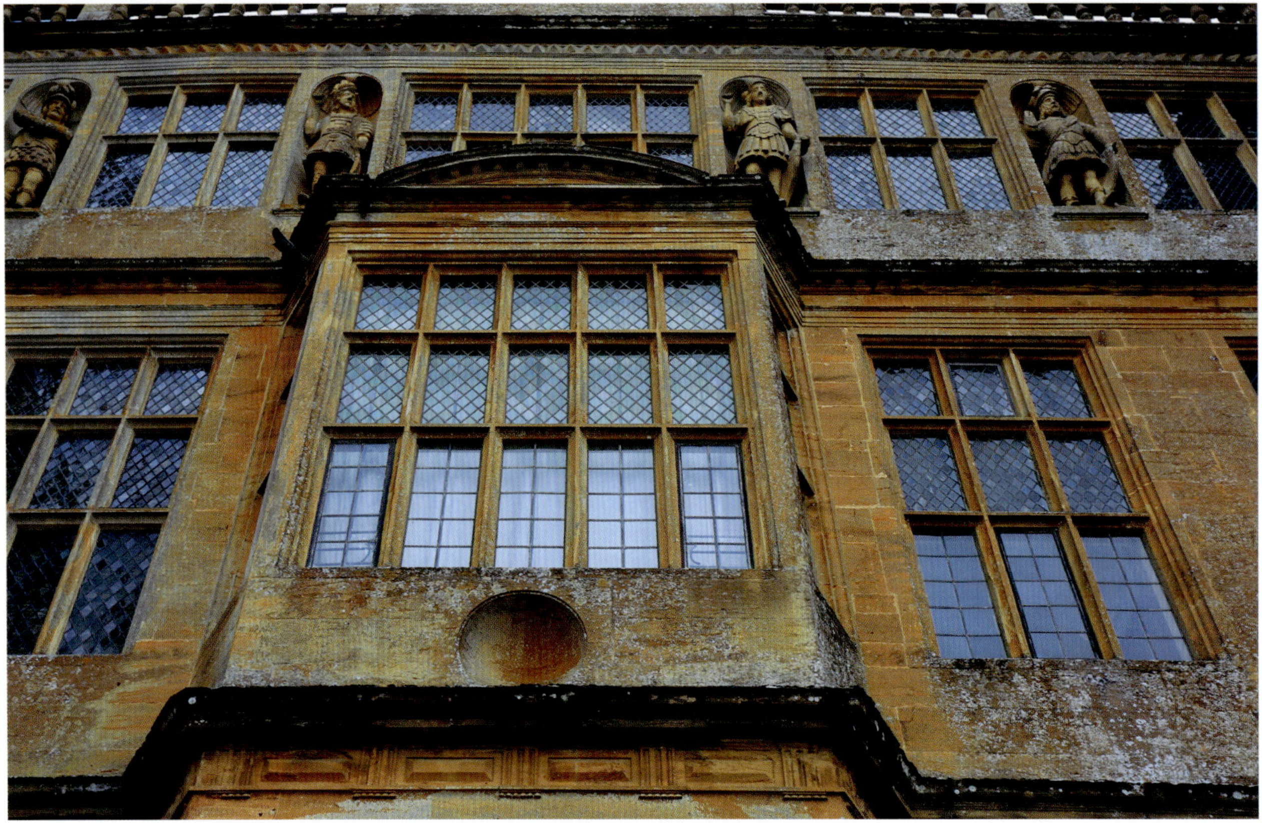

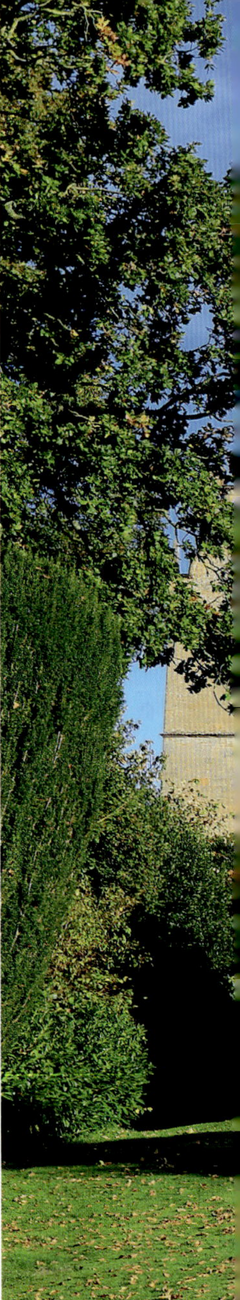

MONTECUTE HOUSE – LOOKING UP AT THE WINDOWS
Oliver's favourite

"I like the colour on the wall and I love all the windows to look at. I looked up and they're all different in their own way."

MONTECUTE HOUSE, SOMERSET

A great frontage to this Elizabethan mansion.

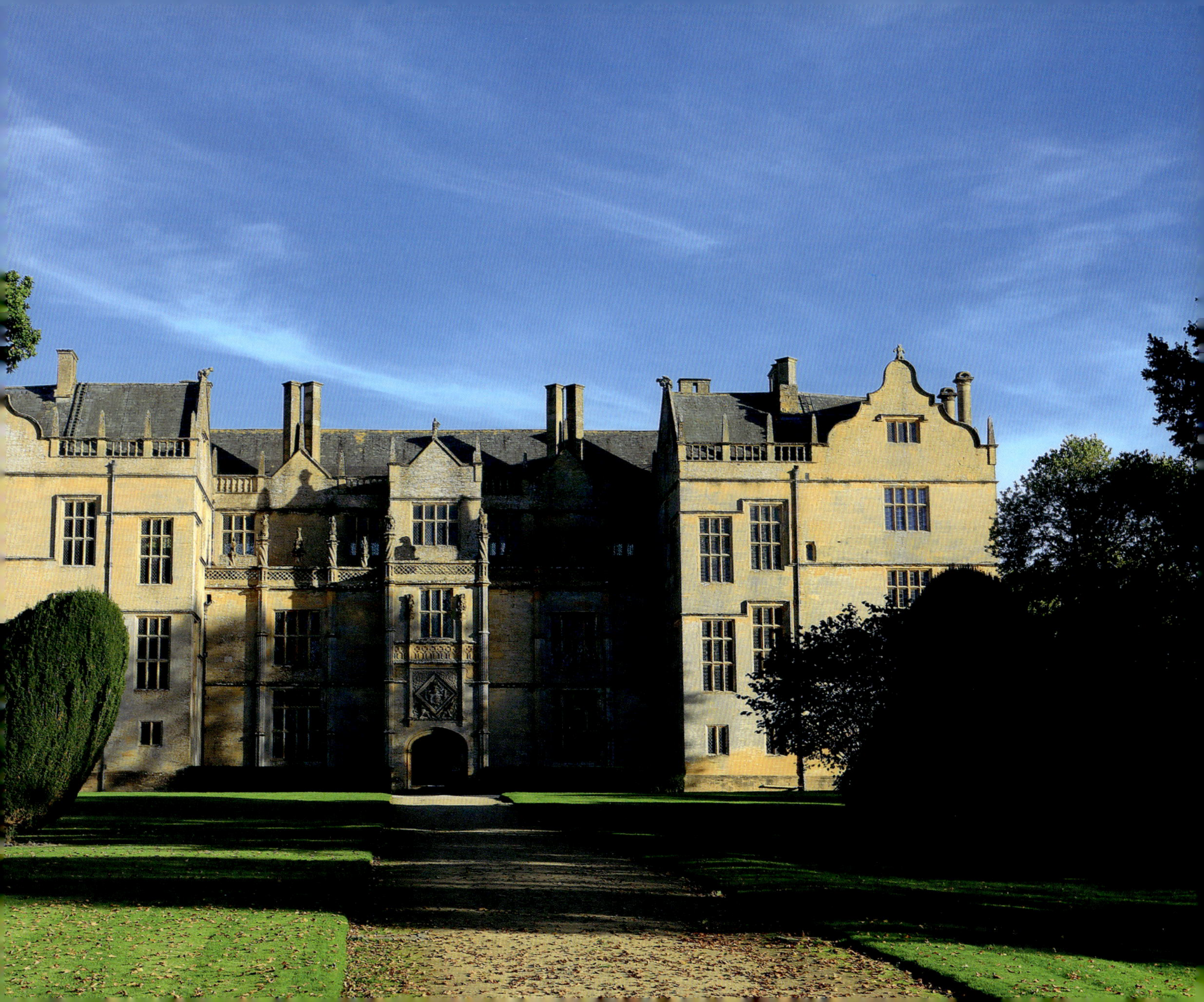

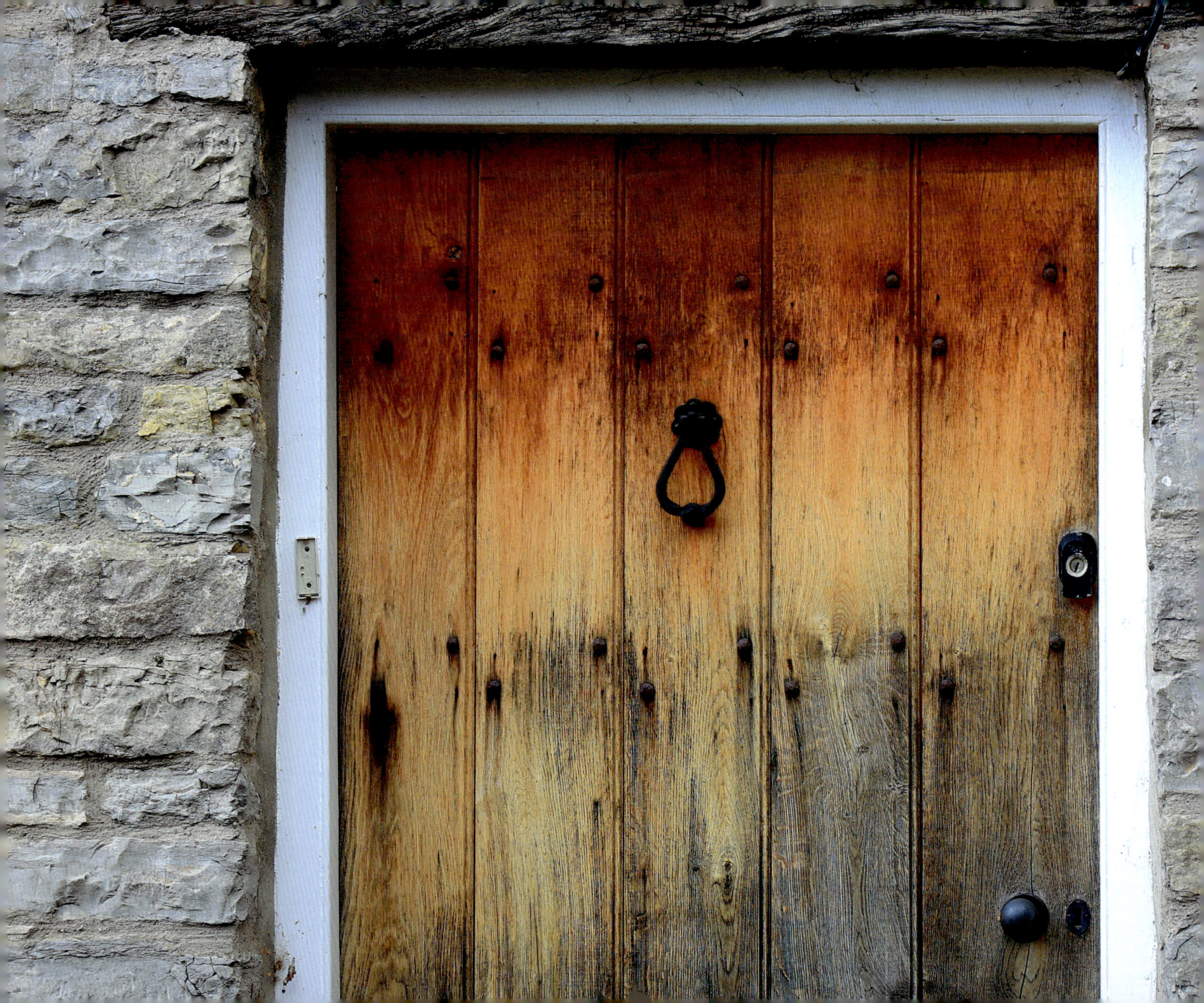

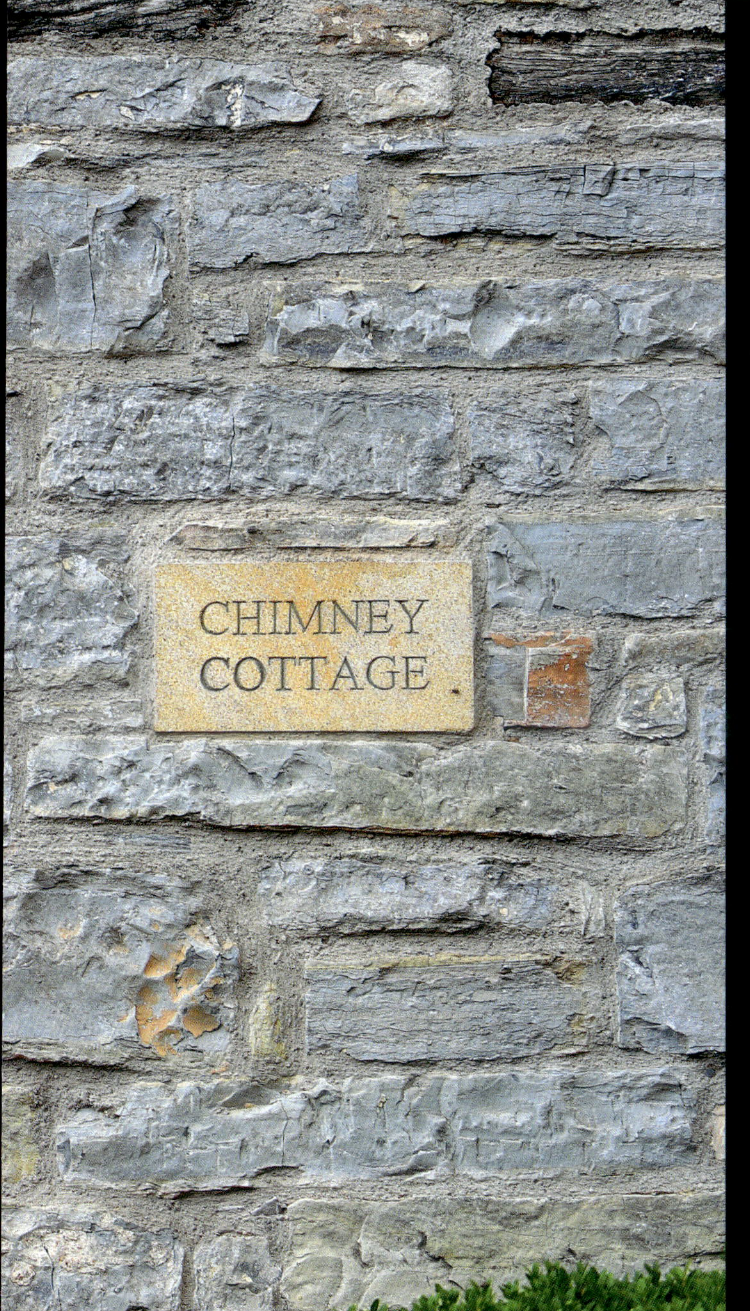

DOORS and POSTBOXES

"I like taking pictures of doors, and my fans like them too. It's actually my mum who likes postboxes, so I take them for her really! They don't have red postboxes like ours in other countries."

Oliver's followers love the door pictures. As well as individual images, they particularly like 'montage collections' of both doors and post-boxes as photographic prints. Oliver enjoys capturing images of doors and often returns from a photographic outing announcing, "Well I got some *great* doors today!" The red post-boxes are such iconic images and provide such a lovely splash of colour – along with our red telephone boxes, which are unfortunately fast disappearing. If you look at the initials on a post-box, you can tell which monarch's reign they were produced in. Ones produced in Queen Victoria's reign (VR) are the earliest.

When Oliver's followers found out he was going to do a book entitled *Oliver's Britain*, hundreds of them commented, "Oh you *must* do a chapter on doors and postboxes!"

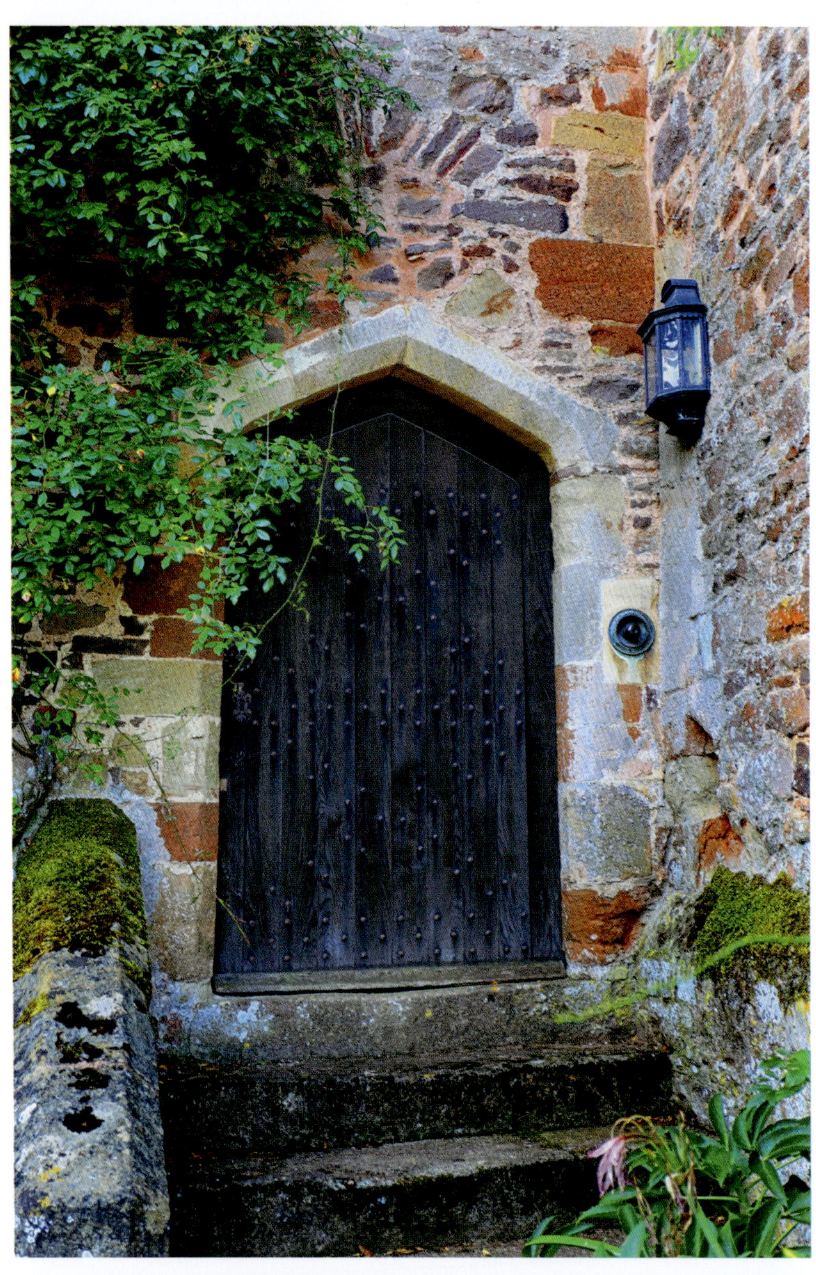

OLD WOODEN DOOR AND DOORBELL
Oliver's favourite

"I really like the wall with the moss on it, and the steps, and the green leaves. The door is an interesting shape and I like the old wood. I like all the colours and the stones in the walls, too."

COTTAGE DOOR AND GARDEN GATE, BISHOPSWOOD

This image was captured in Oliver's home village in the Blackdown Hills.

COTTAGE PORCH AND DOOR

A beautiful example of a front door and porch found on a stone-built thatched cottage in rural Britain.

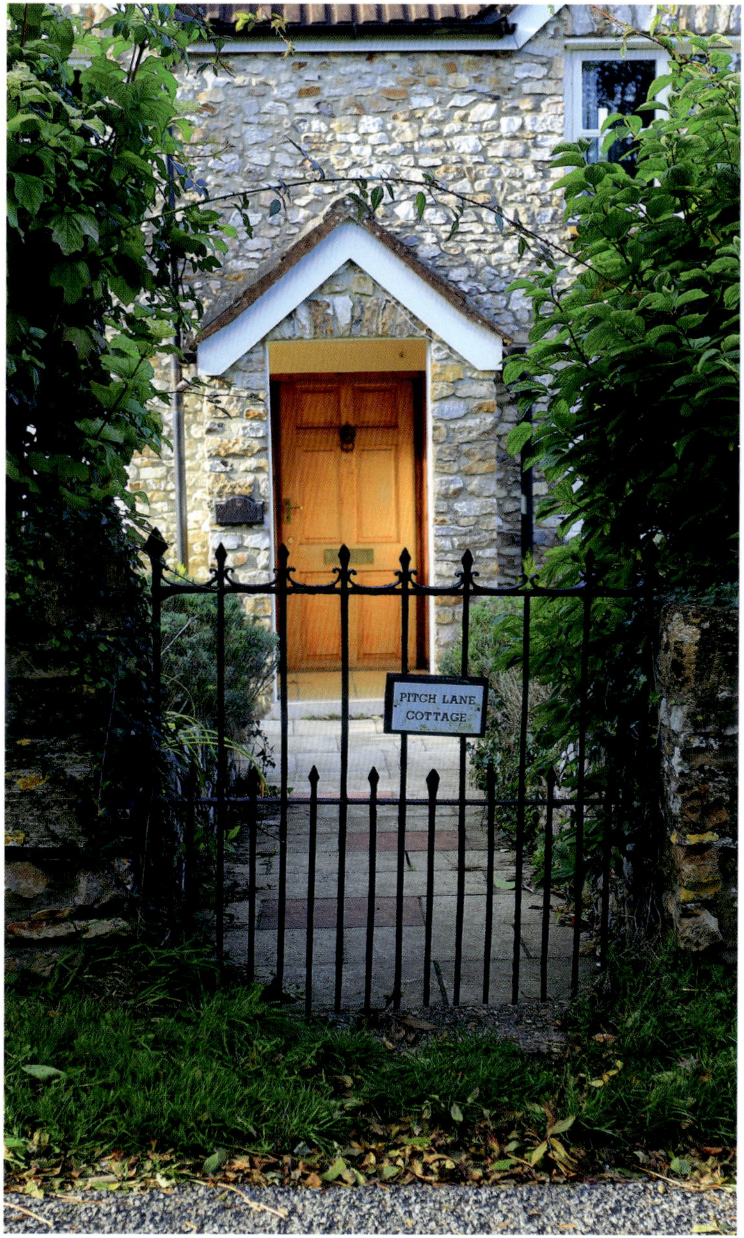

PITCH LANE
COTTAGE

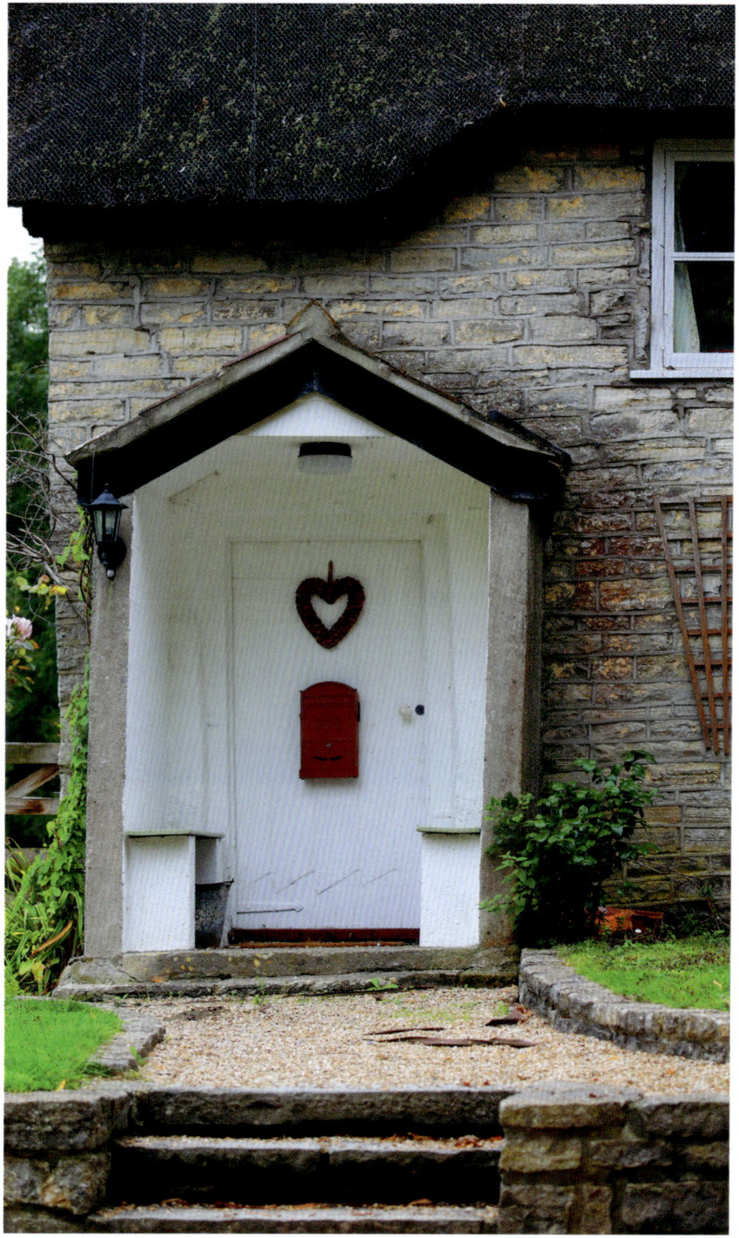

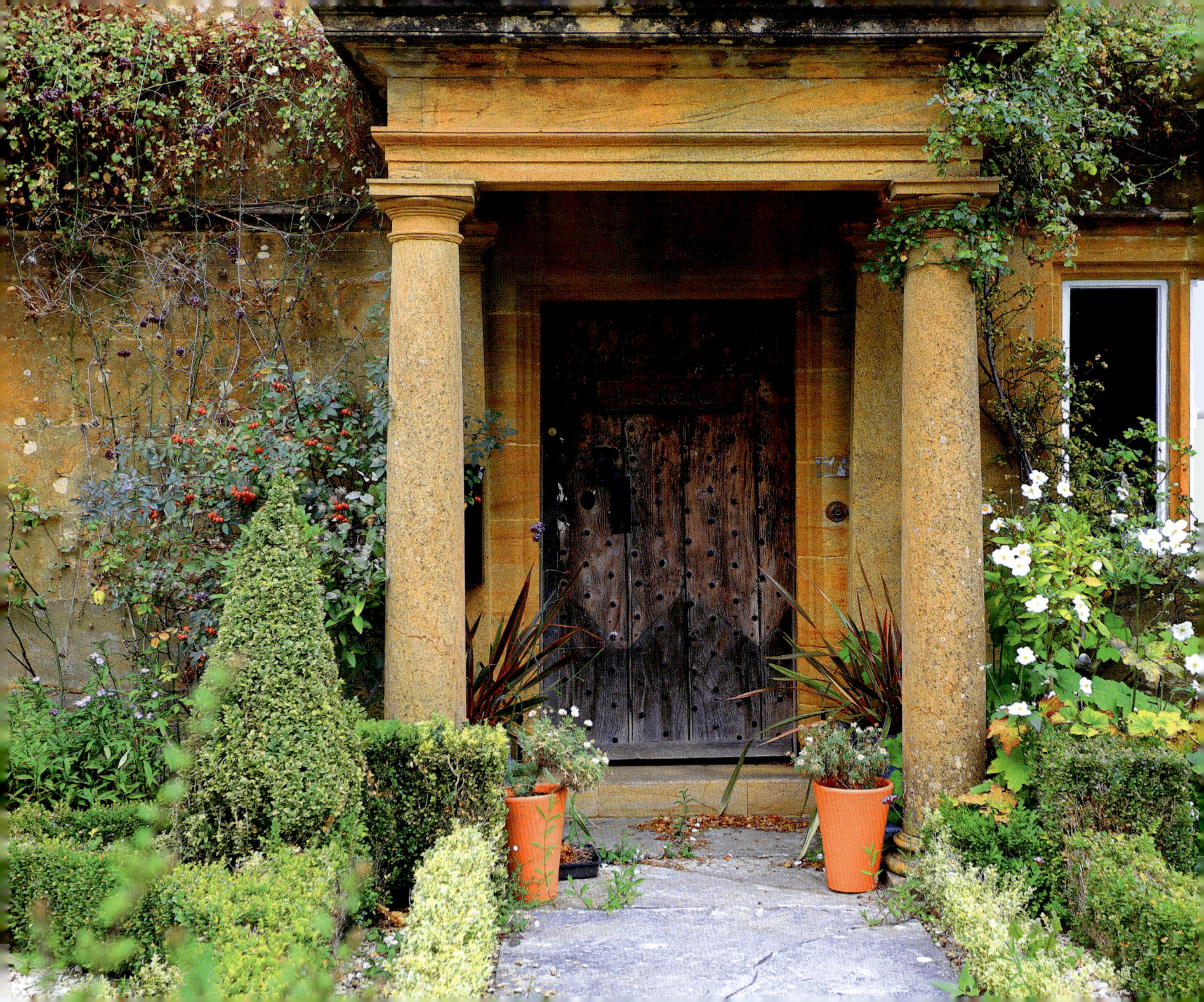

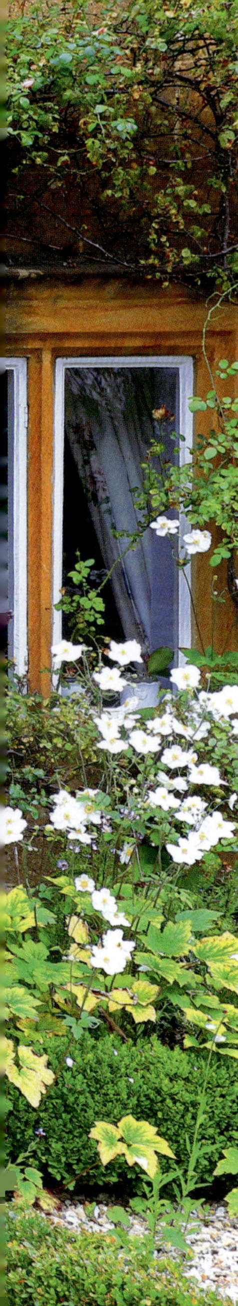

BEAUTIFUL OLD OAK DOOR AND PILLARED PORCH – HOUSE BUILT OF HAMSTONE IN THE 1600S

Oliver's favourite

"There's a place called Martock in Somerset and it's got some lovely houses and doors – and I *do* like doors. I like the flowers in this picture, and the wooden door is really old. The stone pillars are cool; they make it look like a grand entrance."

THATCHED COTTAGE PORCH

Oliver's favourite

"I liked the house because it was gorgeous. I wanted to get the right image so that it's 'cottagey', with its little thatched roof on the porch. I like the green leaves against the wall and the wild bits as well. I like the red poppy on the black door."

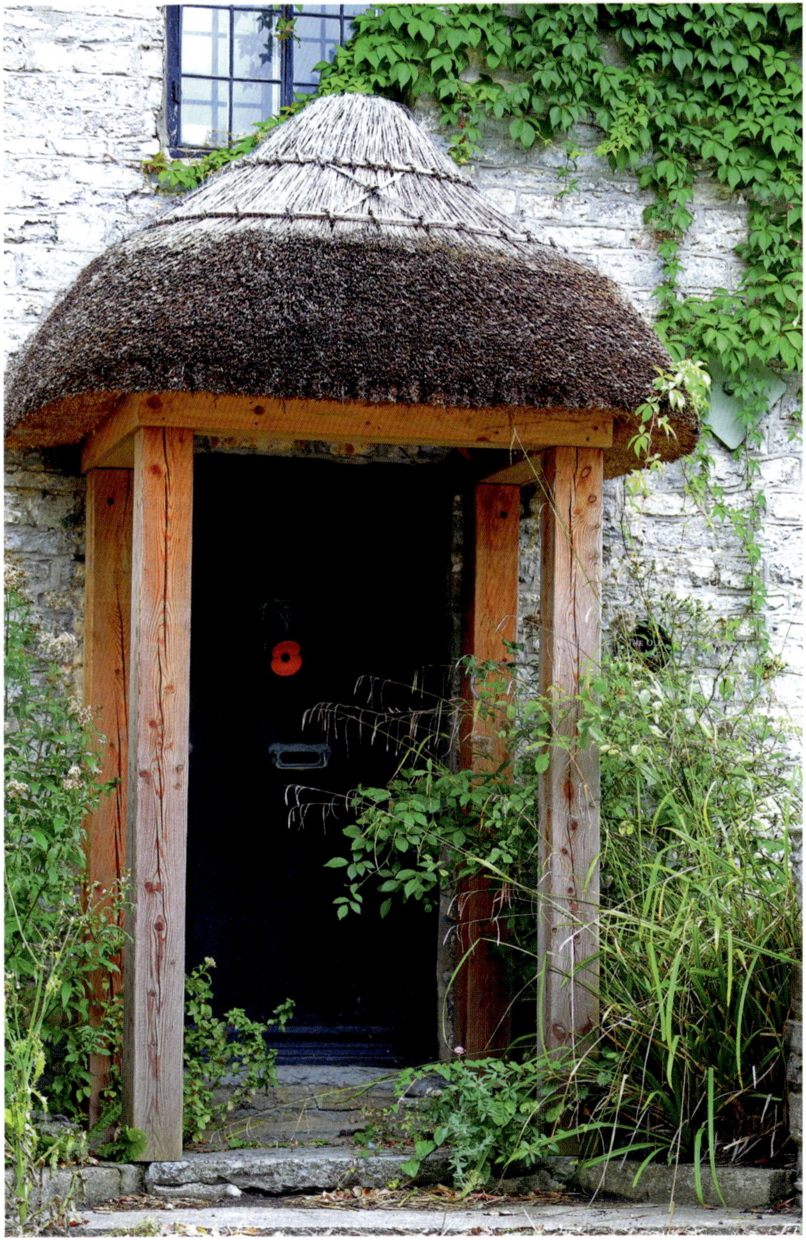

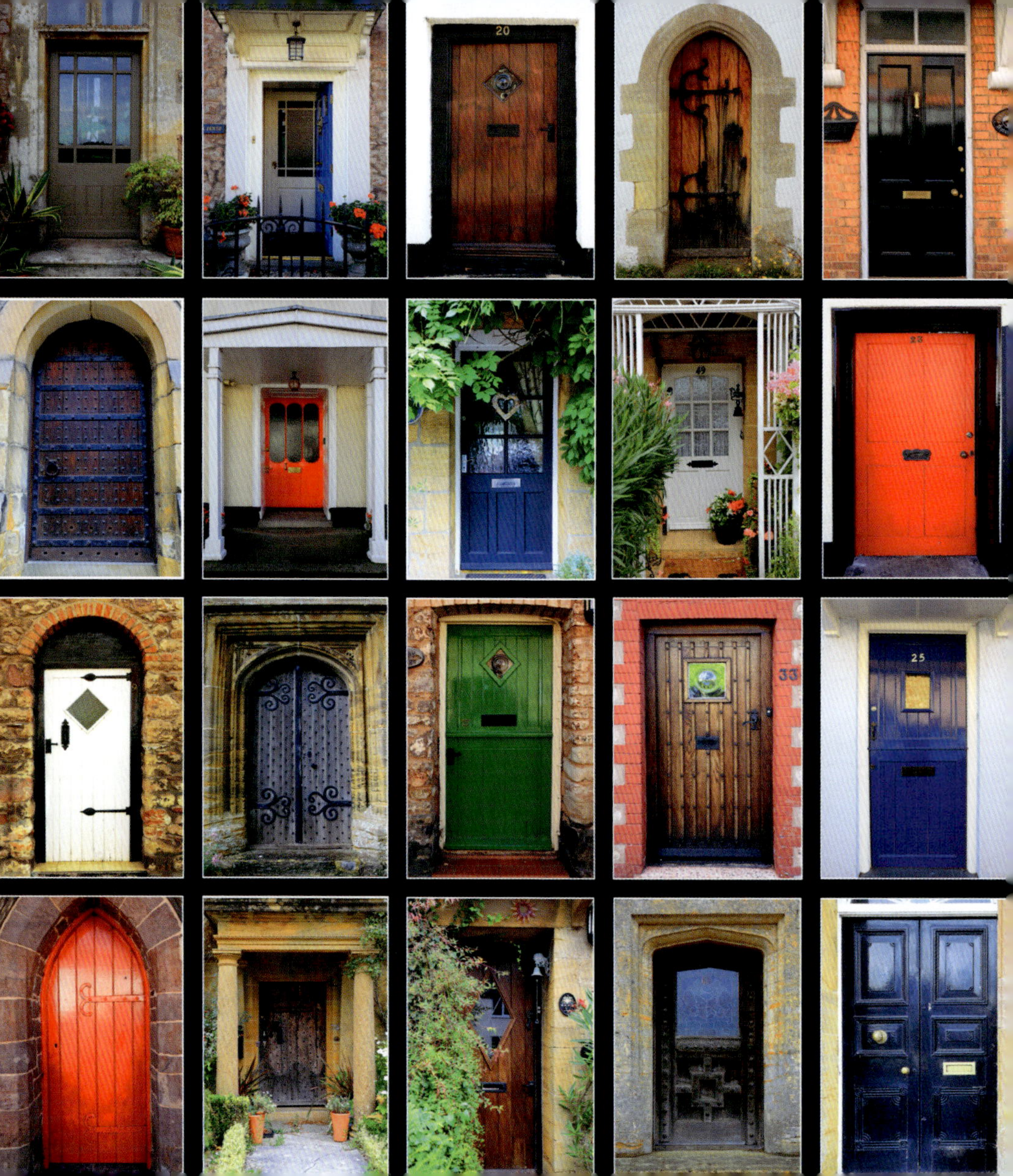

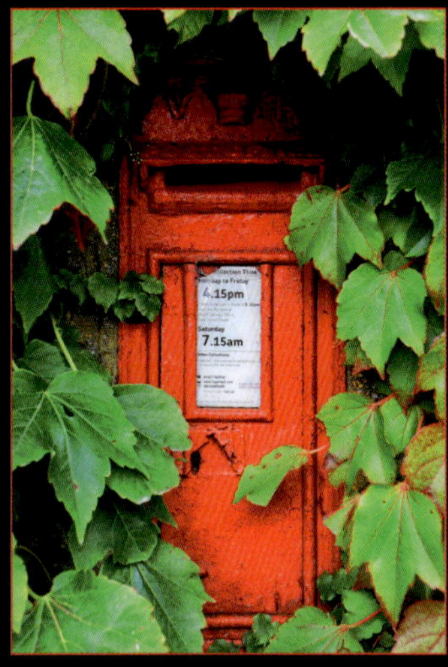

VICTORIA

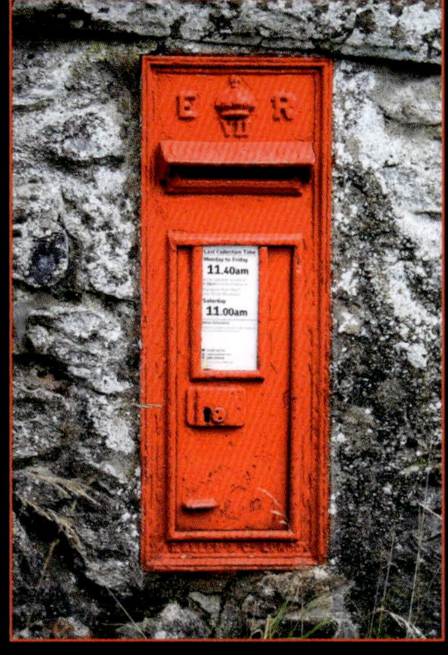

EDWARD VII

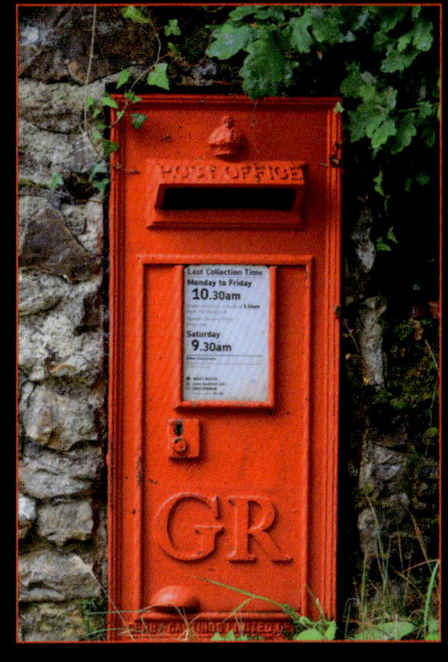

GEORGE V

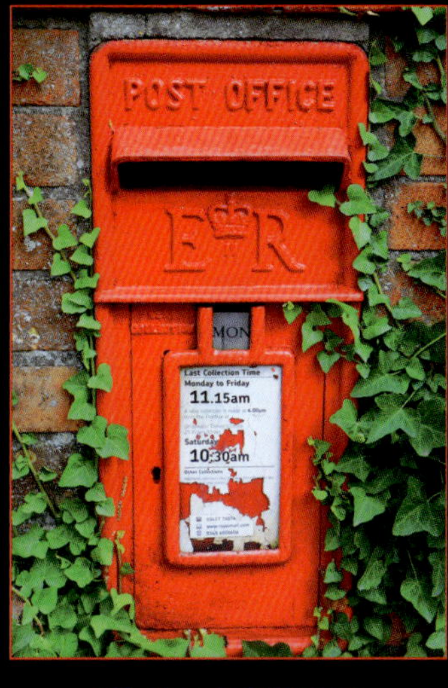

ELIZABETH II

DOORS

A small collection of some of Oliver's favourite doors from across the country. When this image was put up on Oliver's Facebook page, this was one of our favourite comments:
Melanie Gallatin Nightingale: "As a teacher of students with Cognitive Impairments, Oliver is such a great reminder and constant inspiration that an amazing future lies ahead for each of my kids, I just have to help them unlock the right doors."

These four old red postboxes bear the initials of the four different British monarchs who were reigning at the time of their production and installation.

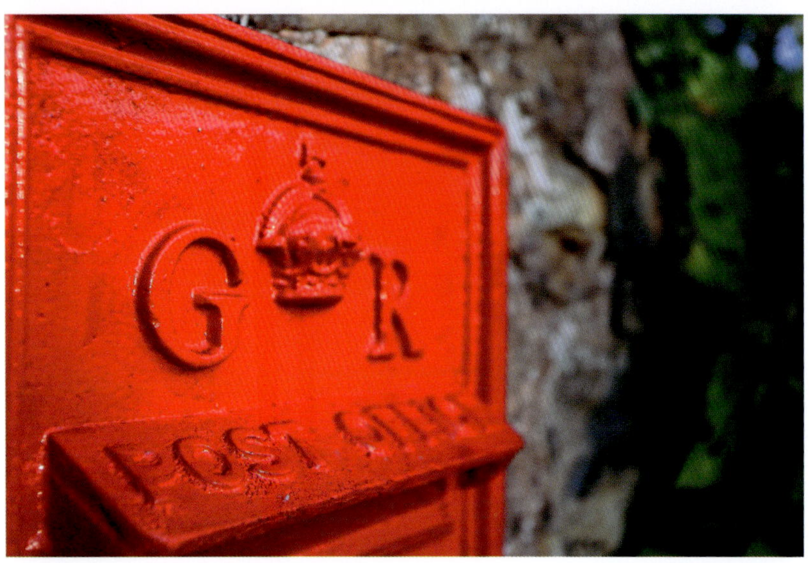

GR POSTBOX

Post-box from the reign of George V, built into a stone wall.

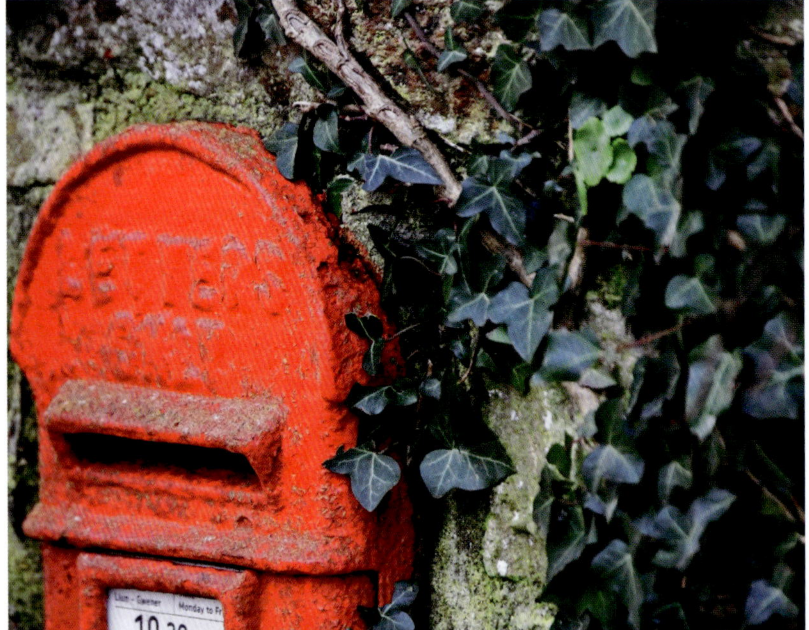

OLD WALL POSTBOX, WALES

Noticed whilst on holiday in Wales. Oliver particularly liked the ivy in this picture.

TRADITIONAL RED TELEPHONE BOX

With the modern reliance on mobile phones, our old red telephone boxes are fast disappearing – although some rural ones are now used to contain free tourist information leaflets or even as small 'free libraries', where you can leave books you've read on the shelves and borrow others.

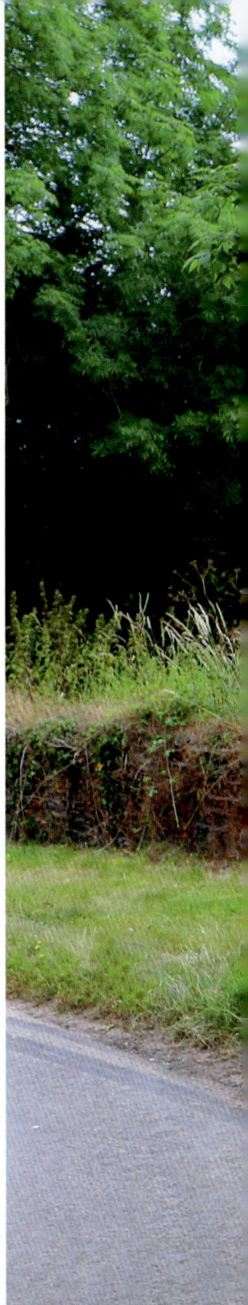

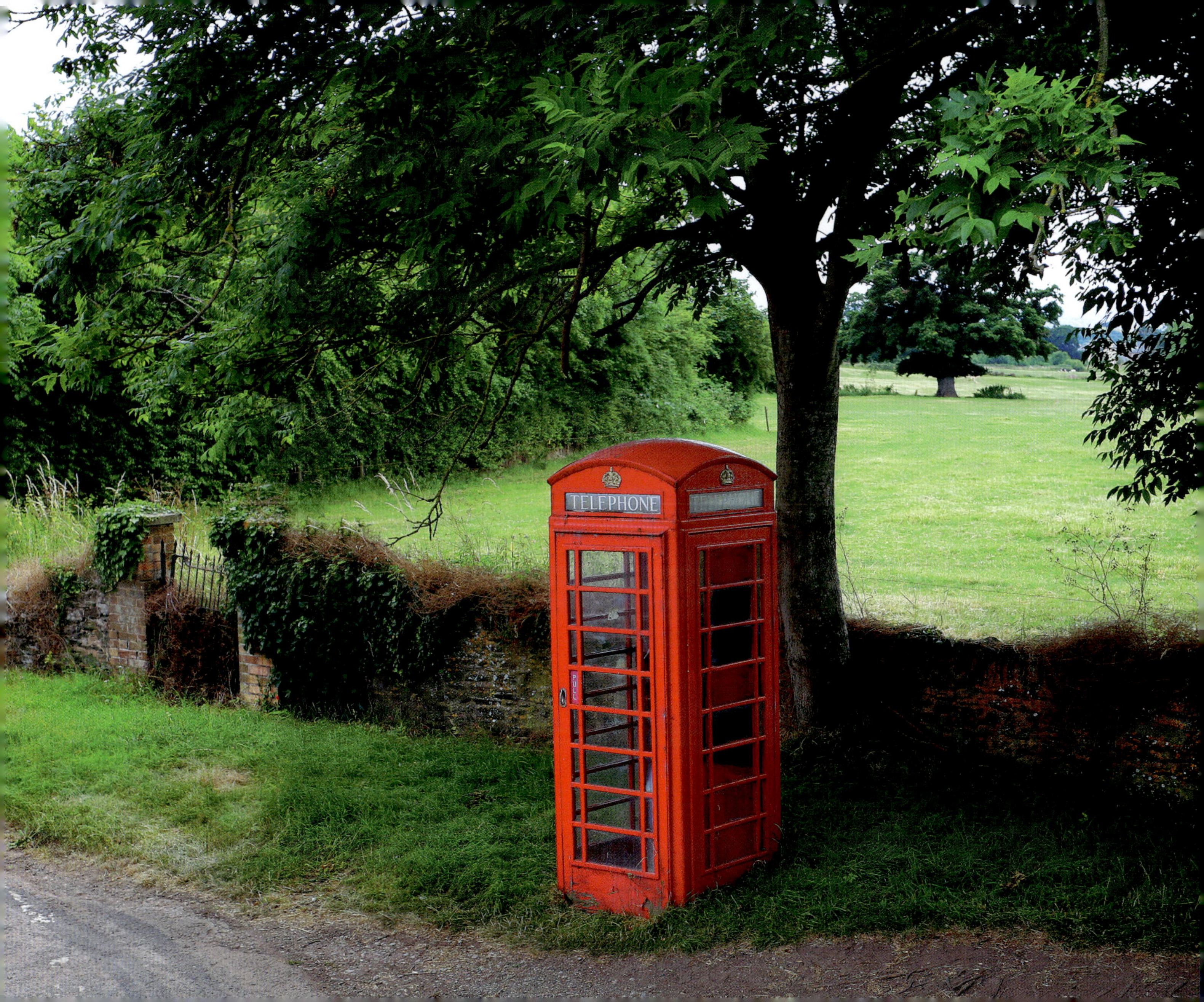

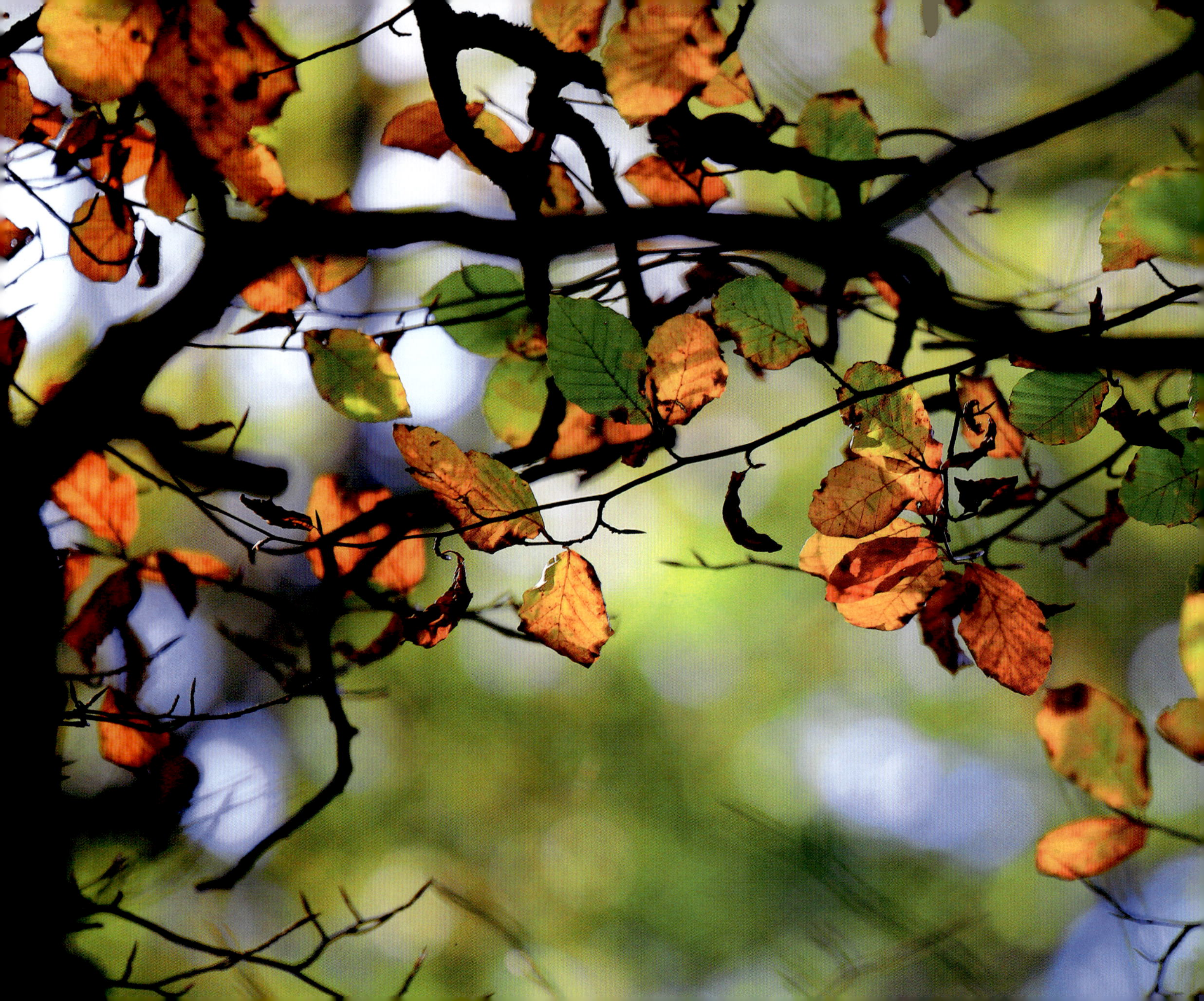

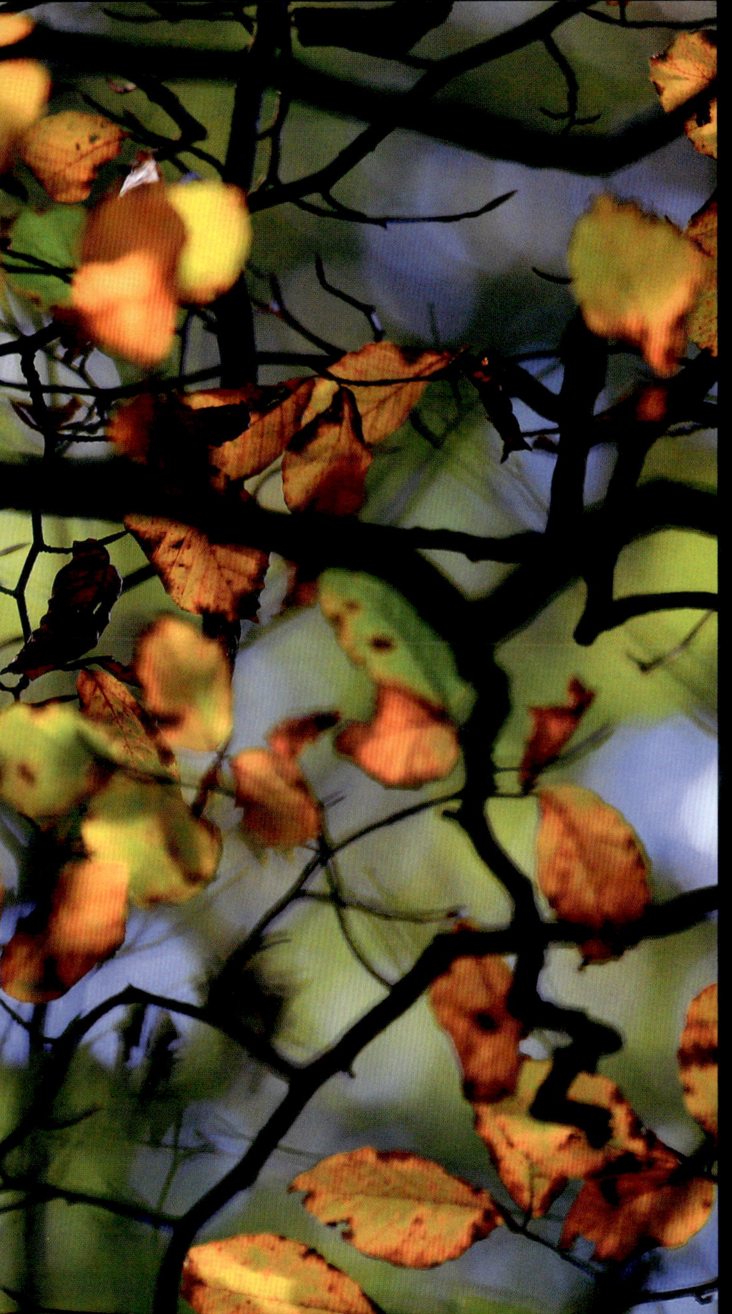

RANDOM COLLECTION

This chapter contains images that didn't seem to fit in any of the other categories, but which Oliver wanted to feature in his book of Britain.

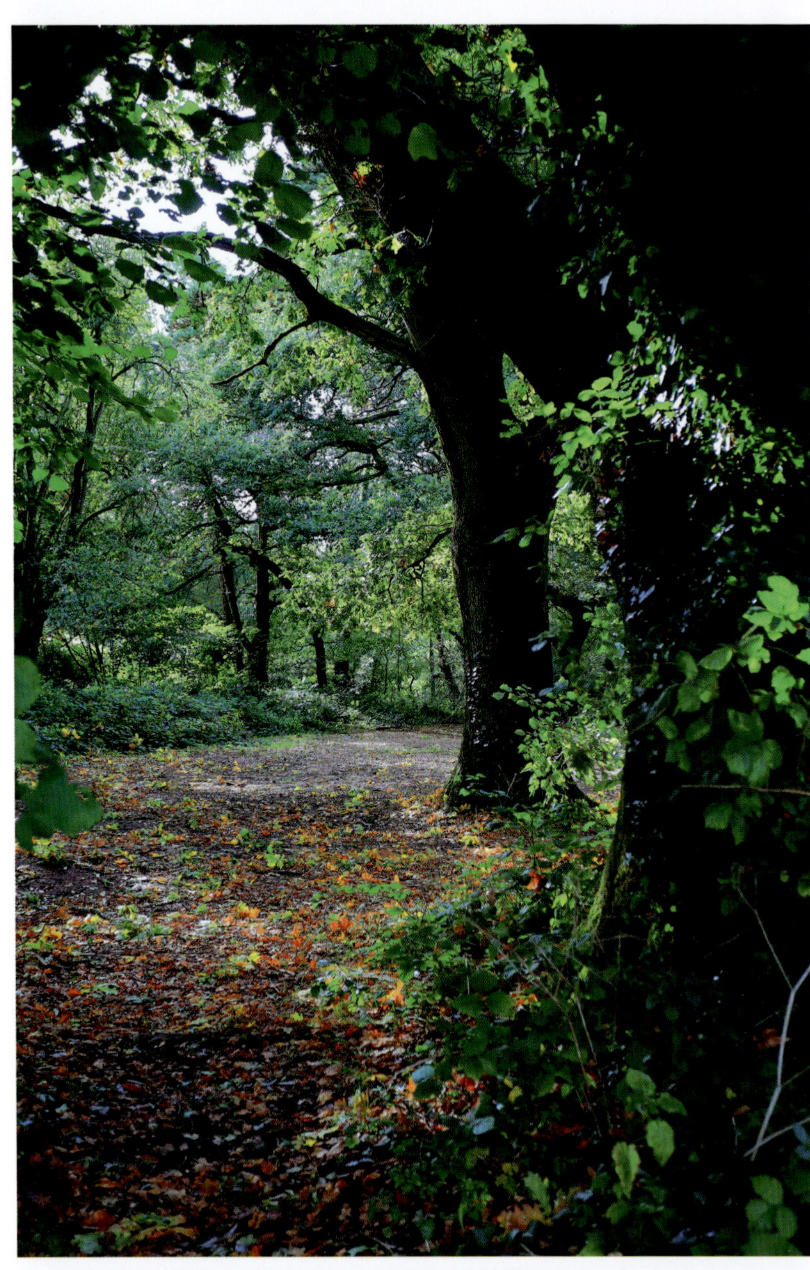

TYPICAL MIXED WOODLAND
Oliver's favourite

"I am always taking pictures in the woods. The woods is one of my most favourite places to go. I love being in the trees. I use trees to frame my pictures a lot. I think people will want to walk into this picture."

LOOKING UP INTO THE BRANCHES OF A MAJESTIC OAK

Britain is renowned for its elderly oak trees – many of them hundreds of years old. This old gent had a very wide and gnarled trunk with lots of interesting sections that Oliver took many detailed shots of, but as he had to narrow it down to one for this book, he chose this view looking up into the branches and leaves.

VIEW FROM THE GROUND – FYNE COURT

Taking pictures from the ground is one of Oliver's specialities and this is a great example.

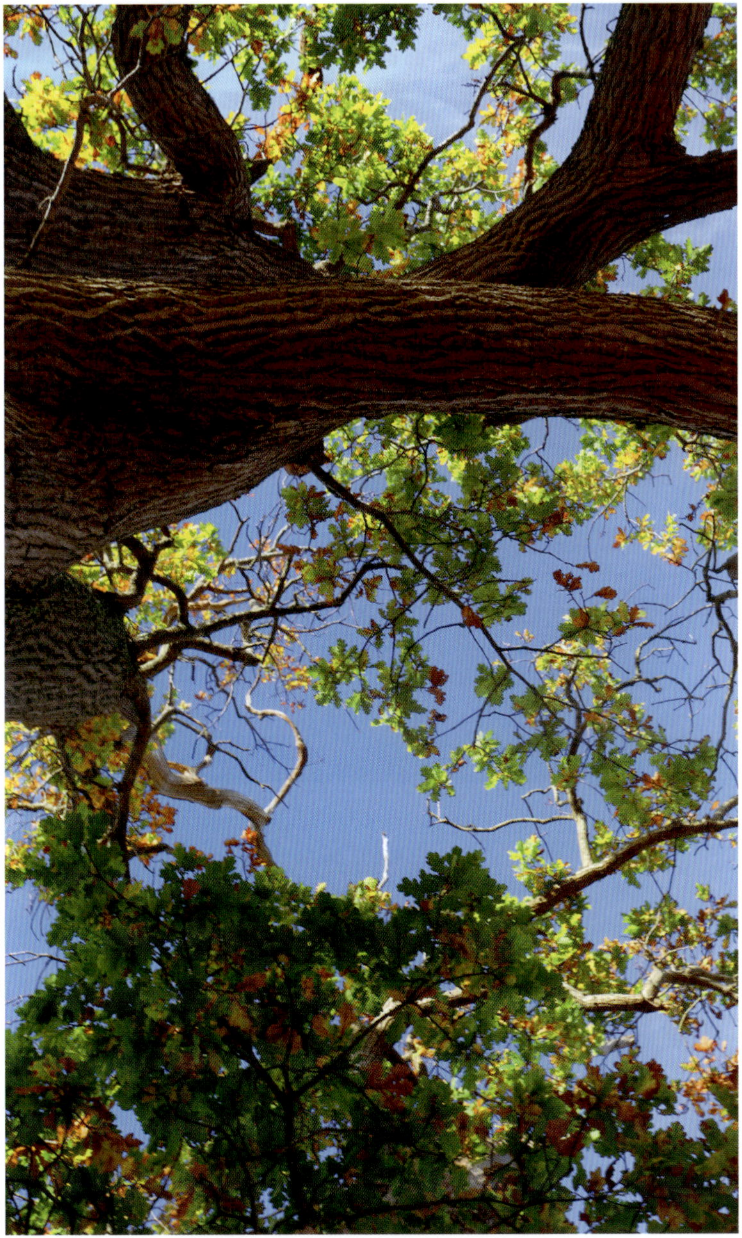

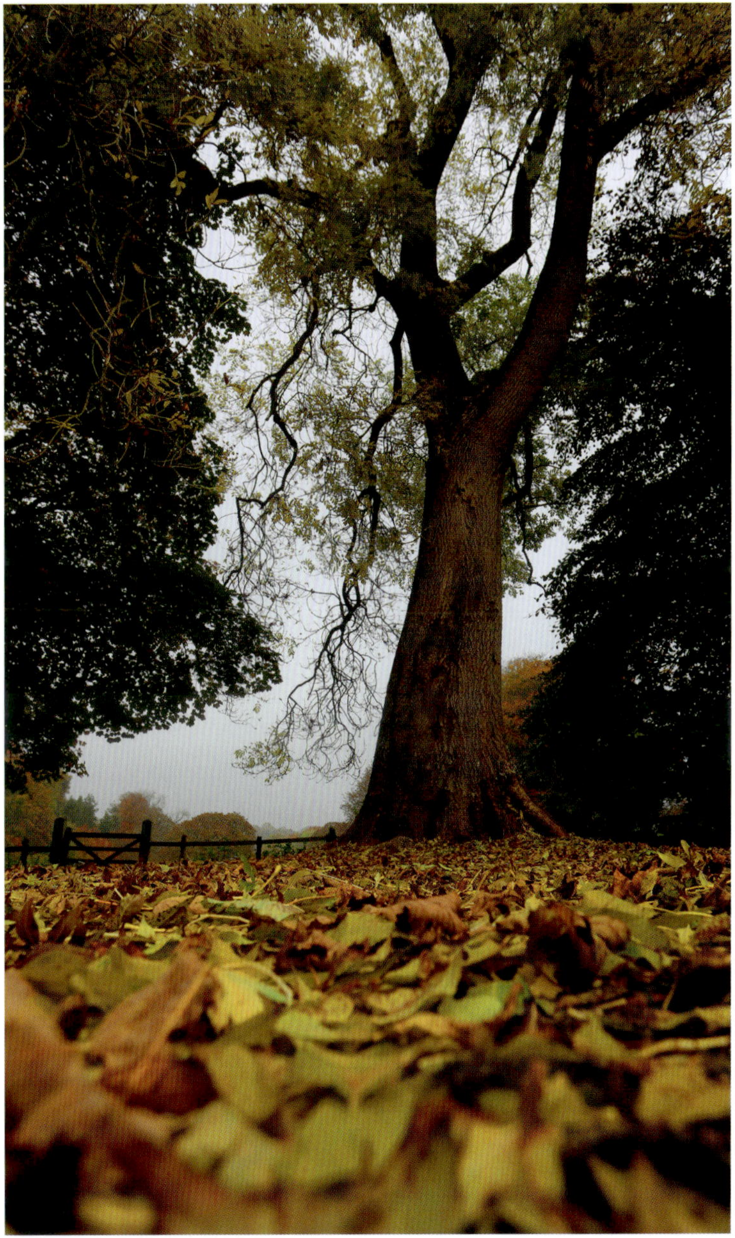

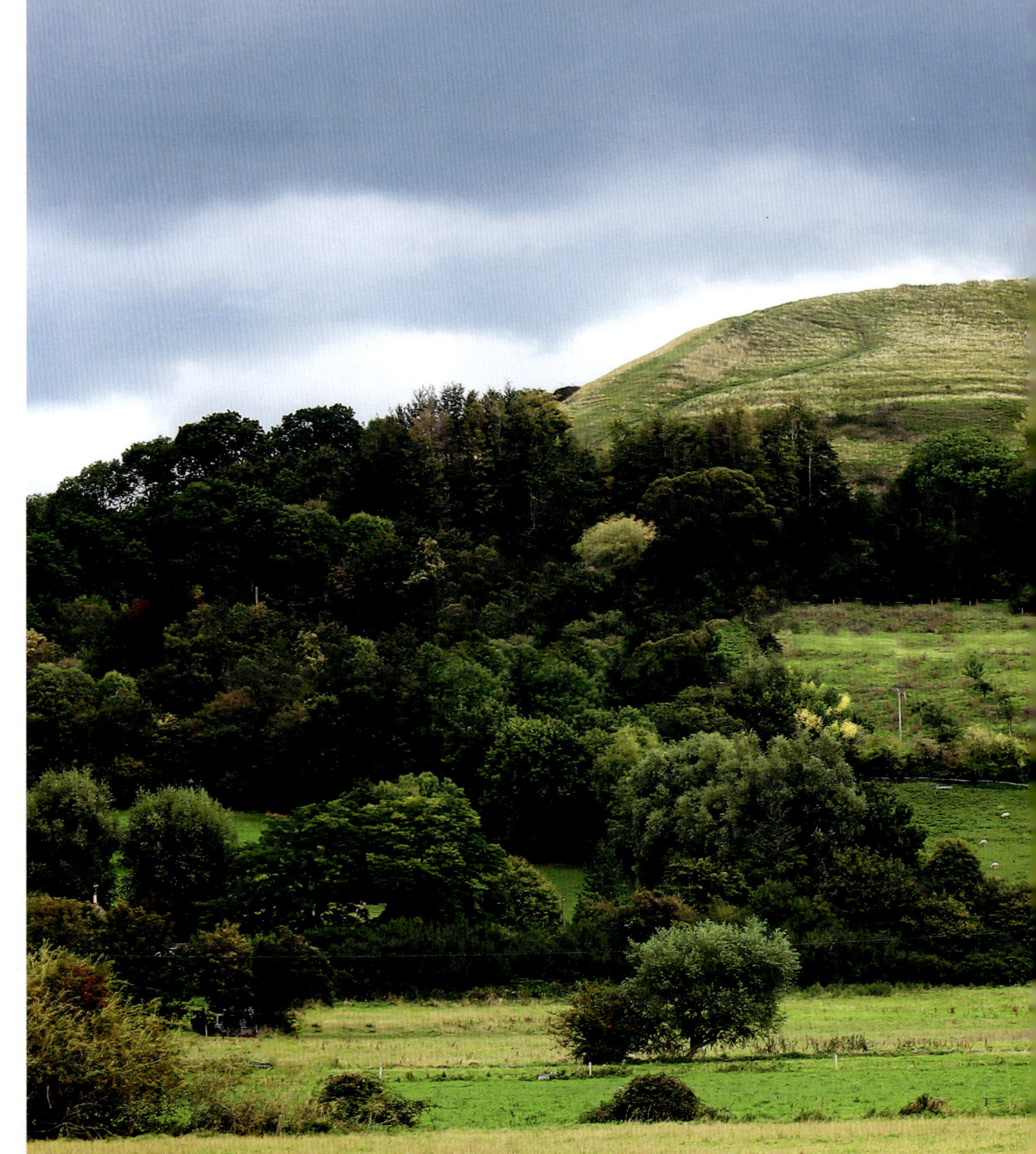

THE ICONIC
GLASTONBURY TOR
Oliver's favourite

"This is Glastonbury Tor. I love
the trees and the Tor. It's a good
view. I like the wavy lines and
the colour."

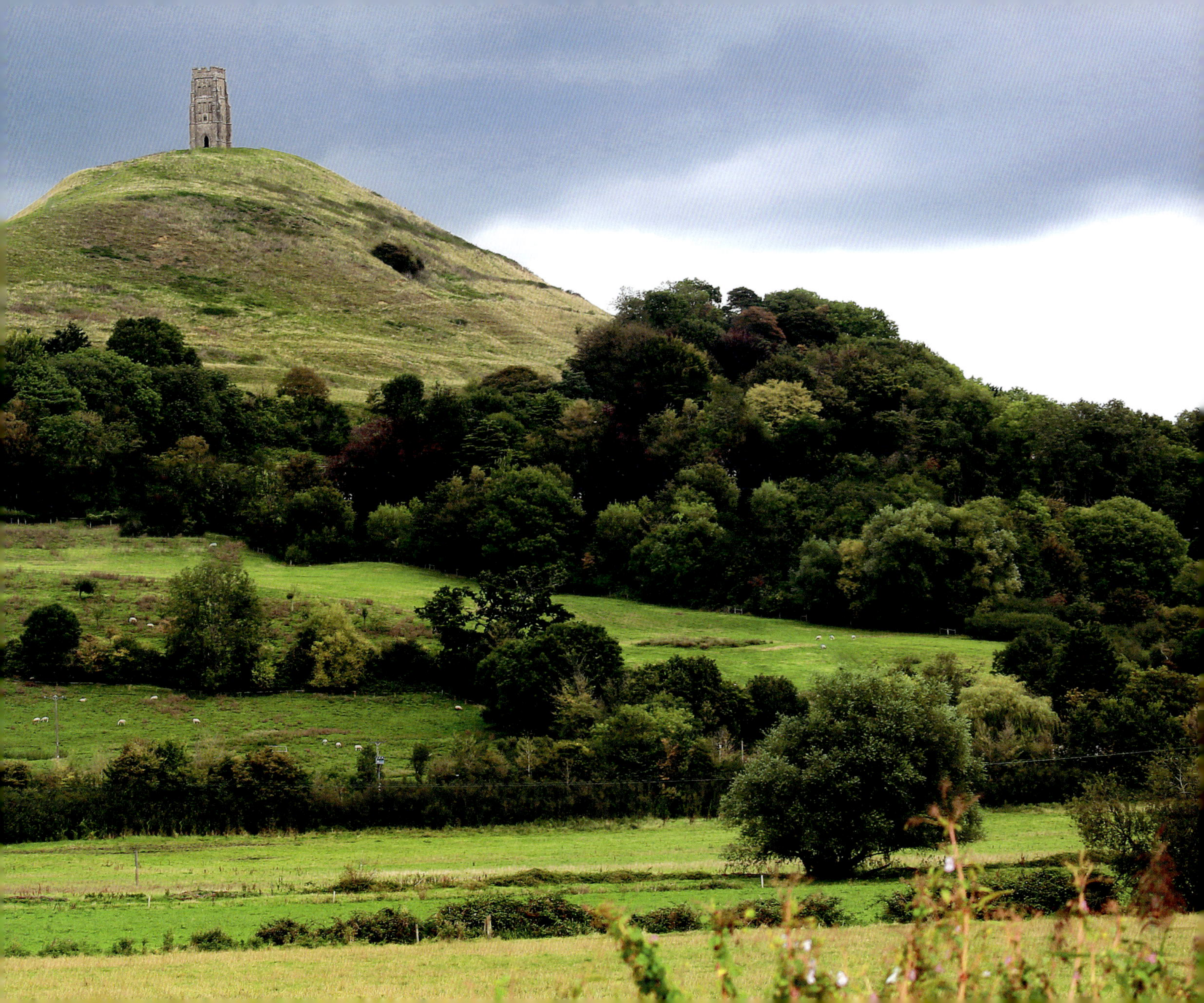

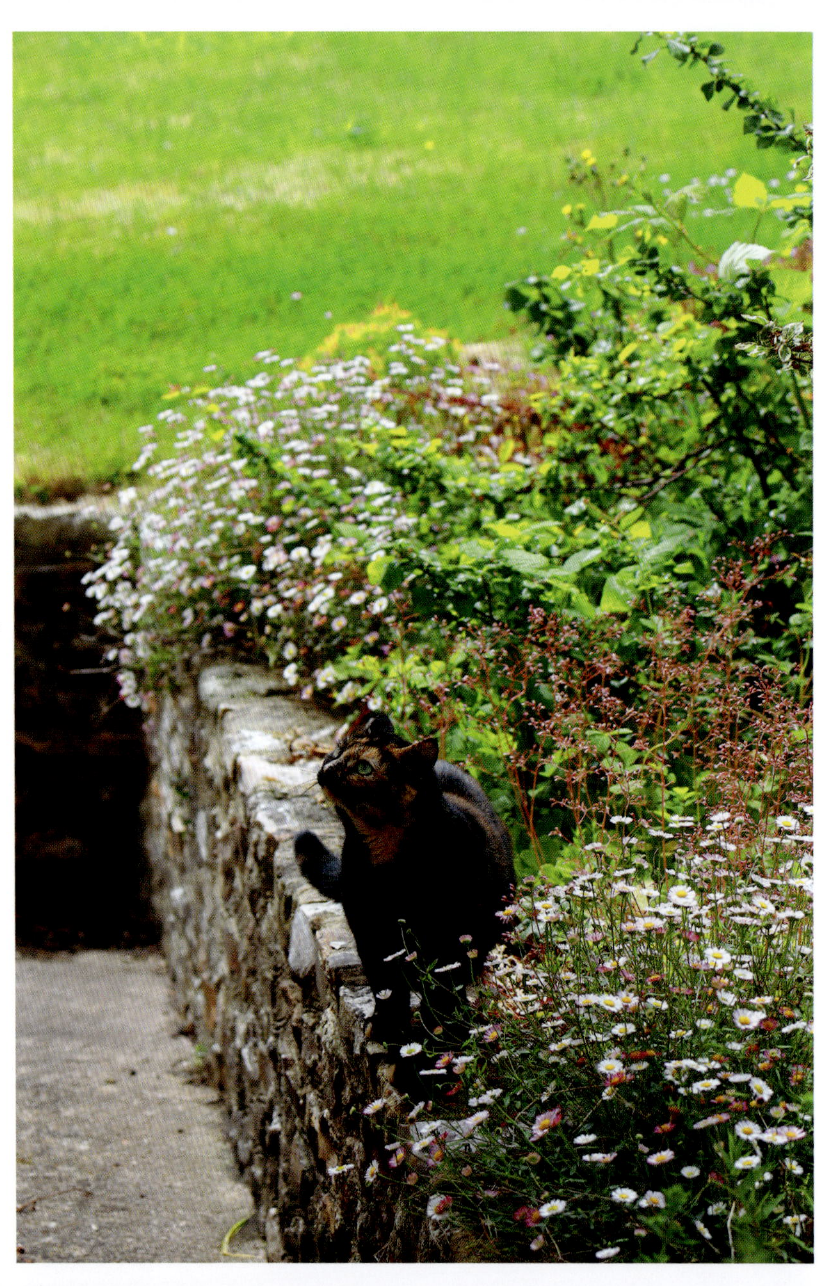

OLIVER'S CAT IN HIS GARDEN
Oliver's favourite

"My cat was perched on the wall in my garden in the perfect position to get a picture. I wanted her to look at me but she didn't. I love my little cat – she's so gorgeous!"

VILLAGE SIGN FOR SPAXTON

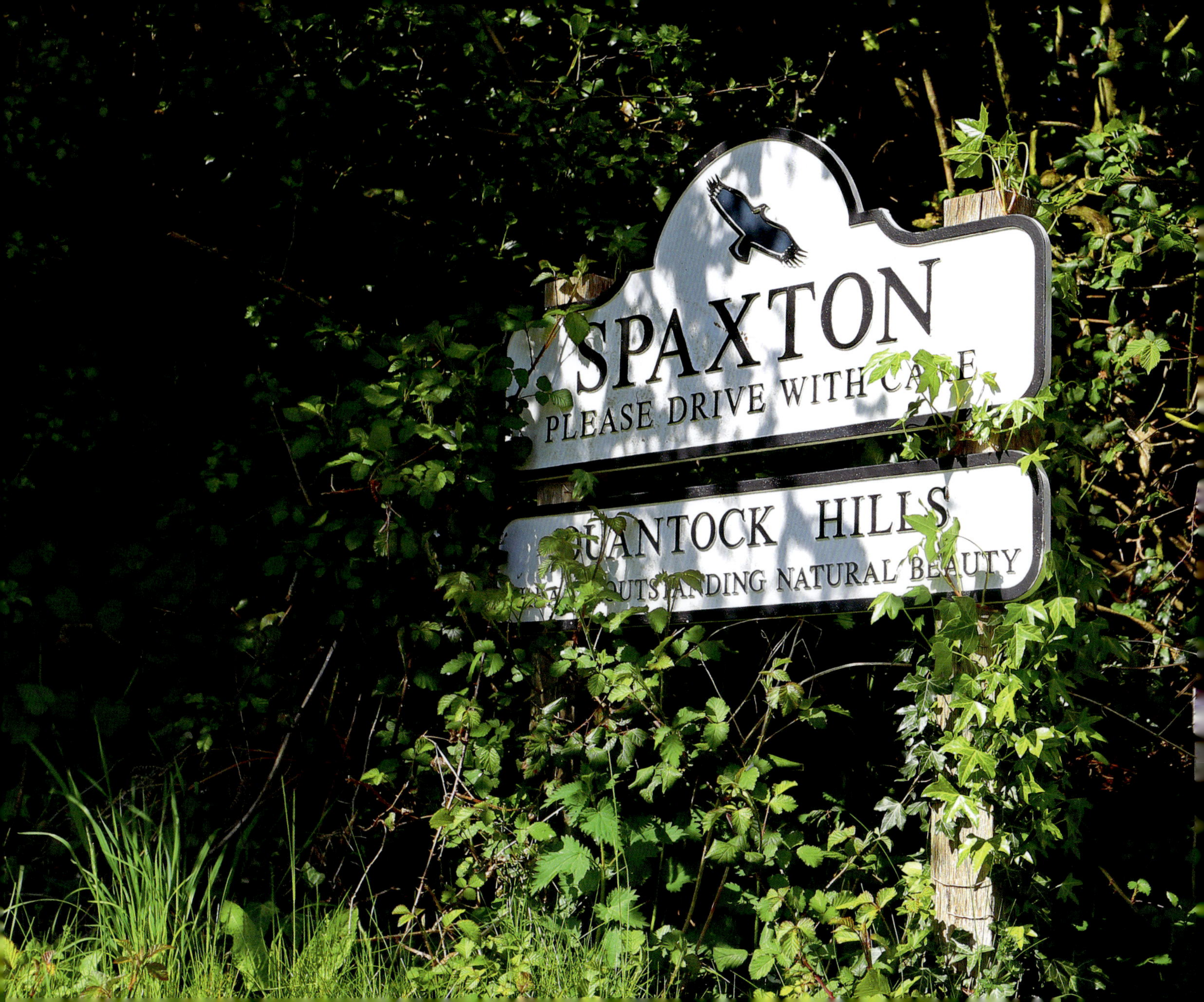
SPAXTON
PLEASE DRIVE WITH CARE
QUANTOCK HILLS
AREA OF OUTSTANDING NATURAL BEAUTY

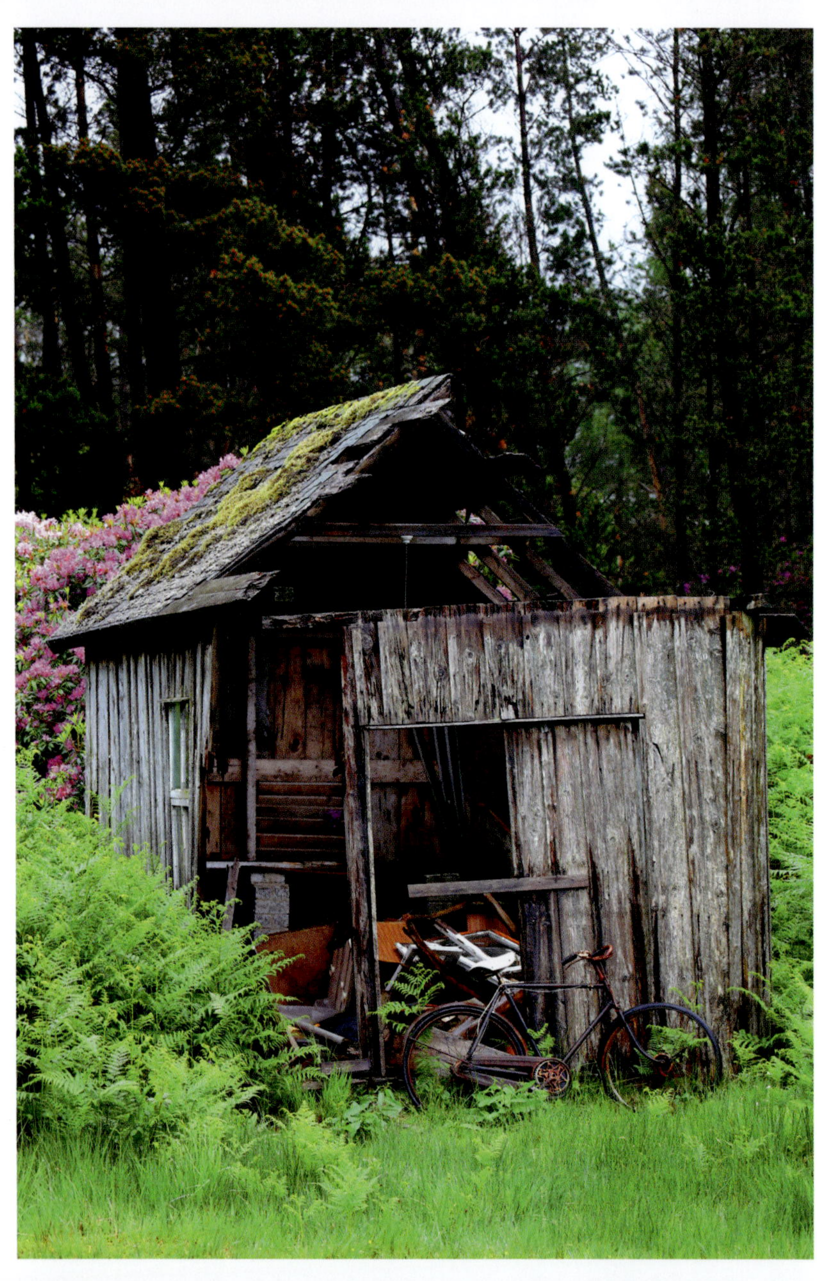

THE OLD BIKE SHED – GLEN ETIVE, SCOTLAND

Oliver came across this dilapidated shed during a wet and misty holiday in the Scottish Highlands.

THE OLD MILK CHURN

This old milk churn, with its brightly coloured nasturtiums, really caught Oliver's attention.

FLY AGARIC

Oliver takes *lots* of pictures of fungi and mushrooms and was rather pleased to spot an intact red and white 'fly agaric' at the bottom of a tree in the woods in Wales.

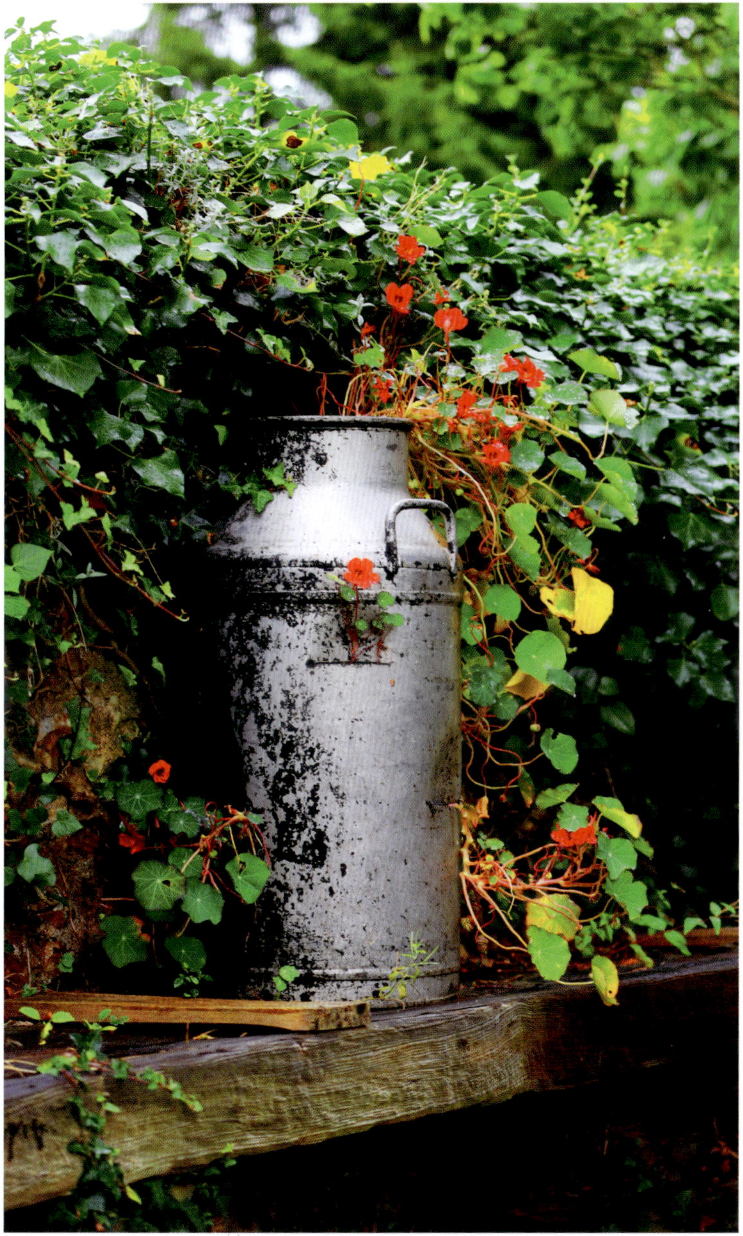

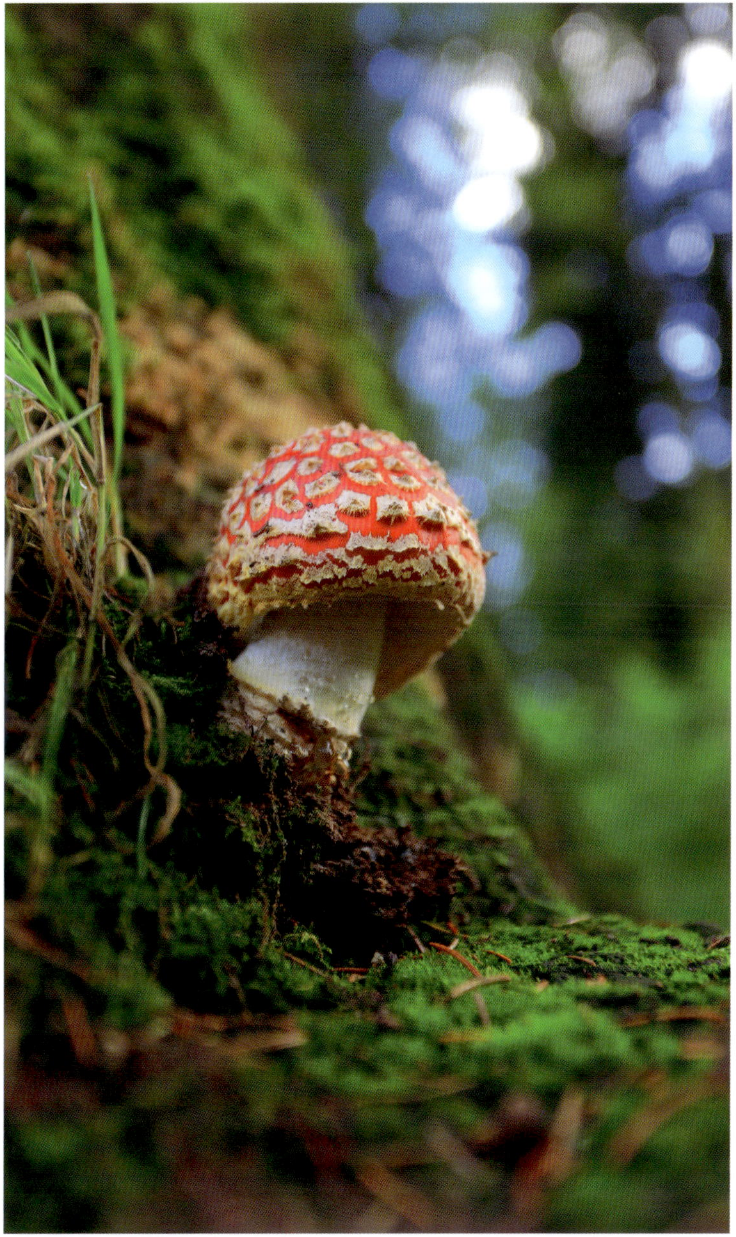

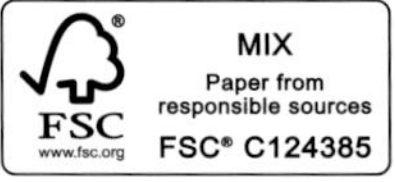

Printed in China
for ACC Art Books Ltd., Woodbridge, Suffolk, England

www.accartbooks.com

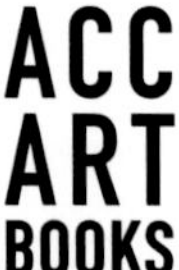

ACC ART BOOKS

Front cover: 'Walking Around Castle Drogo', Devon.
Back cover: Oliver catching the evening light © Mike O'Carroll

All photographs © Oliver Hellowell except the following:

p6 Oliver and his sister Anna © Anna Coles

p8 (top) Oliver with his stepdad Mike © Wendy O'Carroll

P8 (bottom) Oliver with his mum Wendy © Mike O'Carroll

p9 Oliver in the snowdrops © Mike O'Carroll

p10 (top) Oliver on the set of the BBC's The One Show with presenters Matt Baker and Alex Jones having just presented Matt with the first copy of Oliver's Birds © Mike O'Carroll

p10 (centre) Oliver with Ellie Harrison on the BBC's Countryfile © Mike O'Carroll

p10 (bottom) Oliver with his USA/UK Media Award for 'Photographic Travel Feature', 2019 © Mike O'Carroll

p11 (top) Oliver catching the evening light © Mike O'Carroll

p11 (centre) Oliver enjoying the woodland and river © Mike O'Carroll

p11 (bottom) Oliver at work © Mike O'Carroll

p13 Oliver with his friend naturalist and wildlife presenter Iolo Williams © Mike O'Carroll

p31 (top) Oliver photographing a grey seal pup © Mike O'Carroll

p61 (right) Oliver loves waterfalls © Wendy O'Carroll

p72 Oliver capturing 'Reflections of Scotland', his sister Anna's favourite photograph © Mike O'Carroll

www.oliverhellowell.com
www.facebook.com/OliverHellowellPhotographer